T0351119

MACHINE LEARNING FOR CRIMINOLOGY AND CRIME RESEARCH: AT THE CROSSROADS

Machine Learning for Criminology and Crime Research: At the Crossroads reviews the roots of the intersection between machine learning, artificial intelligence (AI), and research on crime; examines the current state of the art in this area of scholarly inquiry; and discusses future perspectives that may emerge from this relationship.

As machine learning and AI approaches become increasingly pervasive, it is critical for criminology and crime research to reflect on the ways in which these paradigms could reshape the study of crime. In response, this book seeks to stimulate this discussion. The opening part is framed through a historical lens, with the first chapter dedicated to the origins of the relationship between AI and research on crime, refuting the "novelty narrative" that often surrounds this debate. The second presents a compact overview of the history of AI, further providing a nontechnical primer on machine learning. The following chapter reviews some of the most important trends in computational criminology and quantitatively characterizing publication patterns at the intersection of AI and criminology, through a network science approach. This book also looks to the future, proposing two goals and four pathways to increase the positive societal impact of algorithmic systems in research on crime. The sixth chapter provides a survey of the methods emerging from the integration of machine learning and causal inference, showcasing their promise for answering a range of critical questions.

With its transdisciplinary approach, *Machine Learning for Criminology and Crime Research* is important reading for scholars and students in criminology, criminal justice, sociology, and economics, as well as AI, data sciences and statistics, and computer science.

Gian Maria Campedelli is a Postdoctoral Research Fellow in Computational Sociology and Criminology at the University of Trento, Italy. In 2020, he earned a PhD in Criminology from Catholic University in Milan, Italy. From 2016 to 2019, he worked as a researcher at Transcrime, the Joint Research Center on Transnational Crime of Catholic University, University of Bologna, and University of Perugia. In 2018, he was also a visiting research scholar in the School of Computer Science at Carnegie Mellon University, in Pittsburgh, the United States. His research addresses the development and application of computational methods – especially machine learning and complex networks – to the study of criminal and social phenomena, with a specific focus on organized crime, violence, and terrorism.

ROUTLEDGE ADVANCES IN CRIMINOLOGY

For more information about this series, please visit: https://www.routledge.com/Routledge-Advances-in-Criminology/book-series/RAC

MACHINE LEARNING FOR CRIMINOLOGY AND CRIME RESEARCH

At the Crossroads

Gian Maria Campedelli

Routledge
Taylor & Francis Group

LONDON AND NEW YORK

First published 2022
by Routledge
4 Park Square, Milton Park, Abingdon, Oxon OX14 4RN

and by Routledge
605 Third Avenue, New York, NY 10158

Routledge is an imprint of the Taylor & Francis Group, an informa business

© 2022 Gian Maria Campedelli

The right of Gian Maria Campedelli to be identified as author of this work has been asserted in accordance with sections 77 and 78 of the Copyright, Designs and Patents Act 1988.

All rights reserved. No part of this book may be reprinted or reproduced or utilised in any form or by any electronic, mechanical, or other means, now known or hereafter invented, including photocopying and recording, or in any information storage or retrieval system, without permission in writing from the publishers.

Trademark notice: Product or corporate names may be trademarks or registered trademarks, and are used only for identification and explanation without intent to infringe.

British Library Cataloguing-in-Publication Data
A catalogue record for this book is available from the British Library

Library of Congress Cataloging-in-Publication Data
Names: Campedelli, Gian Maria, author.
Title: Machine learning for criminology and crime research: at the crossroads/Gian Maria Campedelli.
Description: First Edition. | New York, NY: Routledge, 2022. |
Series: Routledge advances in criminology | Includes bibliographical references and index.
Identifiers: LCCN 2021059992 (print) | LCCN 2021059993 (ebook) |
ISBN 9781032109190 (hardback) | ISBN 9781032109282 (paperback) |
ISBN 9781003217732 (ebook)
Subjects: LCSH: Criminology–Research. | Artificial intelligence–Research. | Machine learning–Statistical methods.
Classification: LCC HV6024.5 .C336 2022 (print) | LCC HV6024.5 (ebook) | DDC 364.072–dc23/eng/20211210
LC record available at https://lccn.loc.gov/2021059992
LC ebook record available at https://lccn.loc.gov/2021059993

ISBN: 978-1-032-10919-0 (hbk)
ISBN: 978-1-032-10928-2 (pbk)
ISBN: 978-1-003-21773-2 (ebk)

DOI: 10.4324/9781003217732

Typeset in Sabon
by KnowledgeWorks Global Ltd.

THIS BOOK IS DEDICATED TO MY FAMILY AND TO MARTA, THE BREEZE IN THE HEAT AND THE FLAME IN THE COLD OF ALL THE DAYS SPENT ON THESE PAGES, AND BEYOND.

CONTENTS

CONTENTS

FIGURES

TABLES

FOREWORD

Criminology and crime research have made tremendous progress in the last decades in answering many critical questions about crime and criminal behaviors. Important results have been achieved in a number of different areas, concerning many different problems. For example, developmental and life-course criminology has provided us with theories and empirical findings demonstrating how individuals get involved in delinquency, and how certain policies, life-events, or historical factors may modify criminal trajectories substantially (Piquero, 2008; Piquero et al., 2003; Sampson & Laub, 1995). Research on crime concentration unveiled significant spatial and temporal patterns that characterize where and when crime occurs in many different contexts, both urban and rural, around the world (Johnson, 2010; Weisburd, 2015; Weisburd et al., 2012). Scholarship on the link between crime and punishment has also revealed the effects that certain policies can have on individuals' concerning desistance and re-offending, as well as in terms of health, economic status, and civic involvement (Kirk & Wakefield, 2018; Loeffler & Nagin, 2022; Sampson, 2011). These selected examples cannot meaningfully summarize the amount of discoveries and the impact of the advances made by scholars interested in researching crime over the last 50 years, especially as data sources and methodological tools advance.

Nonetheless, there are still many questions that are yet to be asked and answered. To continue their mission toward the understanding of crime in all its facets, criminologists and crime researchers need to exploit all the tools, approaches, and techniques that are available today and will be available tomorrow.

One thing that has been often overlooked in research on crime is the systematic application of modern, sophisticated types of computational techniques, in spite of previous calls to embrace such approaches (Berk, 2013). One that holds much promise, artificial intelligence (AI), has been used widely in various disciplines as well as industry more generally. Yet, criminologists know little about these approaches and the power they can provide to study crime.

Fortunately, the book in your hands, Campedelli's *Machine Learning for Criminology and Crime Research: At the Crossroads* provides readers with the most complete, authoritative, and accessible discussion on the perspectives and challenges of the use of AI in criminology and crime research.

By offering a historical account of trends, ideas, and paradigms, Campedelli walks the reader through the foundations of AI, how it is distinguished from other types of computational and quantitative modeling, and then introduces the main concepts in machine learning, a branch of AI that has become particularly popular in the last decades and is slowly starting to be used in criminological research. Additionally, the book presents a quantitative analysis of the current state of the art in the use of AI methods for studying crime and further discusses ways forward and strategies to increase the positive societal potential of this technology in this sphere. The book ends by proposing a crucial overview on methods integrating perspectives from econometrics and machine learning for causal discovery, discussing and highlighting the important perspectives they pose for addressing many of the unanswered problems in criminology and crime research.

I learned a lot by reading this book and believe that you will too. AI is a powerful tool, and one more tool in the toolbox for criminologists to use as we seek to better understand and predict criminal behavior and crime patterns.

Alex R. Piquero, PhD
*Professor of Sociology and Criminology and
Arts & Sciences Distinguished Scholar, University of Miami
Professor of Criminology, Monash University*

References

Berk, R. (2013). Algorithmic criminology. *Security Informatics*, 2(1), 5. https://doi.org/10.1186/2190-8532-2-5.

Johnson, S. D. (2010). A brief history of the analysis of crime concentration. *European Journal of Applied Mathematics*, 21(4–5), 349–370. https://doi.org/10.1017/S0956792510000082.

Kirk, D. S., & Wakefield, S. (2018). Collateral consequences of punishment: A critical review and path forward. *Annual Review of Criminology*, 1(1), 171–194. https://doi.org/10.1146/annurev-criminol-032317-092045.

Loeffler, C. E., & Nagin, D. S. (2022). The impact of incarceration on recidivism. *Annual Review of Criminology*, 5(1). https://doi.org/10.1146/annurev-criminol-030920-112506.

Piquero, A. R. (2008). Taking stock of developmental trajectories of criminal activity over the life course. In A. M. Liberman (Ed.), *The long view of crime: A synthesis of longitudinal research* (pp. 23–78). Springer. https://doi.org/10.1007/978-0-387-71165-2_2.

Piquero, A. R., Farrington, D. P., & Blumstein, A. (2003). The criminal career paradigm. *Crime and Justice*, 30, 359–506. https://doi.org/10.1086/652234.

Sampson, R. J. (2011). The incarceration ledger. *Criminology & Public Policy*, *10*(3), 819–828. https://doi.org/10.1111/j.1745-9133.2011.00756.x.

Sampson, R. J., & Laub, J. H. (1995). *Crime in the making: Pathways and turning points through life*. Harvard University Press.

Weisburd, D. (2015). The law of crime concentration and the criminology of place. *Criminology*, *53*(2), 133–157. https://doi.org/10.1111/1745-9125.12070.

Weisburd, D., Groff, E. R., & Yang, S.-M. (2012). *The criminology of place: Street Segments and our understanding of the crime problem*. Oxford University Press.

PREFACE

Back in the days when I was in high school, I used to dream about becoming a novelist. Nonetheless, I never really found a good story that deserved to be written down or never had a sufficient level of perseverance to seriously try to achieve that goal. Over those years – the ferocious years before one turns 18 – poetry then suddenly became the most appealing and fascinating dream to catch, the intellectual alternative to becoming a football player. Poetry's immediacy and its anarchic attitude seemed to fit my lack of rigor in unfolding narrative structures and devoting months (or even years) to writing novels. When we are young, we often tend to sacrifice long-term commitment for faster returns – or at least this applied to me – and poetry matched that compromise. Hence, I tried my end with short and long poems, some motivated by love, some other by anger, all by those existentialist forces that continuously roam inside us during youth and adolescence in their entirety.

The poetry career did not last that long: the world's attempt to inject in me – mostly indirectly rather than directly – the belief that being enrolled in a university program means starting to walk fast in the direction of the adult age drained all my inspiration, intellectual creativity, and fascination for writing. I kept my passion for reading – both novels and poems – but lost that need for translating thoughts into sentences, fantasies into paragraphs, and desires into lines or chapters. My life kept going, and I must admit it has not spared torments and the like, but that need never really came back. I got my undergraduate and graduate degrees, and then my doctorate, and finally during my doctorate I experimented with another completely different way of thinking about writing. Scientific writing forced me to a transition I initially struggled to adapt to. Writing down papers in a dry, unemotional, objective style almost seemed like a betrayal of myself at age 16. Then, I slowly understood that scientific writing can be creative too: creative but objective, engaging but rigorous, passionate but precise. I still feel I was more promising as a very young aspiring poet rather than as a relatively young scientist, but I guess I will save this opinion for myself without sharing it with the small group of people that will read this book (or with my Editor!).

It feels now odd to realize that I am writing the preface to what will become my first published book, and that this book won't be about a thriller story, it won't be a *bildungsroman*, and it won't be a collection of short poems, either. Yet, it is vaguely captivating to think that the topics of this book possess some of the traits that can be found in thousands of novels or poetry collections. It will describe the tension between the past, the present, and the future. It will address the challenges of multiple communities. It will pose questions that will be tightly connected to intellectual and practical change. It will be a book about disruption, reform, reconstruction, and about opportunities. Also, speaking of connections, while my graduate education went in a completely different direction, I find it funny to remember that my high school graduation project was about the link between neuroscience and philosophy in Artificial Intelligence. I guess at this point I am firsthand a man constantly at the crossroads. I do not know whether the younger version of myself would have read this book, what I know is that I finally found that methodical perseverance and rigor that I lacked during those long-gone days. That methodical perseverance and rigor that brought me here, at the beginning of what I wish will be a very long professional journey.

I hope you will enjoy my company while you walk your road.

ACKNOWLEDGMENTS

This book was made possible by the continuous support of Lydia De Cruz, my Editor at Routledge. Thank you for having believed in my proposal from the very first day, and having assisted me in every step during the writing and production phases. I also owe thanks to the entire Routledge staff, including Assistant Editors and members of the production team for their work and invaluable cooperation.

I am indebted to Alberto Aziani, Francesco Calderoni, and Gianmarco Daniele for their precious comments on earlier versions of this manuscript, and three anonymous reviewers for their thoughtful suggestions and critiques on my initial book proposal.

I would also like to thank Alex Piquero for having participated in this book by writing its Foreword. Finally, I am grateful to many people outside academia who relieved the pressure of days without inspiration through their tireless love. I owe heartfelt thanks to Marta, my family - my mom Daniela, my dad Samuele and my sister Elisa - and to all my dear friends. A sincere mention goes also to Marco, my saxophone maestro and friend, who has helped me galvanizing my writing creativity through the study of music.

1

THE "NOVELTY NARRATIVE"

An Unorthodox Introduction

The Mythical "Novelty Narrative"

One of the most common ways to advertise a scientific product, be it an idea, an article, or a book, is to describe it as "novel." Novel theories might encounter resistance, yet they attract curiosity, and curiosity is enough to make it spread, intellectually and commercially, provided of course that such theories are sufficiently engaging, and plausible. The same goes for research applications, granted that they are not only "novel" but also interesting to a considerable portion of the audience to which they are directed. Addressing "novel" research problems through a given methodology fosters the interest of peers in our research community, leading to wider dissemination, and discussion. This also applies to "novel" methods. If they are to some extent even slight demonstrated to be useful and provide even slight advantages over alternative methodological approaches, branding the empirical approaches we develop in our scholarship as "novel" can help us captivate the attention of our colleagues. In contemporary science, "novelty" is many times used as a marketing strategy to increase the attractiveness of a scientific product, and it is often one of those features upon which one work is judged. On the low-end of a seniority spectrum, graduate students' dissertations are also judged in terms of novelty. On the opposite end, even Nobel prizes are awarded taking into consideration the novelty of their contributions to the study of certain problems.

It is therefore undoubtedly tempting to construct a "novelty"-based narrative around the contents of this book. Most readers or commentators would not argue otherwise. My strategy would not be seen as a marketing one alone, but rather as a motivated, perfectly reasonable decision. In fact, criminologists and crime researchers[1] may have already heard or read several times that "machine learning" represents a novel methodological toolbox to address crime-related problems. This is the dominant narrative depicting the relationship between research on crime and artificial intelligence (AI). Dazzled by the increasing availability of digital data and by the hype around research and practice in machine intelligence virtually spread across every scientific field, readers would easily fall into the novelty trap,

DOI: 10.4324/9781003217732-1

proving the effectiveness of such marketing strategy of scientific communication, not necessarily leading to more lenient evaluations of my work but quite certainly achieving a higher level of attractiveness.

Yet, as tempting as this might be, the truth is different. In fact, the relationship between machine learning and research on crime is not novel at all. And the same goes for the broader relationship between AI and the Social Sciences. Although many papers, reports, contributions to the fields of criminology or crime research have been pictured as "novel" precisely because they rely on the use of machine learning or similar approaches from the AI literature, this "novelty" narrative rests on a – deliberated or no – fabrication of history.[2]

Of course, elements of novelty emerge, including for instance in the type of data that are used or the specific algorithmic approaches that are tested. However, the relationship between these two areas has now quite a long history. Differences between the present and the past as well as important developments in this relationship exist, but dismissing the epistemological discussion around the ways in which research on crime and AI are linked by invoking an alleged "novelty" oversimplifies a scientific process that has longstanding roots.

Acknowledging these roots not only is important for mere historical and chronological reporting, giving credit to the reflections of pioneers that moved the first steps into this line of inquiry. It is also critical to contextualize the challenges that we are facing today, the trends we are witnessing, and the perspectives we are unfolding. The "novelty" narrative obscures early debates in this area of research and severely limits our critical reasoning on the possible future scenarios resulting from the progressively tighter connection between criminology, crime research, and the nuances of AI.

The introduction to this book hence precisely starts with a call to reconnect with the decades-long past that precedes us, refusing the novelty narrative as a cheap marketing strategy to make our works more palatable. Novelty and innovation are essential aspects of science: they are the engine of progress, the forces leading humanity into the future, and they should be therefore invoked cautiously and, most importantly, after cognition and recognition of our past. It takes an appreciation of the process of knowledge-building started decades ago to discriminate advances from selling strategies, true innovation from rebranding, and real novelty from noise.

The immaturity of the dialogue between research on crime and AI, an element that will be discussed in this book, also passes from here: from the inability (or lack of interest) to frame our present in perspective, moving beyond the impromptu logic of publication and dissemination of ideas for the sole purpose of being cited more, selling more book copies, acquiring more grants, pretending to be the elected representatives of a new wave of world-changing research. The "novelty narrative" pushes us all to think of a process that starts from square zero every time we work on an idea or a project, hence refusing a cumulative (and therefore comparative) approach to scientific discovery. However, criminology and crime research – and AI as well – require a cumulative and comparative approach to finally address and respond to pressing questions that go well beyond the abstract task of finding someone willing to publish our research. The "novelty narrative" works perfectly fine for our tenure-track goals and our run for academic prestige, but all the implications it poses severely impair our possibility to make a change in the real world. I will leave to the reader to decide whether this is an acceptable trade-off decision to make.

Being Novel before Being Novel

In Chapter 2 of this book, I will delineate a compact history of developments in AI. One of the first facts that will be highlighted is that AI is nothing short of a long journey: its beginnings date back to centuries and centuries ago. The history of the relationship, dialogue, and blending of AI for research on crime is of course much more recent, but given the "novelty narrative" that dominates most of the extant literature on the topic, one might be surprised to discover that such relationship is now more than three decades old. If one cares to maintain a broader perspective on this dialogue, namely, including also the antecedent literature on the use of computers for research and practice on crime, this relationship becomes even older.

As an example, in 1963 Reed C. Lawlor published an article in the American Bar Association Journal in which he reviewer and discussed the possibilities introduced by computers for the analysis and prediction of judicial decisions (Lawlor, 1963). Lawlor represents one of the few pioneers of computerized legal sciences. Actuarial approaches to criminal justice were already in place in the 1920s in the US system, as already pointed out by Berk (2019), yet the promises of computing in the 1960s fueled an optimistic wave of discussion about how machines could be used to assist judges in their decisions. However, in 1986, Susskind noted how in the two decades before his article was written, computers were primarily used for facilitating information retrieval rather than for data-driven recommendations (Susskind, 1986). Many difficulties limited Lawlor's prediction about computer-assisted predictions, including modest computational power of machines produced at the time and their prohibitive cost. Yet, in reading Lawlor, we can already find the precursors of those tools that have become widespread today and that, over the course of the decades, have become increasingly complex in their nature, ultimately embracing machine learning approaches.

Lawlor's article further elaborates on the applicability of the scientific method to the law and to its inherent decision-making processes. By highlighting the parallels between the pitfalls of uncertainty of mathematical modeling in social and biological-physical research settings, discarding the idea of "exact sciences," Lawlor argues that certain doctrines of law, and particularly "stare decisis," can create patterns that are as computable and as discoverable as those emerging from the uniformity characterizing

3

biology or physics. Contrarily, without such regularities, Lawler warns that machine-aided prediction becomes impossible.

The article does not mention AI or machine learning (the field, as we will see, was "officially" labeled AI less than ten years before the manuscript was published), but it is easy to appreciate the parallelisms between nowadays criminal justice applications and the abstract idealization of tools exploiting the capability of logical and mathematical techniques for informing individual's legal decision.

It is with the popularity of expert systems in the 1980s that the promises of computational approaches for addressing crime research problems found more fertile ground for the development and diffusion of ideas in this direction. While symbolism was moving its last steps as the dominant paradigm in AI, symbolism-driven reflections on the linkages between AI and the social sciences emerged with more frequency, gaining increasing attention.

In this context, I find two different angles to be particularly intriguing to be reviewed today, as they are helpful to force us rethinking about the history of the strange relationship between AI and research on crime. The first angle, the narrower of the two, regards the origins of the literature that saw AI as a mean to a set of specific ends. The second, which is broader, concerns instead the early discussions about the role of AI in sociological theorizing.

A Mean to an End: The Dawn of Artificial Intelligence as a Tool in Research on Crime

Machine learning methods in criminology and crime research are generally seen as tools to achieve a set of limited, specific goals. As most statistical methods are deployed to infer relationships between covariates and a dependent variable, either through causal discovery or mere correlational scrutiny, machine learning approaches are associated to the concepts of prediction or forecasting.

On the one hand, this tendency is a legacy of the "two cultures" dichotomy that was described by Breiman (2001), and that will be part of an extended discussion in Chapter 5. To briefly anticipate it, Breiman critically outlines the existence of two cultures in statistical modeling – the data modeling and the algorithmic cultures – which are inherently distinct because of the different statistical and conceptual approaches they take to data and problems. While the data modeling culture (which can be associated with the fields of statistics and econometrics) is concerned with theorizing and emphasizes the data generating process at the core of a certain problem, the algorithmic culture (that refers to the computer science and AI communities) is much more concerned with the concrete resolution of problems through prediction. In this book, I will show that this scenario has partially changed today, as recent developments in the relationships between the two

4

cultures have emerged, but it is unquestionable that this idealistic division between different approaches to statistical modeling has also permeated the conception of machine learning and AI concerning research on crime.

On the other hand, however, the idea that AI and related subfields are means to an end cannot solely be regarded to the broad conceptualization of the "two cultures" dichotomy. The other relevant cultural and intellectual influence in this sense is the history of actuarial risk-assessment models and the tradition of computerized legal studies.

The longstanding presence of data-driven tools for decision-making in the American criminal justice system has become a natural ancestor of the idea that more sophisticated, powerful, performing methods could be game-changers in building a safer society through empirics. The legacy of data-driven tools is not confined to criminal justice risk assessment alone but has spread across different types of applications and problems, such as policing and intelligence profiling.

The "science of prediction" (Ridgeway, 2013) has been (and, although things are taking a different direction, continues to be to date) the central frame within which machine learning has been positioned in criminology and crime research. Especially in light of the increasing availability of relevant digital data and the democratization of open-source programming languages (or the diffusion of commercial software), researchers and practitioners interested in these techniques zeroed in on predictive accuracy, somehow deliberately overshadowing the importance of causal discovery and interpretation (R. A. Berk & Bleich, 2013). Antecedents of this view can date back to the 1980s already.

As an example, David J. Icove, a former member of the FBI's Behavioral Science Unit, wrote a piece in 1986 in which he described the management and functioning of an AI-based computer system in the FBI's National Center for the Analysis of Violent Crime. The system addressed a triptych of goals, namely, detection, prediction, and prevention of violent crime: crime pattern analysis and classification were carried out through a set of different preliminary steps, such as the analysis of the crime scene, and allowed for the identification of likely suspects through matching with historical data for previous offenders (Icove, 1986). Interestingly, the system was not only engineered for classification purposes but also for unsupervised learning tasks, such as clustering, to identify groups of similar events based on specified sets of characteristics, such as crime motive. The computational architecture of the project rested on a knowledge-based expert system that was highly dependent on the expertise of the analyst to construct a knowledge thesaurus that was consequently transformed into decision rules.

Only a few years later, Ratledge and Jacoby published the *Handbook on Artificial Intelligence and Expert Systems in Law Enforcement* (1989). In the book, which was mostly addressed to practitioners and police officers, the authors engage in an optimistic view of the diffusion of AI-based tools for helping police forces in their investigative duties. Among other things, they analyze a case study of an expert system deployed in Baltimore County, Maryland, that targeted residential burglary in an attempt to convince skeptics about the practicability and feasibility of such technological applications. Additional examples are provided, some of which precisely referring to the works of Icove and colleagues at the FBI. The *Handbook on Artificial Intelligence and Expert Systems in Law Enforcement* reveals two things in retrospective. First, that in the 1980s AI-based systems were to a certain extent already diffused across the US criminal justice institutions. Second, it tells us that the attitude toward these systems was highly optimistic in terms of their potential. Although, as pointed out by Tafoya (1991), a great deal of reluctance characterized members of the law enforcement in embracing technological advances between the 1960s and the 1980s, the general sentiment of notable representatives of the police community was highly positive with regard to the benefits that expert systems could offer to the profession (and to society as a whole).

Optimistic, hopeful visions about the future of policing and criminal justice were not only expressed by members of criminal justice and policing institutions. Favorable tones came from academia as well. Hernandez (1990) for instance detailed a set of significant strengths of expert systems in reference to criminal justice and policing. These included (a) the ability to draw inference; (b) the interpretability of results through what he called a "metaknowledge facility;" (c) the presence of interactive user-friendly interfaces; (d) their expandability, which in his terms refer to adaptability to other contexts and adaptivity of inferences; (e) the simplicity in their engineering; and (d) their module-based architecture. I would not be surprised at all to find these characteristics listed as benefits of a specific machine learning application in a paper published today. The article additionally adventures into predictions about expert systems in the 2000 – clearly miscalculating the importance of connectionism – that unravel an extremely futuristic as well as optimistic assessment of their potential.

This optimism not only marked the policing community but also the fields of law and legal science. Donald H. Berman and Carole D. Hafner have been two of the most prominent and acute scholars investigating the link between AI and the law. Particularly, their contributions to this area between the 1980s and the 1990s have been deeply influential concerning both computational and legal doctrine dimensions (Berman, 1989; Berman & Hafner, 1987, 1988, 1993, 1995). At the time, most critiques of the role of computer and computing in judicial and legal decisions referred to the works of Wiener (1962) and Weizenbaum (1977), who completely rejected the ideas that computers could be used to assist (or predict) judicial decisions. While concurring on the impossibility to substitute human decision-making in such contexts, Berman and Hafner viewed this technology instead as an opportunity to construct a fairer criminal justice system (1989).

By calling out the many dysfunctionalities of the American criminal justice system and the obstacles that it posed to most people, both in terms of economic costs and procedural complications, Berman and Hafner argued that AI could transform the system into a more accessible, inclusive, and less discretionary one. They provided two examples to sustain their claim. The first regarded the use of a predictive expert system used to help a middle-income homebuyer assess its legal position after having been misled by the statements of a real-estate broker. The second concerned a case in which, by porting methods that were already diffused in the medical domain, an expert system could be used to build consensus on sentencing norms in criminal cases, helping decision-makers to understand, evaluate, and communicate the rationale of their decisions.

Unfortunately, we know now that most of these hopes have gone unfulfilled so far. The reasons are multifaceted but are mostly related to the concept of "bias," which permeates different aspects of decision-making and knowledge production in criminal justice. Bias is present in human decisions, from the very first contact between citizens and law enforcement up to the sentencing stage, and bias is crucially embedded also in the data that are used to feed the algorithmic systems that courts and prosecutors are utilizing today. In the past years, increasing attention has been paid to these issues by researchers across different disciplines. Many inputs came from computer and statistical sciences (Barabas et al., 2018; Dressel & Farid, 2018; Fogliato et al., 2020; Green, 2018, 2020; Tolan et al., 2019), but contributions have been made also by criminologists (R. Berk & Elzarka, 2020; Browning & Arrigo, 2021; Ugwudike, 2020), although the inquiry into the ethical dimensions of these systems remains marginal, especially in top-tier journals (see Chapter 3). Some may even argue that, contrary to the expectations of Berman and Hafner (and several others besides them), these technological innovations have contributed to reinforcing inequalities, discrimination, and disparities between strata of the population, with some communities and groups – such as racial or sexual minorities – being negatively affected. Moreover, this broken optimism not only concerns the criminal justice and law enforcement sphere but also many other domains, such as education (Baker & Hawn, 2021) and hiring processes (Raghavan et al., 2020).

Later in this book (Chapter 4), I will try to elaborate on structural ways in which academic research can contribute to increase the positive societal impact of machine intelligence tools in research on crime. In general, it is imperative that all the communities that focus on this intersection recognize the needs to move beyond simple prediction, addressing the pitfalls posed by human-in-the-loop biases. One direction entails recasting the way in which data are generated, collected, and elaborated (Douglas et al., 2017). Another one relates to the shift toward prevention rather than prediction by incorporating causal knowledge besides correlational evidence (Barabas et al., 2018; Ridgeway, 2013).

Ridgeway pointed out the importance of linking prediction with prevention already in 2013, yet to date the benefits of extant projects are controversial. For instance, the "Chicago Heat List"[3] application mentioned in his article has been shown to be almost useless in reducing homicides, leading instead to disproportionate police targeting of certain individuals (Saunders et al., 2016). On the other hand, additional applications involving predictive modeling, such as predictive policing, have been highly criticized for a number of ethical reasons (see Chapters 3 and 4 for a more detailed overview). It is impossible to disagree with Ridgeway's call for a blending of prediction and prevention, yet so far the attempts have been inconclusive or, to put it simple, simply did not work. The goal remains, but it may require structural changes in the ways in which computational models, based on AI principles, are taught, developed, and deployed.

Artificial Intelligence and Sociological Theorizing

As we saw, the association between research on crime and machine learning generally prompts ideas that refer to the analytical resolution of certain problems, such as predicting whether a certain individual will reoffend in the future. Regardless of the sentiment we have about this (and similar) type of applications, the idea that machine learning is only a mean to solve a specific task is generally by far the most common to describe the machine learning/research on crime relationship. Nonetheless, this reductionist view overlooks another aspect: the contribution on sociological theorizing on both humans and machines. This line of inquiry has favored vivid investigations that are still relevant today which spread across areas such as digital humanities and computational social science. Emphasizing this dimension is relevant for criminology, given the intertwined connections between sociology and crime. The eminently social component of crime as a human behavior thus calls for broadening the scope of this retrospective review in order to embrace historical developments that emerged beyond the strict borders of criminology itself.

In a recent article, Molina and Garip (2019) argue that machine learning can be useful in theory testing and development starting from algorithms' predictive ability and their power in discovering regularities. Further, they highlight how machine learning offers solutions to the problem of causal complexity that is often encountered in traditional quantitative approaches based on deductive reasoning, with researchers deriving certain hypotheses from a theory to be tested on available data. Similarly, and even more radically, Grimmer and coauthors (2021) criticize the deductive model of social science as limitative to the possibility to discover new insights about phenomena when analyzing data and pose an emphasis on the benefits of more inductive strategies that are often found in qualitative approaches. Particularly, while the deductive approach offers some important virtues, it significantly impedes to develop new theories or refine existing ones. In light of this, Grimmer and colleagues set forth an agnostic approach to machine learning methods, refusing for instance the aprioristic existence of a correct data generating process. In their view, machine learning methods become essential devices to guide researchers in the definition of their hypotheses due to their ability to provide us with patterns that might be missed when assuming beforehand particular empirical representations of the social phenomena under scrutiny.

Contemporary viewpoints on the importance of theory when combining machine learning with social sciences are the offspring of reflections that also started in the 1980s and the 1990s. In this respect, one of the first proponents of theory building by means of AI has been Bo Anderson. Anderson wrote an interesting manifesto on theory development in sociology through the aid of AI: the modernity of many of his intuitions and positions is remarkable. One of the elements of this modernity is Anderson's call to sociologists for engaging more with the field of AI, reporting a tendency toward intellectual isolation of sociology. In his view, in fact, sociology appeared to be less influenced by the advances made in AI compared to other behavioral sciences and particularly cognitive science, which at the time was closely connected with machine intelligence (Anderson, 1989). These words somehow resonate with many contemporary appeals from social scientists, including very notable criminologists (R. A. Berk & Bleich, 2013) and less popular ones (myself later in this book).

Besides the elements of modernity, Anderson discusses how conceptual analysis and the modeling of complex systems as borrowed from the AI tradition of the time could be relevant contributors to theory development in sociology. Concerning the first aspect, Anderson focuses on the "role" concept, which he describes as one of sociology's most central and controversial topics, connecting it to Minsky's concept of "frame" as a description of domains of interconnected structures of knowledge including a variety of objects, pointing out that the "role" concept used in sociology precisely refers to these Minskian domains. The frame conceptualization proposed by Minsky was a useful tool to represent particular situations composed of different objects, rules, behavioral patterns, and events that could be analytically studied. These situations would range from simple seller-customer relationships to international wars. AI research further refined and formalized Minsky's conceptualization of frames. In this context, Anderson saw the possibility for sociologists to step out of the often-blurred definition of "roles" to practically analyze them through dedicated formalisms and notations. In his view, the need for descriptive completeness required by ad hoc computer languages would push sociologists to think about truthful representations of roles. Moreover, when a role structure is effectively organized, this approach would allow sociologists to directly investigate new research problems. Anderson, in the remainder of his article, provides in this sense a proof-of-concept example focusing on complex political systems. Given the typology of AI described in the article, Anderson's reasoning had many parallelisms with contemporary transdisciplinary research in complex systems to investigate social phenomena.

This type of symbolic and logic perspective, which is of course very different from the current idealization of AI mainly as a data-driven strategy for pattern recognition, was also embraced by Brent (1988). His review of AI contributions to sociological theorizing focused on the representation of knowledge structures to explain social processes and on the expert systems operating through an inductive approach to assist scholars in interpreting data and favoring theoretical reasoning.[4] In this regard, parallelisms with recent calls for a redefinition of the model of social sciences as those made by Grimmer and colleagues (2021) are straightforward. Additionally, Brent posited that AI holds distinctive advantages over mathematical and statistical modeling for exploring qualitative theories, as symbolic AI could in principle check the logical rigor of extant theoretical prepositions. Importantly, Brent not only recognized the importance of expert systems for sociology but also highlighted the relevance of natural language processing, an area that is particularly active in today's computational social science (Bail, 2016; Cardie & Wilkerson, 2008; Edelmann et al., 2020; Goldenstein & Poschmann, 2019). Another common trait between Anderson and Brent is the emphasis given to the translation of sociological concepts into formalisms and, in turn, programming languages. Today, modern languages and software demand little or no effort at all from researchers in reasoning about how to translate qualitative evidence and complex sociological constructs into machine-readable information. During the 1980s and 1990s, however, a combination of factors that included the founding characteristics of the symbolic AI approach and the much lower availability of organized digital data forced researchers to invest considerable amount of intellectual energy on the definition of social entities, mechanisms, dynamics, and behaviors at their very core, as descriptive completeness represented a fundamental gateway to reliable analytic scrutiny via coding formalism.

The progressive evolution from symbolic to connectionist AI is first found in a seminal paper written by Bainbridge and coauthors (1994). In coining the term "Artificial Social Intelligence" – which did not find much fortune over the years – as the field concerned with the applications of machine intelligence methods to the study of social phenomena, the authors provide an overview of state-of-the-art approaches of the time for both theory building and data analysis. This overview is an illuminating retrospective portrait of the paradigmatic shift in AI as, along with applications of symbolic processing and expert systems, we find extensive mentions of AI-aided strategies that we are quite familiar with today. These include "AI-enhanced statistical analysis" by means of neural networks and genetic algorithms for regression and classification purposes. The authors provide a list of advantages of these techniques over traditional statistical methodologies and earlier AI systems based on expert systems, including their higher predictive performance and their ability to handle nonlinearity. Nonetheless, and importantly, they also point out that neural networks come with significant limitations, especially from the perspective of sociological theorizing. Specifically, these are related to the issue of overfitting in presence of scarce amount of data and the low level of interpretability that is an inherent effect of the complex internal mathematical functioning of these algorithms. Again, the connection with our present days is clear-cut: the demand for higher interpretability, transparency, and accountability of algorithmic approaches has longstanding roots.

Furthermore, scholars did not see AI solely as a tool for developing or constructing theories about humans. Interestingly, for instance, Woolgar (1989) criticized the dismissal of a sociological dimension in the study of machine intelligence and proposed to reason about a sociological interpretation of AI as a field. He first called out the tendency to put sociology at the margins of the AI discourse, refusing the attitude of the time to confine the "social" aspects of AI as the mere assessment of societal impacts of intelligent algorithms. Further, he highlighted the importance of a sociology of machines in two directions. First, Woolgar argues that AI could be an interesting area in which to extend the theories and principles of the sociology of scientific knowledge to a technology involving machine entities. Second, the AI phenomenon would allow researchers to discuss and scrutinize one of the "basic axioms of sociology," namely, the fact that human behavior can be represented and viewed as "distinctively social." Albeit AI research in the 1980s was mostly interested in porting human knowledge into machines, Woolgar saw the opportunity to use AI for reassessing our understanding of human behavior and action. Through this dichotomy of directions, Woolgar provocatively asks whether intelligent machines could be treated as subjects of sociological inquiry, somehow paving the way to many topics that are discussed today concerning human-machine interactions (Andras et al., 2018; Muhle, 2016).

Criminology and crime research, unfortunately, lag behind in the theoretical reflections favored by the continuously increasing popularity of machine learning and similar computational methods in the social sciences, because – as I have outlined in the previous subsection – they have mostly seen the machine intelligence framework as a mean to an end. Hopefully, this chapter will help us all revamp the possibilities offered by machine intelligence in this direction. Furthermore, the contents of Chapter 5, which revolves around the mixture of machine learning and causal discovery, will offer in this direction several technical strategies that can be valuable in theory testing and development in the criminology literature of the future.

Seeing machine learning and AI only as a medium for predictive or forecasting purposes means embracing a reductionist approach. Scholarly production on sociological theorizing, and the connections binding the past with the present, should teach us to pay more attention to the possibilities that these methods offer for theoretical reasoning, as their existence pose serious questions that ramify across different dimensions. Not only they can be important for corroborating or falsifying a specific theoretical preposition: machine learning and AI can force us to question the model of the social science and even initiate a discussion on the sociological nature of intelligent machines in a world where machines are increasingly present in criminal justice, policing, and surveillance.

This Book

Rationale

Much has changed since the first contacts between AI, computational sciences, and research on crime. As already mentioned, the shift from symbolic AI to connectionist AI has been decisive for the often-impressive advances made by the field through the years. It has been such a clear and stark shift that we may hardly recognize the systems that were discussed in the 1980s as part of the same field we know today. Yet, they are part of a common story. Perhaps in a less evident fashion, criminology as well has changed in its methodological and often theoretical foundations.

Is then this book only an account of the historical trends that converged from time to time to give rise to nowadays applications, techniques, and problems? Not at all. I started the introduction to this volume with some reflections on the past, and the past will also be central in the second chapter, dedicated to the history of AI. But this book is not a mere historical reconstruction of the legacies we hold today, it is an investigation into the fundamental tension that binds together the past, the present, and the future.

The early days influenced through many different ways and disciplines, the tools, paradigms, theories we govern and exploit today, and the current evolving shape of the relationship between AI and research on crime somehow indicates to us the promises and challenges of the future.

This book hence aims to stimulate a discussion on how to design the future of research on crime by taking advantage of advances in machine intelligence. It does so by transcending the borders of research in the United States and in the Western world, and transcending the borders set by disciplinary boundaries, in the attempt to create stronger connections between all the fields and communities involved in this space.

Structure

The reminder of this book is as follows. The first chapter, entitled "A Short Overview of Artificial Intelligence," will aim at providing the reader with a short but comprehensive historical summary of the heterogeneous field of AI. The first section will draw a historical picture of AI and portray the field as the outcome of centuries (if not millennia) of scientific and philosophical inquiry. A specific focus will be given to the twentieth century, which is the decisive century for the development and engineering of most contemporary AI paradigms and tools. After the historical portray, the section will define AI and review the concepts of Strong AI (known also as Artificial General Intelligence) and Weak AI (also labeled Artificial Narrow Intelligence). These two represent critical concepts for the reader (in particular, the reader who is not familiar with AI) in that they clarify what AI currently stands for in the context of crime research and criminology in general. The second section will build on the concepts detailed in the previous one, defining machine learning and presenting the distinction between Supervised Learning and Unsupervised Learning, providing examples of fundamental techniques used to solve the most typical tasks in this domain, including classification, regression, and clustering. Finally, the second section will also address the most recent developments in AI beyond machine learning, including the success and progresses in deep learning approaches (e.g., object recognition) for offering to the audience an up-to-date summary of the most important trends and breakthroughs achieved by AI.

After having portrayed the main concepts and definitions related to AI, Chapter 3 will picture the evolution of criminology as a discipline now marked by an increasing use of statistical and computational methods that go beyond traditional quantitative methods. The Increasingly Computational Nature of Criminology section will explicitly cover this topic, addressing three main areas that saw significant developments in the past years: crime and geospatial modeling, crime and networks, and crime and simulation methods. In the second section, a quantitative account of the state of the art in the application of AI for studying crime will be provided. The focus will be on the extant literature published in the most important criminology journals and in the most relevant AI and data science venues with the aim to concretely measure trends, topics, and methods in this growing area of research.

Chapter 4 ("To Reframe and Reform: Two Goals and Four Pathways for Increasing Positive Social Impact of Algorithmic Applications in Research on Crime") explicitly reviews two goals and proposes four potential pathways aimed at increasing the positive social impact of approaches to study crime relying on AI. The two goals concern the elimination of the discrimination and disparate impact caused by current algorithmic decision-making systems in criminal justice and policing and the reframing of the focus of computational crime research toward problems, practices, and governance mechanisms that are more inclusive and more effective in protecting weaker strata of the population. The four pathways are instead reflected in four sections.

The first will elaborate on the necessity to create more synergy between the criminology and the computer science communities and beyond, including also all the other disciplines that are contributing to the development of this field of research (e.g., statistics and applied mathematics), providing examples of positive collaborations found in other domains.

The second will instead outline the need for restructuring educational curricula to meet the need for forming and equipping the next generations of scholars, policy-makers, entrepreneurs, and practitioners with critical tools to understand the power and risks associated with algorithmic approaches in the study and prevention of crime. This need will be discussed for what concerns both students enrolled in criminology and computer science programs.

The third will argue that research at the intersection of AI and criminology should expand its scope outside the United States and the Western world, embracing a truly global approach. Technologies deployed to predict crime locations and timings and assess the risk of recidivism first emerged in the United States but have rapidly spread in many countries and regions of the world, including non-democratic contexts. Notwithstanding, research that focuses on such contexts is scant, with most published articles and reports only using US cities as case studies. This subsection will indicate why this represents a shortcoming and a weakness in terms of theory and practice.

The fourth will finally outline the necessity to invest more efforts in trying to study human knowledge and perceptions about the real-world use of algorithmic approaches in crime prevention and criminal justice. Are people aware of their existence? What are the attitudes of people regarding such systems? Can we find sociodemographic, political, economic, and cultural variations in such attitudes? Answering these questions becomes crucial in the pursuit of predicting the future societal trajectory of such technologies.

Chapter 5, entitled "Causal Inference in Criminology and Crime Research and the Promises of Machine Learning," will deal with the potential promises and perspectives offered by machine learning methods (and algorithmic approaches in general) in helping criminologists to detect causal relationships across phenomena of interest. This chapter will be specifically divided into three sections.

In the first, the relationship between criminology and causal discovery will be reviewed, with a discussion building upon Sampson's call against the idea that randomized controlled trials represent the silver-lining for detecting causality in crime-related research problems. The section will also present the main alternatives to pure experimental methods, namely, matching, regression discontinuity design, difference-in-differences, and instrumental variables.

The second section will instead be devoted to the longstanding debate revolving around the idea that machine learning is the ensign of a culture of prediction overlooking inference, explanation, and causal discovery. It will revolve around Leo Breiman's "Two Cultures" argument and will put it into perspective in light of the evolution occurred in the last two decades. In fact, the section will highlight how recent efforts in the AI, statistics, and social science communities led to significant improvements in model explainability and in the ability of algorithms to help to investigate causality.

The third will converge to a unified discussion on the potential of AI, and particularly of machine learning models, in aiding criminologists in their quest for causal discovery. Several recent breakthroughs will be covered to offer an exhaustive horizon of possibilities to the reader, mostly concentrating on heterogeneous causal effects, the promises and pitfalls of simulation methods for causality, and causality tools for temporal and network data.

Finally, Chapter 6 will offer some final remarks and reflections concerning what are (or should be) the main takeaways of this book, hoping that beyond the events that will characterize the future, some of the messages will remain to the readers of this book.

Notes

1 The hendiadys "criminology and crime research" and "criminologists and crime researchers" will be maintained throughout this book: they serve the purpose to consider together core criminological works and problems and all the scholarship that deals with crime from other disciplinary perspectives, such as economics, sociology, political science, and, inevitably, statistics and computer science. When the reader encounters the generic expression "research on crime," this will instead intend both criminology and crime research, to syntactically alternate references throughout the volume. While theoretical prepositions or methodological traditions may differ, the contents here presented should be of interest to a heterogeneous audience. This book is not aimed at criminologists only, it seeks to favor instead a more comprehensive approach to the study of crime: strict boundaries between disciplines that share the same interests are only detrimental to the ability to initiate an organic discussion.

2 Interesting discussions on the pitfalls of the concept of "novelty" in scientific production can be found in Cohen (2017), Rehman (2018), Oreskes (2021), and Burghardt and Bodanski (2021).

3 The program, deployed in 2013 by the Chicago Police Department, was called "Strategic Subject List": it provided estimates for a list of people that were deemed to be at high risk of gun violence, aiming at preventive intervention by law enforcement.

4 Some of the works reviewed by Brent include the interplay between social structures and cognitive structures in knowledge acquisition and decision-making (Carley, 1986a, 1986b), inductive theoretical development through expert systems (E. E. Brent, 1986; Garson, 1987), theory development and causality (Glymour et al., 1987), as well as logic programming and theory development, testing, and expanding (Sylvan & Glassner, 1985; E. E. Brent et al., 1989).

References

Anderson, B. (1989). On artificial intelligence and theory construction in sociology. *The Journal of Mathematical Sociology, 14*(2–3), 209–216. https://doi.org/10.108 0/0022250X.1989.9990050.

Andras, P., Esterle, L., Guckert, M., Han, T. A., Lewis, P. R., Milanovic, K., Payne, T., Perret, C., Pitt, J., Powers, S. T., Urquhart, N., & Wells, S. (2018). Trusting intelligent machines: Deepening trust within socio-technical systems. *IEEE Technology and Society Magazine, 37*(4), 76–83. https://doi.org/10.1109/MTS.2018.2876107.

Bail, C. A. (2016). Combining natural language processing and network analysis to examine how advocacy organizations stimulate conversation on social media. *Proceedings of the National Academy of Sciences, 113*(42), 11823–11828. https://doi.org/10.1073/pnas.1607151113.

Bainbridge, W. S., Brent, E. E., Carley, K. M., Heise, D. R., Macy, M. W., Markovsky, B., & Skvoretz, J. (1994). Artificial social intelligence. *Annual Review of Sociology, 20*(1), 407–436. https://doi.org/10.1146/annurev.so.20.080194.002203.

Baker, R. S., & Hawn, A. (2021). Algorithmic bias in education. *EdArXiv.* https://doi.org/10.35542/osf.io/pbmvz.

Barabas, C., Virza, M., Dinakar, K., Ito, J., & Zittrain, J. (2018). Interventions over predictions: Reframing the ethical debate for actuarial risk assessment. In *Proceedings of the 1st conference on fairness, accountability and transparency,* 62–76. https://proceedings.mlr.press/v81/barabas18a.html

Berk, R. (2019). *Machine learning risk assessments in criminal justice settings.* Springer International Publishing. https://doi.org/10.1007/978-3-030-02272-3.

Berk, R. A., & Bleich, J. (2013). Statistical procedures for forecasting criminal behavior. *Criminology & Public Policy, 12*(3), 513–544. https://doi.org/10.1111/1745-9133.12047.

Berk, R., & Elzarka, A. A. (2020). Almost politically acceptable criminal justice risk assessment. *Criminology & Public Policy, 19*(4), 1231–1257. https://doi.org/10.1111/1745-9133.12500.

Berman, D. H. (1989). Cutting legal loops. In *Proceedings of the 2nd international conference on artificial intelligence and law,* 251–258. https://doi.org/10.1145/74014.74046.

Berman, D. H., & Hafner, C. D. (1987). Indeterminacy: A challenge to logic-based models of legal reasoning. *International Review of Law, Computers & Technology, 3*(1), 1–35. https://doi.org/10.1080/13600869.1987.9966251.

Berman, D. H., & Hafner, C. D. (1988). Obstacles to the development of logic-based models of legal reasoning. In C. Walter (Ed.), *Computer power and legal language: The use of computational models in linguistics, artificial intelligence, and expert systems in the law.* Quorum Books.

Berman, D. H., & Hafner, C. D. (1989). The potential of artificial intelligence to help solve the crisis in our legal system. *Communications of the ACM, 32*(8), 928–938. https://doi.org/10.1145/65971.65972.

Berman, D. H., & Hafner, C. D. (1993). Representing teleological structure in case-based legal reasoning: The missing link. In *Proceedings of the 4th international conference on artificial intelligence and law,* 50–59. https://doi.org/10.1145/158976.158982.

Berman, D. H., & Hafner, C. D. (1995). Understanding precedents in a temporal context of evolving legal doctrine. In *Proceedings of the 5th international conference on artificial intelligence and law,* 42–51. https://doi.org/10.1145/222092.222116.

Breiman, L. (2001). Statistical modeling: The two cultures (with comments and a rejoinder by the author). *Statistical Science, 16*(3), 199–231. https://doi.org/10.1214/ss/1009213726.

Brent, E. (1988). Is there a role for artificial intelligence in sociological theorizing? *The American Sociologist, 19*(2), 158–166.

Brent, E. E. (1986). Knowledge-based systems: A qualitative formalism. *Qualitative Sociology, 9*(3), 256–282. https://doi.org/10.1007/BF00988401.

Brent, E. E., Glazier, J., Jamtgaard, K., Wetzel, E., Hall, P. M., Dalecki, M., & Bah, A. (1989). Erving: A program to teach sociological reasoning from the dramaturgical perspective. *Teaching Sociology, 17*(1), 38–48. https://doi.org/10.2307/1317923.

Browning, M., & Arrigo, B. (2021). Stop and risk: Policing, data, and the digital age of discrimination. *American Journal of Criminal Justice, 46*(2), 298–316. https://doi.org/10.1007/s12103-020-09557-x.

Burghardt, J., & Bodansky, A. N. (2021). Why psychology needs to stop striving for novelty and how to move towards theory-driven research. *Frontiers in Psychology, 12,* 67. https://doi.org/10.3389/fpsyg.2021.609802.

Cardie, C., & Wilkerson, J. (2008). Text annotation for political science research. *Journal of Information Technology & Politics, 5*(1), 1–6. https://doi.org/10.1080/19331680802149590.

Carley, K. (1986a). Knowledge acquisition as a social phenomenon. *Instructional Science, 14*(3), 381–438. https://doi.org/10.1007/BF00051829.

Carley, K. (1986b). An approach for relating social structure to cognitive structure. *The Journal of Mathematical Sociology*, 12(2), 137–189. https://doi.org/10.1080/0022250X.1986.9990010.

Cohen, B. A. (2017). How should novelty be valued in science? *ELife*, 6, e28699. https://doi.org/10.7554/eLife.28699.

Douglas, T., Pugh, J., Singh, I., Savulescu, J., & Fazel, S. (2017). Risk assessment tools in criminal justice and forensic psychiatry: The need for better data. *European Psychiatry*, 42, 134–137. https://doi.org/10.1016/j.eurpsy.2016.12.009.

Dressel, J., & Farid, H. (2018). The accuracy, fairness, and limits of predicting recidivism. *Science Advances*, 4(1), eaao5580. https://doi.org/10.1126/sciadv.aao5580.

Edelmann, A., Wolff, T., Montagne, D., & Bail, C. A. (2020). Computational social science and sociology. *Annual Review of Sociology*, 46(1), 61–81. https://doi.org/10.1146/annurev-soc-121919-054621.

Fogliato, R., Chouldechova, A., & G'Sell, M. (2020). Fairness evaluation in presence of biased noisy labels. In *Proceedings of the twenty-third international conference on artificial intelligence and statistics*, 2325–2336. https://proceedings.mlr.press/v108/fogliato20a.html

Garson, G. D. (1987). The role of inductive expert systems generators in the social science research process. *Social Science Microcomputer Review*, 5(1), 11–24. https://doi.org/10.1177/089443938700500102.

Glymour, C., Scheines, R., Spirtes, P., & Kelly, K. (1987). *Discovering causal structure: Artificial intelligence, philosophy of science, and statistical modeling* (pp. xvii, 394). Academic Press.

Goldenstein, J., & Poschmann, P. (2019). A quest for transparent and reproducible text-mining methodologies in computational social science. *Sociological Methodology*, 49(1), 144–151. https://doi.org/10.1177/0081175019867855.

Green, B. (2018). "Fair" risk assessments: A precarious approach for criminal justice reform. In *5th workshop on fairness, accountability, and transparency in machine learning (FAT/ML 2018)*. https://www.fatml.org/media/documents/fair_risk_assessments_criminal_justice.pdf

Green, B. (2020). The false promise of risk assessments: Epistemic reform and the limits of fairness. In *Proceedings of the 2020 conference on fairness, accountability, and transparency*, 594–606. https://doi.org/10.1145/3351095.3372869.

Grimmer, J., Roberts, M. E., & Stewart, B. M. (2021). Machine learning for social science: An agnostic approach. *Annual Review of Political Science*, 24(1), 395–419. https://doi.org/10.1146/annurev-polisci-053119-015921.

Hernandez, A. P. (1990). Artificial intelligence and expert systems in law enforcement: Current and potential uses. *Computers, Environment and Urban Systems*, 14(4), 299–306. https://doi.org/10.1016/0198-9715(90)90004-D.

Icove, D. J. (1986). Automated crime profiling. *FBI Law Enforcement Bulletin*, 55(27), 27–30.

Lawlor, R. C. (1963). What computers can do: Analysis and prediction of judicial decisions. *American Bar Association Journal*, 49(4), 337–344.

Molina, M., & Garip, F. (2019). Machine learning for sociology. *Annual Review of Sociology*, 45(1), 27–45. https://doi.org/10.1146/annurev-soc-073117-041106.

Muhle, F. (2016). Embodied conversational agents as social actors? Sociological considerations on the change of human-machine relations in online environments. In *Social bots and their friends*. Routledge.

Oreskes, N. (2021). Why bad science is sometimes more appealing than good science. *Scientific American*. https://www.scientificamerican.com/article/why-bad-science-is-sometimes-more-appealing-than-good-science/

Raghavan, M., Barocas, S., Kleinberg, J., & Levy, K. (2020). Mitigating bias in algorithmic hiring: Evaluating claims and practices. In *Proceedings of the 2020 conference on fairness, accountability, and transparency*, 469–481. https://doi.org/10.1145/3351095.3372828.

Ratledge, E. C., & Jacoby, J. E. (1989). *Handbook of artificial intelligence and expert systems in law enforcement*. Https://delcat.worldcat.org/title/handbook-on-artificial-intelligence-and-expert-systems-in-law-enforcement/oclc/19554021. New York : Greenwood Press. https://udspace.udel.edu/handle/19716/21756

Rehman, J. (2018). Novelty in science – Real necessity or distracting obsession? *The Conversation*. https://theconversation.com/novelty-in-science-real-necessity-or-distracting-obsession-84032

Ridgeway, G. (2013). Linking prediction and prevention. *Criminology & Public Policy*, 12(3), 545–550. https://doi.org/10.1111/1745-9133.12057.

Saunders, J., Hunt, P., & Hollywood, J. S. (2016). Predictions put into practice: A quasi-experimental evaluation of Chicago's predictive policing pilot. *Journal of Experimental Criminology*, 12(3), 347–371. https://doi.org/10.1007/s11292-016-9272-0.

Susskind, R. E. (1986). Expert systems in law: A jurisprudential approach to artificial intelligence and legal reasoning. *The Modern Law Review*, 49(2), 168–194.

Sylvan, D. J., & Glassner, B. (1985). *A rationalist methodology for the social sciences*. Blackwell Pub.

Tafoya, W. L. (1991). Book review: Handbook on artificial intelligence and expert systems in law enforcement. *Criminal Justice Review*, 16(1), 134–136. https://doi.org/10.1177/073401689101600133.

Tolan, S., Miron, M., Gómez, E., & Castillo, C. (2019). Why machine learning may lead to unfairness: Evidence from risk assessment for juvenile justice in Catalonia. In *Proceedings of the seventeenth international conference on artificial intelligence and law*, 83–92. https://doi.org/10.1145/3322640.3326705.

Ugwudike, P. (2020). Digital prediction technologies in the justice system: The implications of a 'race-neutral' agenda. *Theoretical Criminology*, 24(3), 482–501. https://doi.org/10.1177/1362480619896006.

Weizenbaum, J. (1977). *Computer power and human reason: From judgement to calculation* (new edizione). W H Freeman & Co.

Wiener, F. B. (1962). Decision prediction by computers: Nonsense cubed—and worse. *American Bar Association Journal*, 48(11), 1023–1028.

Woolgar, S. (1989). Why not a sociology of machines? An evaluation of prospects for an association between sociology and artificial intelligence. In *Intelligent systems in a human context: Development, implications, and applications* (pp. 53–70). Oxford University Press, Inc.

2

A COLLECTIVE JOURNEY

A Short Overview on Artificial Intelligence

Introduction

The task of summarizing the history of artificial intelligence (AI) in few pages is one of those challenges that face the risk of becoming insulting. I will do my best to condensate decades – centuries, or even millennia, actually – of developments in a compact way, aiming at offering an overall description, especially to those who do not have a background in computer science and other disciplines more closely related to AI.

This task is coupled with another one: the attempt to go beyond the historical perspective to meaningfully introduce the reader to the main guiding concepts behind AI and machine learning, further presenting the current state of the field. AI is so tremendously quick in its evolution that the "current state of the field" might be outdated by the time this book is published, and each topic, concept, breakthrough, or failure touched throughout the next pages would easily require an entire library to be studied properly. I hence ask the reader to keep in mind that none of what will be read in this chapter should be regarded as exhaustive or comprehensive.

Nonetheless, this book is centered around the peculiar and rapidly evolving relationship between AI and research on crime and it is thus necessary to provide at least an overview of the pathways that led to the stage(s) in which we are today, as they are critical to facilitate a broader reasoning on the complexity and multifaceted nature of AI, both in absolute terms and in conjunction with research on criminal behaviors and phenomena. The aim at the core of this chapter is to provide the reader with a roadmap constellated by key ideas and concepts that can help in orienting a curious mind in this fascinating (and intellectually demanding) space.

Describing current trends or discussing future perspectives without having a remote idea of the many pieces that contributed directly and indirectly to the rapid diffusion of algorithms and the explosion of hype around machine learning would be useless, or even deleterious.

This chapter will therefore first provide an overview on the history of AI, followed by a discussion of the conceptual and factual separation between weak and strong AI as the outcome of the mixture between breakthroughs

DOI: 10.4324/9781003217732-2

and failures in the field during the twentieth century. After that, the ideas behind machine learning will be presented, with a specific focus of two distinct sets of approaches, namely, supervised and unsupervised learning. Finally, the concluding section will be dedicated to major advancements in deep learning as the most recent and most enduring frontier in artificial intelligence, trying to summarize the most promising developments and accomplishments in AI at large.

A Long Journey – An Historical Account of AI

A Tale of Many Tales

Trying to map and describe the tumultuous history of AI cannot be done without acknowledging the many different scientific souls contributing to this quest. AI as a field of inquiry cannot be reduced to a singular entity: as often happens in science, the creation of ideas, their consolidation, and the formation of a field result from collective efforts. This "collectivity" not only regards scientists at the individual level, through their scholarly cooperation, but also concerns the higher level interconnections between disciplines, fields, and schools of thought. This is, after all, valid also for criminology. Criminology and crime research as we know them now are undoubtedly the resulting process of decades of dialogues, exchange, and discussion between many different souls, including sociology, psychology, political science, economics, and statistics. AI, in this context, is probably one of the supreme testimonies to the importance of contamination in reading, understanding, and describing the scientific process.

The twentieth century – and particularly the second part of the twentieth century – is generally seen as the timeframe in which the most important ideas in AI emerged and the pioneers came together to create the field from the ground up. I tend to believe – as many others that are more influential than me – that solely focusing on the twentieth century rather limiting. Disregarding what happened before leads to an incomplete and myopic view on what AI actually is and what AI crucially seeks to accomplish.

In this sense, Russel and Norvig, in the first pages of their "Artificial Intelligence – A Modern Approach" – one of the most relevant, read, and inspiring books that have been written on AI – list which disciplines have most contributed to AI as a field. These are philosophy, mathematics, economics, neuroscience, psychology, computer engineering, control theory and cybernetics, and linguistics. One might even argue that other disciplines should be added, especially in light of the most recent milestones in AI (what about physics?), but I agree with them that these represent those disciplines that contributed most to the formation, consolidation, and exploration of the key questions and the key perspectives in the field.

The intricated patchwork defined by all these disciplines places the origins of the intellectual journey that led to nowadays AI thousands of years before the moment this book is written. Goodfellow, Bengio, and Courville even cite Galathea, Talos, and Pandora as examples of artificial lives, dating back to ancient Greece (Goodfellow et al., 2017). Russell and Norvig (2010) instead report how Aristotle first proposed a set of laws that govern the rational dimension of the mind, becoming the first contributor from the philosophical side to the AI journey, and how Ktesibios of Alexandria was the first to create a self-controlling machine, becoming the first pioneer from the control theory and cybernetics barricade. When we think of both the philosophical position of Aristotle and the engineering solution of Ktesibios of Alexandria and we put their efforts and achievements in comparison with the current state of AI, the link between the present and the past might not result immediately self-explanatory. However, if one frames this link in the context of millennia of collective efforts to satisfy the human interest in understanding what governs, defines, and constitutes intelligence and what can be created and simulated using intelligence, its relevance should become much more evident.

It took some time to move from the laws of Aristotle to the idea that an artifact of mechanical nature could produce reasoning, and in this sense, Russell and Norvig highlight the role that Lull, Hobbes, and Leonardo da Vinci all had in connecting reasoning with numerical computation, paving the way to the actual construction of calculating machines by Schickard, Pascal, and Leibniz in the seventeenth century.

The tangible attempts to produce artifacts for reasoning do not exhaust the contribution of philosophy. In fact, centuries of history are adorned with intellectual wrestling on the nature of mind, the relationship between mind and matter, and the principles of knowledge. From rationalism to dualism, materialism, empiricism, and up to logical positivism in the twentieth century, many schools of philosophical inquiry have helped stimulate the debate and build the intellectual premises for the study of algorithms, the proposal of computational theories of mind, and the origins of knowledge. It would be wrong to confine philosophy's contribution to AI in the past. Philosophy is still continuing to foster new questions and open new perspectives to the investigation of profoundly critical issues, including algorithmic ethics, singularity, and existential threats (Bostrom & Yudkowsky, 2014; Eden et al., 2012; Müller, 2020).

While Russell and Norvig acknowledge the role of philosophy as a fundamental engine for generating relevant questions and producing cornerstone ideas for AI, they also point out that a sophisticated level of formalism was (and is) needed to move from theory – or, say, a certain type of theory – to practice. Mathematics, and particularly logic, computation, and probability, have filled this void, becoming the fundamental alphabet of AI as a science. Gödel and Russell have deeply influenced the "logical" dimension of mathematics in AI. The former, through his incompleteness theorems, has been the first to show that there exist functions that cannot be computed (Gödel, 1931). And there comes the link between the "logical" dimension of mathematics in AI and the "computational" one, as Gödel contributions pushed Turing to investigate what functions can be deemed as computable and what instead are not. Computability, moving from logic, led to the problem of tractability, which posed the question of studying what problems can only be solved in exponential time. Tractability, and the theory of NP-completeness, fueled profound scientific efforts around the theoretical and practical limits posed by problems that are intractable, forcing the AI community to rescale expectations and excessive optimism. The third dimension, namely, "probabilistic" mathematics, represents nowadays the core essence of the functioning of virtually every algorithm developed and deployed in AI. The necessity of algorithms to make decisions with incomplete information and, in general, the necessity to deal with uncertainty in every learning mechanism requires the probabilistic paradigm in contrast with deterministic approaches that are inherently ineffective in capturing the complexity of every process that deals with knowledge.

Mathematics contributed to shed light on the required formal mechanisms to draw valid conclusions, investigated the limits of computation, and reasoned on the strategies to deal with uncertainty and its related complexity. In relation to this last aspect, economics had an irrefutable influence to connect uncertainty with utility, and, more in general, with the need for agents (both natural and artificial) to maximize the payoffs deriving from their actions. Notably, decision theory (which integrates utility theory and probability), game theory, and operations research strongly advanced our understanding of the behaviors of "rational" agents. The intellectual perspectives posed by breakthroughs in these three areas increased the attention and interest of scientists on many new problems, including those arising in multi-agent systems and reinforcement learning, where artificial agents are programmed to take rational decisions and maximize certain objective functions (or minimize cost ones), mimicking strategic reasoning of animals, including humans.

The study of reasoning in animals has been a core topic in the quest for AI, and neuroscience offered in this regard the opportunity to grasp insights on how nervous systems work. How brains process relevant information for making decisions and taking actions is a central problem in neuroscience that has become more and more central also in AI, especially in the twentieth century, where the first mathematical and computational models trying to reproduce brain functioning were proposed to the scientific community (McCulloch & Pitts, 1943; Rashevsky, 1936; Rosenblatt, 1958), building on earlier work on brain neuronal structure (Ramón y Cajal, 1899). Although still many questions remain unsolved, the amazing advancements in neuroscience during the last century helped AI researchers in their efforts to recreate artificial entities that resemble the functioning of human brains, culminating with the emergence of artificial neural networks which, albeit with alternating fortune, finally become central in the AI landscape.

Closely related to neuroscience, psychology primarily influenced AI through research in cognitive psychology, which incorporates an information processing dimension in the study of brains. Decades of debates, experiments, and discussions, coupled with the increasing diffusion of computers and the consequent growing use of computer modeling, gave birth to cognitive science, which Russell and Norvig link to three seminal studies by Miller (1956), Chomsky (1956), and Newell and Simon (1956) - what a year, right? Cognitive science has addressed topics such as memory, language, and logical reasoning, shedding light on the potential of computational models to define and imitate psychological processes effectively.

Computers represent the artifact through which investigating AI problems. Without computers as a means, we could not go beyond the mere phases of theoretical speculation of formalization. The history of computer engineering is therefore essential to comprehend the mix of failures and successes achieved by AI research so far. This history has two sides, the hardware and the software ones. The hardware side narrates the evolution from calculating devices such as those designed by Jacquard and Babbage, passing through the first operational computer constructed by Alan Turing in 1940, up to the worldwide diffusion of increasingly powerful machines. Nowadays, computers possess unprecedented levels of speed and memory at accessible costs, with current trends pointing in the directions of parallelization and quantum computing to solve the structural limits posed by power dissipation. On the other side, the software history of computer engineering offered a wide spectrum of languages and tools to transpose formalisms and ideas into programs, libraries, and toolboxes.

The compelling panoramic proposed by Norvig and Russel concludes with the recognition of the impact that control theory and cybernetics and linguistics had on AI. Control theory and cybernetics seek to understand how computers function under their own control and therefore without the need for an animal entity to intervene in a given process. The contributions of Wiener (1961), McCulloch and Pitts (1943), and von Neumann and Burks (1967) have been enormous in this area, along with Ashby (1956), Turing (1937), and Grey Walter (1950). They laid the foundations of modern control theory and stochastic optimal control in which intelligent systems seek to behave optimally and stably, similarly to what − at least in principle − humans do.

Finally, the link between linguistics and AI can be traced back to the opposing views of Skinner (1948) and Chomsky (1957) on language learning, which marked the end of the behaviorist theory of language proposed by the former in favor of the latter's formalized theory of linguistic structure. Chomsky's work had a profound influence on computer scientists, and its formalism resonates with the approaches taken by computational linguistics and natural language processing, two intertwined areas that are currently sparking massive interest in the AI community. The importance of language for AI is explained by its connection with awareness, understanding, and, ultimately, thought.

As this summary borrowed from Russel and Norvig's approach demonstrates, AI is a tale of many, many stories. Furthermore, as already mentioned, I am not entirely convinced this list fully grasps the variety of disciplines that significantly contributes to AI. It is probably safe to say that this is an accurate portrait of those that influenced the field up until the second part of the twentieth century, but nowadays the picture looks even more diverse. The AI relationship with physics, for instance, is having a crucial impact in redefining old problems or discovering new ones, both from theoretical and practical perspectives (Dunjko & Briegel, 2018; Guest et al., 2018; Trabesinger, 2017). At the same time, behavioral and social sciences other than psychology and economics have started to engage more systematically with the kaleidoscope of AI. As this journey is incomplete, I find it hard to exclude a particular discipline as completely useless in the quest of AI. While in most cases we only tend to think in unidirectional terms, meaning that we only see the potential gains or benefits that AI could offer in a specific application field, we tend to overlook the potential hidden in mutual links between AI and such application fields, e.g., the social sciences. In a mutual relationship, a given field of application may give new insights about knowledge and intelligence, then creating a new bidirectional exchange that can ultimately contribute to the evolution of AI in the present. An AI application in fine arts might reveal new insights on how humans perceive beauty, and how this subjective concept leads to tangible decisions. Similarly, an AI application in criminology might offer new perspectives to think about malicious human behaviors, and therefore also malicious machine intelligence. The journey is incomplete and ever-changing. Thus, what the reader should keep in mind is that this book is really about contamination and collective efforts and that AI cannot be simplistically seen as a closed, unitary, homogeneous mission.

The Twentieth Century: In Search of a Unifying Tale

What happened before the twentieth century is surely important to frame, contextualize, and understand more recent developments in AI. However, it is undeniable that the twentieth century represents the fundamental time frame in which AI became a field and in which its backbone of ideas, breakthroughs, and advancements has been engineered. Chanting the achievements only would be a betrayal of the truth: the period that started roughly around 1943 and continued up to the 2000s (and then again up to our days) has been a rollercoaster of monstrous discoveries and thunderous failures. The optimism has been replaced by discomfort and resignation several times, and like an Arab Phoenix, AI returned with new ideas, new perspectives, and new approaches every time.

The community has not reached a universal agreement regarding what should be flagged as the first AI work ever published. Two are usually the most recurring ones, and they have been both published before the term "AI" was even coined.

The first one, in chronological order, has been the seminal paper by McCulloch and Pitts (1943) in which they proposed the first computational model of an artificial neural network functioning on a threshold mechanism. The threshold mechanism – entrenched in Boolean logic – aimed at resembling the way in which neurons are activated in the human brain, and the work in general sought to provide a description of how interconnected neurons work together to produce complex patterns. McCulloch and Pitts also demonstrated that these connected neurons can actually compute every computable function and had the merit to inspire subsequent works on artificial neural networks that are still influential today. Hebb (1949), for instance, advanced the McCulloch and Pitts model based on the threshold mechanism to let neural networks learn. The so-called "Hebbian learning" builds on a neural mechanism for learning, set forth by Hebb himself, that substantially posits that neurons that are activated simultaneously are also connected together. This means that the more a learning stimulus is repeated, the stronger the connection becomes, implying a form of "weight update" rule that becomes the first influential attempt at modeling the concept of "learning" in a computational model.

Besides Hebbian learning, at the beginning of the 1950s, Minsky and Edmonds constructed the first neural network computer simulating a network of 40 neurons (see Knight, 2015). Furthermore, in 1958 Rosenblatt created the "Perceptron," which is generally regarded as the first proper software of an artificial feedforward neural network, with the possibility of involving multiple layers – anticipating the philosophy of deep learning (Rosenblatt, 1958).

The second AI work that is generally regarded as foundational in AI is "Computing Machinery and Intelligence," by Alan Turing (1950). The paper starts with a question that still vigorously resonates to date and that was somehow already roaming across centuries:[1] *"Can machines think?"* In his seminal article, Turing tries to redefine such a question by proposing a way to determine whether machines can act as ourselves, intended as thinking entities. He hence presents the so-called "imitation game," which will be later rebranded "Turing test." The game consists of three main entities: a person, a machine, and an interrogator. The interrogator is located separately from the person and the machine, and the interrogator has to determine which is the machine between the other two subjects. The interrogator poses questions to the two entities, and the object for the machine is to fool the interrogator by making them think it is the person. If a machine passes the test, Turing advances the idea that there is probabilistic support for the intelligence hypothesis. The Turing test has become the object of lively debates across fields and disciplines, beyond the mere boundaries of computer science, and over the decades dozens of researchers have proposed variations to address limitations of the test in its attempt to measure machine intelligence (Epstein et al., 2009; Marcus et al., 2016; Pinar Saygin et al., 2000). Besides introducing the imitation game, however, it is worth noting that the article delves into other fascinating concepts concerning machine intelligence, including a discussion on the promises of digital computers and a review of nine different objections that he anticipates could be made to his view on machine intelligence.

If scholars have not found universal agreement on which one should be regarded as the first "AI" work, there is much less debate around the event that symbolically marked the beginning of the field. In 1955, John McCarthy proposed the name "Artificial Intelligence" to describe the new field concerned with the theory and practice of thinking machines. In the same year, McCarthy, along with Marvin Minsky, Nathaniel Rochester, and Claude Shannon, asked funding for a workshop to discuss topics related to machine intelligence, including neural networks, computers, and theoretical perspectives on computation (McCarthy et al., 1955). The workshop, whose official name was "Dartmouth Summer Research Project on Artificial Intelligence," was held in 1956 at Darmouth College, in New Hampshire, for an estimated period of eight weeks, giving birth – especially from a symbolic point of view – to AI.

The attendees to the workshop included, besides the organizers, Arthur Samuel, Ray Solomonoff, Oliver Selfridge, Trenchard More, Herbert Simon, and Allen Newell. The enthusiasm characterizing those months is well represented by Newell and Simon's presentation of their reasoning program, called the Logic Theory Machine (1956), which was able to prove mathematical theorems. In unfolding the program, Newell and Simon claimed to have finally solved the mind-body problem by creating a software that could think in non-numerical form. Such a position underlines that machines can have minds that are indistinguishable from human ones, paving the way to the "Strong AI" line of thought (see the next section for further details). Decades after, the most important heritage of the workshop does not lie in technical breakthroughs but, rather, in the opportunity for the major figures in computer science, cognitive science, mathematics, cybernetics, and related fields to meet each other, initiating a phase of incredible optimism for the newly created field of AI.

The following two decades were marked by a series of important achievements that ignited unprecedented enthusiasm in AI. Newell, Shaw, and Simon presented the General Problem Solver (GPS), which appeared as a consequence of the Logic Theory Machine work (Newell et al., 1959). The GPS was a computer program that sought to solve problems imitating humans: specifically, its approach consisted in a "means-end analysis" revolving around the resolution of sub-problems. The GPS used the idea of recursion and can be thought of as a sort of hierarchical process built on the sequential resolution of such sub-problems until the final problem is properly solved. Besides the GPS, other notable breakthroughs were the Geometry Theorem Prover, engineered by Gelernter (1959), the checkers programs by Arthur Samuel (1959), the creation of the LISP language (McCarthy, 1960b) which became the standard AI language for the following decades, the invention of time sharing to overcome scarcity of computational resources, and the formulation of the Advice Taker (McCarthy, 1960a), regarded as the first complete AI system. After moving from MIT to Stanford, Minsky also helped advance knowledge on machine intelligence by focusing on general-purpose methods for logical reasoning. In the early 1960s, research on neural networks grew as well, inspired by the early works of McCulloch and Pitts (Widrow, 1960; Widrow & Hoff, 1960).

Starting in the 1960s, AI researchers also started to consistently work on the so-called "expert systems," which were deemed to be computer programs able to emulate the decision-making ability of humans in specific contexts. Proposed as an alternative to the dominant problem-solving philosophy implying the solution of tasks through search mechanisms directed toward the solution of elementary tasks, expert systems worked through the exploitation of knowledge-based mechanisms applied to narrower problems. The areas in which expert systems attracted much interest were biology and medicine. The two applications that first fostered promising interest appeared during the 1970s. The DENDRAL program, for instance, attempted to predict molecular structure using data coming from a mass spectrometer (Buchanan & Lederberg, 1971). MYCIN was instead a program intended to diagnose infections through bacteria identification (Shortliffe, 1977). In addition, the diffusion of knowledge-based approaches fueled interest in language modeling, laying the foundations of research in natural language processing as we know it today (Weischedel et al., 1978; Wilks, 1972).

In spite of these important results, the community faced substantial funding cuts between 1974 and 1980. Most of the optimistic appeals for the imminent creation of machine intelligence indistinguishable from human intelligence were not followed by proper results, and this led major investors – including the US government – to step back from the race toward AI. Some of the major problems faced by researchers working in the field during those years were the absence of machine knowledge on subject matter, computers' limited computational power, and the intractability of many of the problems investigated.

Expert systems, however, largely contributed to the comeback of conspicuous funding by governments and corporations, which saw a revived opportunity in the intelligent systems that were engineered and distributed during the early 1980s. Not long after this new "peak" in the interest in AI, the reinvention of back-propagation prompted a vigorous return of neural networks and particularly the connectionist approach (Rumelhart et al., 1986). This approach rapidly became the alternative paradigm to symbolic AI. Although for long scholars have wrestled around symbolic and connectionist AI, Minsky argued that a complementary approach should be preferred anticipating the current sentiment of part of the AI community on the fundamental question on how to build machine intelligence (1991). It is well worth briefly explaining what symbolic and connectionist AI are to avoid leaving the reader in the dark on this important distinction. These two different paradigms – or perspectives – are rooted in the early debates in cognitive science on how cognition and reasoning happen and how to represent them.

Symbolic AI fundamentally represents information via symbols and their relationships, and it works via propositional calculus in which propositions define features of the world. In turn, relationships between such features are described through connectives. Symbolic AI then aimed to encode human reasoning and knowledge through rules and facts with manipulation of these symbols as the key to achieving machine intelligence (Thomason, 2020).

On the other hand, the connectionist perspective precisely builds upon the distributed representation of information inspired by the organization and relationships between neurons and synapses (Buckner & Garson, 2019). Information is thus processed through connections between collections of simple processing units, enabling parallel computation and adaptive connectivity patterns that ultimately allow one to learn to decode complex representations and solve tasks.

Beyond the alternate fortunes of expert systems and the emergence of connectionism, the 1980s have been important for the history of AI because they marked the moment in which the community started to move significantly in the direction of empirical validation, leaving behind a tradition of theoretical speculation (Russell & Norvig, 2010). It is only with the second part of the 1980s that researchers finally started to evaluate the validity of hypotheses and the performance of algorithms intended to solve specific tasks by means of statistical metrics and robustness protocols. While before works in AI were mostly intended to propose new theories or construct new machines from the ground up, the trends between the 1980s and the 1990s started to change, with more rigorous validation and a deeper focus on the quantitative assessment of algorithmic performance.

In the meantime, the initial spectacular results of expert systems and knowledge-based programs were progressively shadowed by the issues at the very core of their functioning, in spite of major breakthroughs which had a considerable public echo, like Deep Blue, the first computer program able to beat a reigning world chess champion (Campbell et al., 2002). Expert systems needed a massive amount of information and expertise, which was costly to translate into symbolic language in terms of time and resources. Furthermore, expert systems were only good at addressing a specific task, somehow dismissing the original quest for "machines that think" of the AI community.

The fall of interest in expert systems, the increasing power of machines, and the growth in automated and digital data across a wide range of fields all played a role in the evolution of AI occurred from the mid-1990s to date. First came the "intelligent agent" paradigm, facilitated by the integration of AI with decision theory and economics (Russell & Norvig, 2010). One of the works that marked this decisive passage was Judea Pearl's "Probabilistic Reasoning in Intelligent Systems" (1988). After the dissolution of hopes in expert systems, the machine learning revolution occurred, decisively stimulated by the shift from knowledge-based approaches to data-driven ones. Before delving into it, however, we necessarily need to take a step back and finally address the question: "what is AI?"

Defining Artificial Intelligence – Weak versus Strong AI

I cannot recall a single phenomenon I encountered in my journey since the beginning of my university studies that could be described by a single, universally agreed definition. Decades of debates can emerge from the nuances differentiating two definitions of the same concept. Without any surprise, AI is no exception. The number of definitions associated with AI is massive, especially favored by the skyrocketing hype on intelligent algorithms of the last decade, a decade in which the fundamental question of finding a concise answer to the "what is AI?" question saw the increasing participation of people outside computer sciences or even outside academia. Some are elegant and thought-provoking; others only reflect AI's crude business side as an industry. A safe start to avoid the noise and impromptu of hype-dependent and time-dependent definitions is relying on John McCarthy's one, who first coined the term "Artificial Intelligence" in 1955:

> (Artificial Intelligence) is the science and engineering of making intelligent machines.

This definition may appear too broad, leaving the reader to wonder what machines are and, most importantly, what "intelligent" really means. McCarthy (2007) himself helps in clarifying part of our questions and doubts, by specifying that machines have to be intended as "intelligent computer programs," and that intelligence is "the computational part of the ability to achieve goals in the world," noting that "varying kinds and degrees of intelligence occur in people, many animals and some machines." While keeping the scope of the definition broad, McCarthy implicitly instructs us on what AI is not, ruling out the possibility that intelligence can be measured through a binary indicator, indicating instead that mechanisms, degrees, and nuances of intelligence exist and are at the core of research in AI.

The lack of a simplistic intelligent/nonintelligent distinction resonates with the contemporary efforts in AI, moving beyond many of the discussions that characterized pioneers in the field back in the second part of the twentieth century. To me, the modernity of this open-ended definition recognizes the limits of the universal, mutually exclusive approaches that characterized AI in its early days, up until the 1990s at least, where feuds between philosophies and approaches were limiting the scope of machine intelligence through idealistic (or maybe ideological?) barriers. Additionally, I always find the connection between "science" and "engineering" majestically explanatory. AI is not only about constructing, developing, and deploying programs (the "engineering" part), but it also about understanding, evaluating, describing, and inferring (the "science" part). This conjunction seems to anticipate the "empirical" shift that occurred to AI research in the late 1980s and in general crucially reminds scholars that AI cannot be pursued or investigated by only concentrating on one of these two aspects.

The beauty and simplicity of McCarthy's definition also pose considerable questions and problems. For instance, are goals the only objects that intelligence seeks to achieve? What does "making" actually mean? And also, if various degrees of intelligence exist in humans and other animals, is not the range too ample? Nonetheless, I believe this definition is a good basis to meaningfully interpret the trajectory connecting the starting and the current point on research in AI, the initial objectives and promises, and the present results and perspectives.

Interestingly, the absence of boundaries – or the presence of very few of them – in McCarthy's definition enables us to introduce distinctions more easily. Albeit the spectrum of intelligence introduced by McCarthy is broad and heterogenous, we shall not be tempted to think that he was somehow dismissive of the foundational aim of AI research from the beginning of the field: achieving human-level intelligence. Instead, he actually opposed more recent trends in AI, arguing that the lack of ambition of the majority of the research community, which focused on specific applications and narrow tasks, deviated from the ultimate goal of creating thinking machines intended as machines possessing the intelligence to sense the world, make decision, create, and act as we humans do.[2]

But his very definition provides a horizon in which different types of intelligence can be defined, targeted, and ultimately crafted. It is this heterogeneity, as anticipated, that allows us to introduce different layers in surveying AI today, at least from a macro-level perspective. These layers may be porous, and someone might find them overly simplistic, but they are a informative representation of the state in which AI research has come today.

The intricated philosophies, research lines, and experiences accumulated over the decades partially explain the roller-coaster of failures and successes in AI, as we already pointed out. Progressively – I would say starting from the establishment of expert systems – the community has started experiencing a deeper and deeper fracture between two separated sides. If once the main division concerned the debates between symbolism and connectionism, over the years the main divisive issue became the separation between "strong" and "weak" AI (Searle, 1992).

Proponents of strong AI, often linked to the concept of "Artificial General Intelligence" (AGI) or Human-level AI - a term I personally tend to prefer for several reasons, had positions in line with the one offered by McCarthy. In general, their idea was that scientists could finally create a universal algorithm capable of reaching learning and intellectual abilities that are as deep and as performative as those of humans. The emphasis should be placed on the word "universal": researchers seeking to reaching AGI were (and are) not interested in the mere resolution of specific tasks (e.g., correctly classifying pictures or sound signals). They are rather interested in an artificial agent that possesses characteristics such as self-awareness and consciousness that can create, reason, and adapt as animals and humans do. The challenge is massive and prompted a series of vivid discussions about the feasibility of such a mission, as well as enduring philosophical and epistemological debates on the threats posed by this scientific quest (Bostrom, 2016; Eden et al., 2012; Müller & Bostrom, 2016). Equipped by unprecedented hardware resources, information infrastructures, and multi-millionaire funding programs, a consistent number of research institutions and (mostly) companies are currently working on these problems.

While many AI researchers either think that AGI will never be reached or, at best, will be reached in the medium-long term, in the last years particularly we have witnessed several spectacular breakthroughs that revamped enthusiasm on the topic – as well as concerns. One of these is AlphaGo – a program created by DeepMind that won against Go champion Lee Sedol in a five-match game in 2016 (Silver et al., 2016). The complexity of the game required planning and decision-making abilities that were much more demanding than those associated with chess, a game that has been long used as a benchmark in gameplay applications of AI. The neat victory over a human world champion in Go shocked the world. Another important achievement is the release of the Generative Pre-trained Transformer 3 (GPT-3), created by OpenAI. The GPT-3 is a language model exploiting hundreds of billions of parameters, capable of producing human-like text with unprecedented accuracy – although many advanced critics especially on the ethical side of the outputs offered by the model (T. Brown et al., 2020). A third more recent success is AlphaFold, also developed by DeepMind, which solved the 50-year long "protein folding problem" (Jumper et al., 2021). Even though none of these three applications can be directly regarded as an attempt to reach AGI, their impact on the scientific community and the public has revitalized the never-ending questions regarding the actual landscape of research in machine intelligence. More generally, it can be said that these attempts lie in the middle of the conceptual continuum that goes from narrow problem-solving tasks to a more comprehensive, far-reaching machine intelligence, identifiable with AGI.[3]

The lower bound of this continuum is concerned with the study, development, and deployment of learning systems that are capable of carrying out very specific tasks and is generally referenced with the term "weak" (or "narrow") AI. Recognizing digits, classifying anomalous transactions, or interpreting the meaning of sentences are all examples of weak AI applications. In this sense, it is appreciable why systems such as AlphaGo lie in between a hypothetical continuum from narrow AI to AGI: while they lack common sense, consciousness, self-awareness, and other characteristics that are deemed to be foundational for any human intelligence, and while they are generally aimed at achieving a certain specific goal (e.g., winning a Go game), they are nonetheless composed by multiple modules and mechanisms in parallel that go well beyond the boundaries of simple classification or regression problems, showing elements of creativity and adaptivity. AlphaGo surely is not an example of AGI, yet it implies and involves many smaller problems and challenges that make its learning abilities impressive to an unprecedented extent.

As the reader may have intuited by now, everything that is regarded as "AI" today is actually an example of "weak" AI: from the marvelous results of AlphaGo and other equally impressive systems, down to the simplest – and maybe overrated for commercial purposes? – binary classification application buried in the commercial flyers of a small technology company. Listing the differences – qualitative and quantitative – between AlphaFold and the classifier your friend trained with five lines of code in Python last week would be far too easy, and ultimately boring. However, it is interesting to acknowledge that they almost certainly have a thing in common: to a certain extent, they all work using machine learning.

Machine Learning or the Superstar of Our Times

Unless one has been living in a cave with no connection with civilization in the last 10 years, the expression "machine learning" should sound at least vaguely familiar. It is one of those expressions that suddenly become part of the lexicon of people trying to impress other people while sipping wine at a bar, waiting to get on an airplane, or walking out of a theater. This boost of popularity affected the world outside academia, and more so academia itself. The number of funded projects, published articles, advertised positions linked in some capacity with "machine learning" has skyrocketed in the last decade (Brynjolfsson and McAfee, 2017; S. Miller & Hughes, 2017). In our everyday lives, we are surrounded by dozens of machine learning applications that we often take for granted, a fact that well exemplifies the pervasiveness of learning algorithms. Netflix, for instance, uses machine learning-empowered recommendation systems to suggest movies we may like. Smartphones' text autocomplete options run on specific powerful machine learning approaches. Virtual Personal Assistants, like Amazon Alexa, revolve around speech recognition and NLP, two branches of machine learning. And while we scroll our Twitter feed in search of new exciting papers or we navigate through YouTube to enjoy Miles Davis playing "Human Nature" at the 1989 Montreaux Jazz Festival, these social media platforms gather data on our preferences that will be used to show specific contents or ads, almost instantaneously. In spite of the ubiquity of machine learning, both semantically and factually, many times however there appears to be a certain degree of confusion around its definition or description.

As for AI, finding a suitable, concise, informative definition of machine learning that attracts universal agreement is challenging. Furthermore, the hype around machine learning brought chaos and superficiality around a concept that is too often misinterpreted or used interchangeably with "AI." Before digging into its definition, it is necessary to clarify that machine learning is not AI: it is instead a branch of it. The father of the term is Arthur Samuel (1959), who coined it few years after McCarthy "invented" the term "Artificial Intelligence" and the Dartmouth workshop. There are thousands of definitions of "machine learning" available – possibly as many as AI definitions – but Tom Mitchell has proposed one that is among the most quoted. In fact, in the early pages of his 1997 book, Mitchell set forth two distinct ways to define machine learning. The first was more succinct and descriptive, following the minimalistic style of McCarthy's AI one. The second is more formal and can help us shed light on some fundamental aspects of machine learning. Concerning the former, Mitchell (1997) writes:

> the field of machine learning is concerned with the question of how to construct computer programs that automatically improve with experience.

The formal one instead reads:

> A computer program is said to learn from experience E with respect to some class of tasks T and performance measure P if its performance at tasks in T, as measured by P, improves with experience E.

The first element that should be noted is that none of the two mentions "intelligence" in any form: no reference to human, animal, machine, or artificial intelligence is made. Instead, what appears to become central in both is the word "experience." In the shorter definition, Mitchell clarifies explicitly that the goal of machine learning researchers is to create programs that take advantage of experience to improve the outcomes of their actions. In the formal one, experience is the means through which a computer program improves its performance in relation to a given task. Even if the idea of intelligence as the sole byproduct of "trial and error" processes is limiting, I find Mitchell's definitions inspiring because – beyond their clarity – they have the ability to highlight the natural connection between the overall functioning of machine learning algorithms and how we – at least partly – learn.

During the coronavirus pandemic, precisely at the beginning of 2021, I started to learn to play the alto saxophone. Besides a terrible experience with the flute during primary and secondary school, I never had the chance to invest some time and effort in learning a musical instrument, though I love music and spend many hours a day listening to it. At the beginning of my coursework, I could not even read notes on a music sheet, let alone produce them through my alto. Training every day both theory and practice led me to (almost always) correctly read the sheets and even play some tunes. Experience E, here, can be proxied by the hours of training invested in learning the basics of the instrument. My performance P is the increased ability to produce pleasant sounds, rather than monstrous noises annoying my neighbors. The task T, trivially, is being able to play the alto at least decently. There is a clear, consistent, revealing connection between how I am continuing to study music and how a machine learning algorithm works, and even though human intelligence as a whole cannot be certainly limited to a chain connecting together a task, the measurement of a performance and experience, it is indisputable that many actions through which humans learn resemble this process.

Machine learning works in a very similar fashion. Albeit simple and formally elegant, however, Mitchell's definitions do not stress a fundamental aspect of machine learning, which was already in the 1959 definition offered by Arthur Samuel:

> (Machine Learning is the) field of study that gives computers the ability to learn without being explicitly programmed.

The closing part of the sentence is decisive to fully capture the essence of machine learning. A machine learning algorithm automatically carries out a given task without any human assistance: it learns through examples typically contained in a set of data to make decisions on another set of unseen data, finding out associative patterns without external instructions. Keeping this in mind is crucial.

Here is another example to further contextualize Mitchell's definition moving from a real-world example (me playing the sax – or attempting to do so) to a computational one. First, a computer program or machine is an algorithm (or a set of algorithms). A task T is, for instance, predicting whether a picture portrays animals or vegetables. The experience E, as anticipated, is constituted by data inputs in the likely form of photos, and finally performance P generally consists of one or more metrics describing how well the algorithm is doing in correctly separating animals from vegetables.

A reader who was not previously exposed to an introduction to machine learning might be surprised to discover its overall simplicity. Yet, this is just a very general definition that serves the purpose of illustrating the nature of machine learning from a macroscopic perspective. Machine learning is characterized by a myriad of algorithms that could be grouped into different families, which in turn could be grouped into higher level classes. One of the main distinctions that are always made, and are particularly informative for educational purposes, is the one between supervised and unsupervised

34

learning. This dichotomy will be the focus of the following sections, but the reader should keep in mind that dichotomizing implies an intrinsic simplification of the machine learning landscape.

Supervised Learning

Supervised learning refers to all those tasks in which a program learns from labeled examples or, more precisely, supervised learning is concerned with problems for which we have a known target variable. One example is correctly classifying pictures containing dogs or cats using a labeled dataset, in which our variable of interest is known, namely, the images are annotated with the ground-truth label. More formally, assuming that we are given N examples $x_n \in \mathbb{R}$ and N corresponding scalar labels $y_n \in \mathbb{R}$, in a supervised learning setting we obtain the pairs $(x_1, y_1), \ldots, (x_N, y_N)$, matching our features with the target variable. From these pairs, we want to estimate a predictor $f(\cdot, \theta) : \mathbb{R}^D \to \mathbb{R}$ that aims at finding a good parameter θ^* such that:

$$f\left(x_n, \theta^*\right) \approx y_N \ \forall n = 1, \ldots, N$$

The N examples represent the observations in a given dataset, x_n are instead measurements associated to each example, such as the population density, the level of inequality and the average temperature of a certain city, and y_n are our target variables, indicating whether for example the city is situated on the West or East coast of the United States or measuring its overall wealth level. The goal is thus to find a function that works as a satisfactory predictor of y_N given measurements x_n, generalizing well on the available observations.

When we carry out a supervised learning task, data are usually divided into two disjoint sets. These two sets are called "training" and "test" sets – sometimes, when data are sufficiently rich, and the number of observations is considerable, a "validation" set is also created. In other cases, when we do not have many observations or we are interested in obtaining stable predictions, cross-validation (through an array of different variants) is employed, using iteratively different portions of a dataset as train and test sets. The distinction between training and testing is one of the core distinctions between traditional statistics and machine learning. Logistic regression is one of the most common approaches used in statistics and econometrics to estimate associations (mostly) between a binary variable of interest (also called dependent variable or target variable in the machine learning vocabulary) and a set of predictors (or features or, as in econometrics and statistics, covariates or independent variables). But when we traditionally employ logistic regression, we exploit all the data at our disposal. In machine learning, this does not happen: a logistic regression model is first fitted on the training set in order to let the model learn the parameters associating our features with the target variable. Generally, the training occurs utilizing optimization methods such as gradient descent to minimize the error between the model predictions and the ground truth. After having trained our model using the examples in the training set, the algorithmic performance is evaluated on the test set.

One helpful example to translate this into more comprehensible terms is to think about our (long?) gone high school days. Our "training set" was constituted by the mathematics homework we were instructed to complete at home, which were generally similar or comparable to the exercises included in our exams or class tests. The exercises in the class tests represent our "test set": we trained ourselves at home by sweating on differential equations and trigonometry, and our knowledge on those topics was then tested in an (allegedly) unbiased way in class.[4]

A fundamental dichotomy between tasks in supervised learning refers to the distinction between classification and regression. Classification concerns problems in which our target variable is discrete, whereas the target variable is continuous in regression. Therefore, predicting whether an image contains a cat or a dog is a classification problem, as well as correctly predicting to which animal species a set of measurements refer to, like color, weight, and height. Conversely, predicting a person's net income from some sociodemographic variables is a regression task, because net income is expressed in a continuous form that goes from 0 to a very large number. If you read the previous sentences carefully, you might have noticed that we can also introduce a further distinction between classification problems in the three examples provided above. In fact, in the cat-dog problem, we only deal with two separate categories, while in the species one the number of underlying categories is higher. This suggests that there exist different types of classification typologies.

Binary classification is the most common typology, and concerns problems in which we have a discrete target variable that can only take two values, such as the dog-cat dichotomy. Multi-class classification, instead, refers to tasks in which we have more than two labels. Animal species are one example, as well as digit recognition. Finally, we also have a third category, which is multi-label classification. In a multi-label classification, we have more than two labels, and multiple labels can be assigned to an instance. Object recognition is one good example, particularly object recognition in the navigation system of an autonomous vehicle: a machine has to classify, for instance, that a certain object is a person, who is a child, who is riding a bike, and so on. Trivially, multi-label classification problems are very often more challenging than binary and multi-class ones.

This is not a textbook in machine learning nor a technical review, but the reader should keep in mind that supervised learning involves a myriad of different specific approaches, and many of them can handle both classification and regression tasks. Some of the most common supervised learning approaches are logistic regression, Naïve Bayes, Random Forests, Decision Trees, Nearest Neighbors algorithms, Support Vector Machines, and Gradient Boosting Machines. A thorough review of such approaches can be found in Bishop (2006).

Unsupervised Learning

Unsupervised learning represents the other "side" of machine learning. There is a chance that those of you who had attended quantitative courses throughout their lives or worked on projects involving quantitative data of some sort have already encountered unsupervised learning in some fashion, without maybe knowing it.

Contrarily to what happens in the supervised learning setting, in unsupervised learning, the machine is not provided with any annotated target variable but only receive input data $x_n \in \mathbb{R}$. The machine has hence to learn patterns in absence of a "teacher" signal. Hastie et al. (2013) write that the task of the machine is then to describe how the data are organized or clustered. While still being generic, this definition offers a more precise hint on what unsupervised learning actually is, or *does*. Unsupervised learning, in fact, mainly covers four main tasks, which are relatively common in computational sciences as well as in traditional statistics and that is why I would guess that, if you had ordinary statistics coursework, you may have studied or worked with some unsupervised learning approach before. These four main categories of tasks are clustering, dimensionality reduction, anomaly detection, and density estimation.

Clustering refers to an area of computational research that aims to find communities or subgroups of objects that are similar according to a certain criterion. Criteria for finding similar objects in a sample of observations are mainly two: intra-cluster similarity and inter-cluster dissimilarity. The former is more concerned with grouping together objects that are similar to each other, whereas the latter is more interested in organizing groups by maximizing the dissimilarity of objects belonging to different groups.

Taxonomies of clustering algorithms can also be identified (Fahad et al., 2014). One main distinction is between hierarchical and partitional clustering approaches. The two approaches have very different characteristics, but overall the key distinction is that hierarchical clustering consists of a sequence of data partitions that are nested and therefore structured in a hierarchical form. In contrast, partitional clustering divides data into a small number of clusters usually needing a specification of the number of clusters required beforehand. Hierarchical clustering algorithms are thus organized through different levels of decomposition, while in partitional clustering the algorithm produces a single partition.

Clustering algorithms can also be discriminated based on their group assignment procedure (Hartigan, 2001). Particularly, agglomerative algorithms start their procedure by assigning each observation to its own cluster, then iteratively merging similar ones into higher level subgroups. Divisive methods, instead, work the other way around: the entire sample is first labeled as a single cluster, and the algorithm then proceeds to split clusters until a particular criterion is minimized or maximized.

A further discrimination relates to hard and fuzzy clustering approaches (Miyamoto & Umayahara, 2000). In hard clustering, one observation belongs to a single cluster, fuzzy clustering instead entails approaches in which each observation is associated with a certain degree of membership to each of the resulting clusters. More specifically, in a two-cluster case, one item can have a certain probability p to belong to cluster i, and a corresponding probability $1-p$ to belong to cluster j. The term "fuzzy" reflects the possibility of blurred boundaries and the absence of strictly mutually exclusive assignments. A third alternative is overlapping clustering, where an item can simultaneously belong to more than one cluster.

Clustering really is a fascinating area of research. It resembles several actions we perform in our everyday endeavors, like reordering the books in our library (how should I organize them? Contemporary literature on the left, classic on the right? Or should I arrange them by geographical proximity?). I find the associative patterns detected by our chosen algorithms often extremely intriguing, as they show us associations that are often buried under loads and loads of information, offering us new standpoints from which to study certain phenomena. But, as many argue, clustering offers extremely subjective results that are hard to verify or validate.

By having access to the ground-truth grouping of items in a dataset, one can first train a clustering algorithm and then evaluate ex-post how well it has resembled the actual sub-groupings. Most of the times, however, we do not have access to such information, and we specifically ask a machine to perform a clustering task because we search for patterns and associations that are hidden, hard to find in a multidimensional space. For this reason, it is fundamental to be clear about the underlying hypothesis at the core of our analyses and, in general, be conscious about the criterion that we choose as the one to optimize to derive our clusters. Once an instructor at a summer school at Carnegie Mellon University told us that clustering is a form of art. It is so, indeed. The absence of a "teacher" signal opens up almost infinite possibilities for us to detect clusters or develop ad-hoc methods that more precisely capture the complexity of a specific phenomenon. But being an "art" is both the beauty and the curse of clustering, and poses significant challenges concerning statistical validity, stability, interpretability.

Dimensionality reduction is another area within unsupervised learning. There may be cases in which our input data have thousands – or even millions – of different dimensions. This is not often the case in social sciences and criminology, where generally datasets are not as big as in other disciplines, but the increasing interest in natural language processing or nontraditional data structures (such as video streams) has already led to a sensible increase in the amount of data utilized in social sciences research projects. Furthermore, wildly large feature spaces might lead to overfitting, which is the issue arising from models generating an excessive number of parameters leading a model to perform too well on the training set, but poorly on the test set, hence failing to generalize sufficiently.[5] The general goal of dimensionality reduction algorithms is therefore to represent our data in a lower-dimensional space preserving the fundamental information contained in the original dataset, with the intent to find patterns that would be otherwise missed.

Similarly, one may use dimensionality reduction to group closely related variables into composite indicators to avoid the so-called "curse of dimensionality," which refers to estimation problems caused by sparsity or time complexity occurring when analyzing high-dimensional data. Many different dimensionality reduction algorithms have been developed, and some have become particularly popular. Among these are embedding approaches, principal component analysis, factor analysis, singular value decomposition, and autoencoders.

A third area of application of unsupervised learning is anomaly detection. There are cases in which we need to identify observations that significantly deviate from the underlying distribution in our data. Anomalies, in the statistical and computational realms, are generally defined as "outliers." Outliers can occur both in settings in which our data are independent and identically distributed (i.i.d.), such as when we measure the height of soccer players in a team and we seek to detect exceptionally tall players, or when data are temporally dependent, as in the case of time-series. Anomaly detection, for instance, can be useful to identify deviations in crime trends, as those occurred in the aftermath of the policies implemented by governments to contain the spread of the coronavirus. In general, anomaly detection can be used both in the pre-processing step of a certain secondary task and as an exploratory-diagnosing strategy constituting the proper task. Some recurrent approaches are One-class Support Vector Machines, Isolations Forests, Local Outlier Factor, and Generative Adversarial Networks.

The fourth class of unsupervised problems is density estimation. It concerns the issue of learning relationships among attributes in our data and particularly seeks to learn the underlying probability distribution that generates the observed variables. In this way, we can accurately describe our data, gaining insights into their nature. By describing our data, we are then facilitated in identifying unlikely events, such as anomalies, or using learning approaches that are suitable for specific types of probability density estimations. In typical use cases, we should decide between two main different categories of density estimation approaches. We use parametric density estimation strategies when we assume to know a priori the functional form describing the distribution associated with a certain variable. For instance, we may assume that a certain population of interest follows a Gaussian distribution, and we then seek to estimate the relevant parameters in our data. Two examples of parametric density estimation are Maximum Likelihood Estimation (MLE) – a method that estimates the parameters of a given probability distributions by optimizing a likelihood or log-likelihood function – and Gaussian Mixture Model (GMM) – a density estimation technique that seeks to minimize bias between the true and the sample probability by allowing a mixture of different parametric distributions to model the underlying probability density function of a population.

Conversely, when assumptions are too challenging or could not be made, we can apply nonparametric methods. Multi-modal distributions for instance, which are distributions characterized by the presence of several "peaks," are hard to estimate through parametric approaches, and therefore nonparametric methods are preferred. One common nonparametric approach is Kernel Density Estimation (KDE). The bandwidth of the kernel function governs KDE: the estimator attempts to create a curve resembling the distribution of the data by weighing the distance of every point in each location along the distribution, with the bandwidth being the element capable of modifying the shape of the curve.

Besides these four traditional unsupervised learning categories (i.e., clustering, dimensionality reduction, anomaly detection, and density estimation), and more generally perhaps beside the supervised-unsupervised distinction, an additional paradigm that has gained increasing attention in the AI community is self-supervised learning (LeCun & Misra, 2021). Self-supervised learning is said to lie between supervised and unsupervised learning, so the choice of where to mention it in this chapter was somehow tricky. I opted to talk about it here since I think it nicely closes the loop of the quick tour we had in machine learning. Self-supervised learning has a hybrid nature because although the ultimate attempt is to obtain classification outputs from a dataset, the dataset is not initially labeled. This means that the machine itself acts as both the teacher and the learner. There are practical and theoretical reasons behind research in self-supervised learning. The practical ones concern the economic resources and time cost that are required to annotate millions of observations. Given the scale of datasets currently used in many research areas, like computer vision, the expenses associated with data labeling have become unbearable. On the theoretical side, instead, scientists working on self-supervised learning have been inspired by research in psychology and cognitive sciences, which suggests that children learn to navigate and understand the world around them in a similar fashion (Gopnik et al., 2007).

The underlying idea is that to create intelligent machines that go beyond the very limited scope of the tasks they are generally asked to perform, supervised and unsupervised learning are insufficient. In spite of the enormous quantities of labeled data available, and despite the progress in hardware resources, traditional supervised algorithms are still not able to generalize sufficiently well, calling for a new paradigm to get closer to the development of machines that learns more efficiently and – more importantly – effectively.

Deep Learning and Recent Developments

I have already mentioned throughout this chapter that the history of AI, and specifically the history of machine learning in the last decades, has been influenced by the tremendous advances made in software and hardware engineering, as well as the increasing availability of data. Not only data have grown in terms of datasets dimensions (from 1 or very few KB in the 1970s to terabytes today) but also in terms of variety. The digitalization processes that have occurred – or are happening – in many scientific domains, industries, and public sectors[6] made available hundreds of new datasets for the application of machine learning approaches. However, these three advances – software, hardware, and data growth – have not walked in parallel in the last decades. As noted by Zhang and coauthors (2021), the memory capacity of computers has been outpaced by the increasing amount of available data, and at the same time, computational power has surpassed data. This asymmetry called for more memory-efficient models that can now spend more time in the parameter optimization processes due to a higher computational budget. According to the authors, this mix of constraints and new possibilities produced – or, say, inspired – a topical revolution in AI and machine learning research: the deep learning one.

This revolution has built upon research that is decades old. Deep learning is founded in McCulloch, Pitts, and Rosenblatt's attempts to imitate the functioning of brains using artificial neural networks, as well as in more recent work on convolutional neural networks (LeCun & Bengio, 1998), recurrent neural networks (Elman, 1990; Hopfield, 1982; Jordan, 1986; Rumelhart et al., 1986), and in particular long short-term memory nets (Hochreiter & Schmidhuber, 1997). The comeback of neural networks has led to an explosion of new approaches, methods, and mechanisms that significantly changed the landscape in AI (Sejnowski, 2018).

But what exactly is deep learning? Again, providing a fully comprehensive definition is difficult. Goodfellow et al. (2017) tried to address this question by referring to deep learning as a way of constructing representations graph of concepts that are deep, meaning that they comprise different layers, or hierarchies, that have the precise goal of subsetting complex problems into simpler ones. Deep learning is then fundamentally an answer to the long-standing problem of representing learning. A very useful example is a deep neural network trained to recognize an object in a picture. The depth of the network enables the machines to focus on different aspects present in the image, such as the main colors, the contours, the shadows, and so on. By decomposing a picture into distinct representations, mainly distinguishing between a first visible layer tracting the observable parts of the image and hidden layers that capture abstract elements in it, the model exploits connections and nonlinearities between these distinct representations to learn a higher level one, which should lead to an accurate representation, and therefore prediction, of the image itself.

Hence, one of the most intriguing characteristics of deep learning models is that they do not depend on feature engineering carried out by humans, which is costly in terms of time and labor and also prone to errors, miscalculation, and bias.[7] Goodfellow, Bengio, and Courville provide as an example the task of creating a machine that is able to detect cars in photographs (Goodfellow et al., 2017). How can we precisely describe how a car component, such as wheels, looks like in terms of pixels values, which are the fundamental components of data used in computer vision problems? Deep learning addresses this problem through its hierarchy of interconnected representations, which are organized so that simpler ones contribute to more complex ones.

Deep learning has already accomplished numerous missions in the last 15 years. Some of these were already anticipated, such as AlphaGo, AlphaFold, and GPT-3. Another notable achievement in the "game" realm is Libratus, a system developed at Carnegie Mellon that proved to be able to win for the first time ever against human champions in Poker, a game with no information symmetry (N. Brown & Sandholm, 2018), over nearly three weeks of playing. Furthermore, the past decade has seen massive signs of progress in object recognition and estimation: the improvements made in the ImageNet competition,[8] for instance, have been enormous. Improvements in object recognition have contributed to research on self-driving vehicles. Albeit fully autonomous cars and trucks have not yet been developed and deployed – and may likely be still years or decades away from us (Mims, 2021) – a degree of autonomy is already present in the roads and driveways surrounding us. Furthermore, deep learning techniques have sensibly impacted on the performance of virtual assistants, text-autocompletion services as well as machine translation, and applications also cover medical diagnosis, robotics, and even art (Sejnowski, 2018).

Despite the ubiquity of deep learning applications across research domains, both in academia and industry, the social sciences have not yet fully benefited from its promises and power, nor did criminology. The likely reasons are mainly two, and they are interconnected.

First, although social scientists are increasingly trained in quantitative and computational methods, traditional machine learning is generally the extreme sophistication border in a graduate student's education, leaving a gap between theory and implementation of classic supervised or unsupervised approaches and more complex deep learning methods. It is undoubtedly true that the democratization of programming languages provoked a stark increase in the accessibility of libraries and frameworks dedicated to deep learning, making it very simple to implement a deep neural network. Nevertheless, the limits of formal education portfolios somehow curb the reachability of deep learning from a social science perspective.

Second, data in the social sciences are often of limited dimension. Albeit in the last years some disciplines or lines of research have been gifted with larger and larger datasets, usually a byproduct of the internet revolution, most social scientists generally work with datasets that only contain hundreds or thousands of observations, severely restraining the possibilities of deep learning approaches to meaningfully find hierarchical representations. Nonetheless, examples of deep learning applications for addressing social science-related problems do exist.

Particularly, one of the most promising areas of inquiry is poverty prediction through remote sensing and satellite images (Jean et al., 2016;

Piaggesi et al., 2019; Xie et al., 2016), where nontraditional data sources are exploited in combination with deep learning algorithms such as convolutional neural networks to help sustainable development. The study of human mobility is also another fascinating realm in which deep learning is used due to the growing availability of novel data formats, such as GPS signals, phone records, or social media activity, showing promise for tackling issues such as urban planning, pollution monitoring, and epidemics or virus spreading (Luca et al., 2021). Other areas currently being explored are fake news detection (Monti et al., 2019; Popat et al., 2018), terrorism (Campedelli et al., 2021; Johnston & Weiss, 2017), and also crime (Wang et al., 2017).

Conclusions

The AI journey has truly been a collective one and continues to do so. This chapter has drawn a trajectory of milestones, characters, ideas, and trends that – I hope – has helped you, the reader, in familiarizing with some fundamental concepts and paradigms that are crucial to understanding how research in AI changed over the centuries, from the first philosophical speculations of profound thinkers to the prodigious accomplishments of deep learning. The account here provided cannot be considered exhaustive or complete, as this collective journey is so profound that it could barely fit an entire library, but I had to make choices and select those aspects that, to me, more accurately describe how we got here today. However, throughout this chapter, I have included references to many seminal books and papers that I encourage to discover and read if interested in digging a bit more into this compelling human enterprise.

In this chapter, we started by overviewing the disciplines that had the highest influence in the development of AI as a field, borrowing the framing set forth by Russel and Norvig. Subsequently, we have proceeded to discover the history of AI, precisely starting from Aristotle, passing through Turing and the Dartmouth workshop up to the most recent breakthroughs, such as AlphaGo, GPT-3, and AlphaFold. After that, we finally tried to define what AI is, introducing the distinction between Strong AI (or AGI) and Weak AI (also ANI), which took us directly to machine learning. Machine learning has been described in terms of its two most common "souls": supervised and unsupervised learning, with a final mention to self-supervised learning, a hybrid approach that has recently shown interesting properties and promises. Finally, the last section of this chapter has been dedicated to deep learning, a branch of machine learning that has prompted an unprecedented hype around AI in the last decade and a half.

One may have noticed that, throughout this journey, expectations, objectives, and the questions underlying research in AI have changed, sometimes dramatically. High-level, philosophical arguments around the possibility of creating machines that could think as we do, arguments that roamed through human minds and fantasies for millennia, have been first embraced by the strongly optimistic attitude of scientists in the first part of the twentieth century, a period which marked the beginning of AI as a field *per se*. Then, however, a rollercoaster of (shocking) failures and (thunderous) successes compressed in a restricted number of years took form. The rollercoaster led to a rescaling of those expectations and objectives that were at the core of all the endeavors of researchers in AI until that moment, regardless of their preferred approach or paradigm. The shift of sentiment in the community brought to rethink the fundamental goals of AI, as well as its scopes and possibilities. This, in a way, created an intriguing ideological schism, dividing those who were still aiming at creating a form of machine intelligence that could be compared to ours, and those who were more concerned with the theory and engineering of systems that were specifically designed to carry out narrow tasks, somehow putting the orthodox mission of the fathers of AI on hold.

Despite the results achieved by AI systems in a variety of domains, many are still wondering whether we should talk about intelligence at all. Critiques emphasize the fact that the vast amount of computational resources, investments, and information used to train even the more performing and expensive models have not yet led to machines possessing common sense, consciousness, or simply the ability to adapt to endogenous dynamics (Crawford, 2021; Fjelland, 2020). Some have even argued that most applications today, even the most celebrated ones, are profoundly stupid (J. M. Bishop, 2021). They may be able to recognize objects or correctly predict cancer, but they cannot explain why they made a given decision. It is difficult to disagree to such position; it is a piece of irrefutable evidence. Furthermore, most of these systems are overly dependent on the quality of the data they are fed with, and the way in which they work remains highly unintelligible, making them "black boxes." These "black box" characteristics pose problems not only on the full understanding of the mechanisms governing learning in increasingly complex models, but also open discussions related to the ethics of these algorithms, especially when employed in contexts where high stakes are at play (Buolamwini & Gebru, 2018; Eubanks, 2018; Kleinberg et al., 2018; Rudin, 2019; Veale et al., 2018).

These are all true concerns, and they are all aptly addressed by strands of research that attracted more and more attention.

Nevertheless, and in spite of the distance that still separates current AI from human-level AI, it would be myopic – or unfair – to ignore or overlook what research in machine intelligence has achieved over the years, especially over the last decade. There may be a lot of noise out there, a lot of garbage we should all be sufficiently trained to discover to avoid sensationalism or the temptations of jumping on the hype-train. Many are the examples of research in academia and industry that use the machine learning jargon for opportunistic reasons, rather than for the genuine interest in discovering new things about the world we live in or even attempt to go for the big shot, namely, AGI. But beyond this noise, incredible things are happening, which were deemed totally unrealistic just a few decades back. And, most importantly, the journey is not over yet. It is with this precise spirit, a mixture of realism, awareness, critical attitude, and amazement that I fell in love with AI during my graduate studies, and it is with this precise spirit that I tried to condense the highlights of this chaotic and beautiful story in this chapter. The inevitable question running around tirelessly in my mind is: what comes next?

Notes

1 Particularly, Descartes anticipates some of the themes set out by Turing in his "Discourse on the Method" (1637).
2 McCarthy was not alone in criticizing the trends occurring in AI between the 1990s and the 2000s. Some of the pioneers of the field also shared his perplexities and concerns (Nilsson, 2005; M. Minsky, 2007).
3 It should be mentioned that there exists a line of research that not only considers the mission of reaching AGI but also aims at discussing and reaching Artificial Superintelligence, a form of machine intelligence that greatly surpasses human intelligence. This topic will not be considered in this chapter, but readers interested in it are recommended to read Gill (2016) and Bostrom (2016).
4 One would argue that this parallelism is wrong, as it assumes that our younger self was not influenced by stress and pressure during the test, two elements that certainly do not impact algorithmic performance in the test set. This is a reasonable objection: the parallelism was purely intended to exemplify and trace a parallelism between ourselves and a supervised learning setting. While writing it down, I could not help myself in reasoning about the massive underlying differences between human intelligence and its reaction to internal and external stimuli and the stolid behavior of a computational model.
5 Conversely, underfitting concerns the inability of a model to capture the underlying characteristics of the data, failing to perform sufficiently in both the train and test sets.
6 I wish I could say that this "digital revolution" has also occurred regarding the criminal justice and law enforcement sectors in Italy, which are very close to my research and background given that I am trained as a criminologist and I am from Italy. Unfortunately, that is not the case. I hope this will change in the coming years.
7 This does not mean that deep learning ensures bias-free and ethically fair representations, but that it can contrast the direct biases that are the effect of human coding or human-driven feature engineering choices.
8 The annual competition called ImageNet Large Scale Visual Recognition Challenge (ILSVRC) has been run yearly from 2010 to 2017 and is arguably the most important competition concerning large-scale object recognition tasks. It is the successor of the earlier PASCAL VOC Challenge and consists of a public available dataset and a competition along with a workshop. The aim is to assess the state-of-the-art in the field and discuss the progress and advances made by research teams from all over the world.

References

Ashby, W. R. (1956). *An introduction to cybernetics*. Chapman & Hall.

Bishop, C. M. (2006). *Pattern recognition and machine learning* (new ed. edizione). Springer Nature.

Bishop, J. M. (2021). Artificial intelligence is stupid and causal reasoning will not fix it. *Frontiers in Psychology, 11*, 513474. https://doi.org/10.3389/fpsyg.2020.513474.

Bostrom, N. (2016). *Superintelligence: Paths, dangers, strategies* (reprint edizione). Oxford.

Bostrom, N., & Yudkowsky, E. (2014). The ethics of artificial intelligence. In K. Frankish & W. M. Ramsey (Eds.), *The Cambridge handbook of artificial intelligence* (pp. 316–334). Cambridge University Press. https://doi.org/10.1017/CBO9781139046855.020.

Brown, N., & Sandholm, T. (2018). Superhuman AI for heads-up no-limit poker: Libratus beats top professionals. *Science, 359*(6374), 418–424. https://doi.org/10.1126/science.aao1733.

Brown, T., Mann, B., Ryder, N., Subbiah, M., Kaplan, J. D., Dhariwal, P., Neelakantan, A., Shyam, P., Sastry, G., Askell, A., Agarwal, S., Herbert-Voss, A., Krueger, G., Henighan, T., Child, R., Ramesh, A., Ziegler, D., Wu, J., Winter, C., …, Amodei, D. (2020). Language models are few-shot learners. *Advances in Neural Information Processing Systems, 33*, 1877–1901. https://papers.nips.cc/paper/2020/hash/1457c0d6bfcb4967418bfb8ac142f64a-Abstract.html

Brynjolfsson, E., & McAfee, A. (2017, July 18). What's driving the machine learning explosion? *Harvard Business Review*. https://hbr.org/2017/07/whats-driving-the-machine-learning-explosion

Buchanan, B., & Lederberg, J. (1971). The heuristic DENDRAL program for explaining empirical data. In *IFIP Congress*. https://www.semanticscholar.org/paper/The-Heuristic-DENDRAL-Program-for-Explaining-Data-Buchanan-Lederberg/074ae08c6c668ecadea2d9bc90b0165f4bf01c65

Buckner, C., & Garson, J. (2019). Connectionism. In E. N. Zalta (Ed.), *The Stanford encyclopedia of philosophy* (Fall 2019). Metaphysics Research Lab, Stanford University. https://plato.stanford.edu/archives/fall2019/entries/connectionism/

Buolamwini, J., & Gebru, T. (2018). Gender shades: Intersectional accuracy disparities in commercial gender classification. In *Proceedings of the 1st Conference on Fairness, Accountability and Transparency*, 77–91. https://proceedings.mlr.press/v81/buolamwini18a.html

Campbell, M., Hoane, A. J., & Hsu, F. (2002). Deep blue. *Artificial Intelligence, 134*(1–2), 57–83. https://doi.org/10.1016/S0004-3702(01)00129-1.

Campedelli, G. M., Bartulovic, M., & Carley, K. M. (2021). Learning future terrorist targets through temporal meta-graphs. *Scientific Reports, 11*(1), 8533. https://doi.org/10.1038/s41598-021-87709-7.

Chomsky, N. (1956). Three models for the description of language. *IRE Transactions on Information Theory, 2*(3), 113–124. https://doi.org/10.1109/TIT.1956.1056813.

Chomsky, N. (1957). *Syntactic structures*. Mouton & Co.

Crawford, K. (2021). *Atlas of AI: Power, politics, and the planetary costs of artificial intelligence*. Yale University Press.

Dunjko, V., & Briegel, H. J. (2018). Machine learning & artificial intelligence in the quantum domain: A review of recent progress. *Reports on Progress in Physics, 81*(7), 074001. https://doi.org/10.1088/1361-6633/aab406.

Eden, A. H., Moor, J. H., Søraker, J. H., & Steinhart, E. (2012). *Singularity hypotheses: A scientific and philosophical assessment.* Springer.

Elman, J. L. (1990). Finding structure in time. *Cognitive Science, 14*(2), 179–211. https://doi.org/10.1207/s15516709cog1402_1.

Epstein, R., Roberts, G., & Beber, G. (Eds.). (2009). *Parsing the Turing test: Philosophical and methodological issues in the quest for the thinking computer.* Springer Netherlands. https://doi.org/10.1007/978-1-4020-6710-5.

Eubanks, V. (2018). *Automating inequality: How high-tech tools profile, police, and punish the poor.* St Martins Pr.

Fahad, A., Alshatri, N., Tari, Z., Alamri, A., Khalil, I., Zomaya, A. Y., Foufou, S., & Bouras, A. (2014). A survey of clustering algorithms for big data: Taxonomy and empirical analysis. *IEEE Transactions on Emerging Topics in Computing, 2*(3), 267–279. https://doi.org/10.1109/TETC.2014.2330519.

Fjelland, R. (2020). Why general artificial intelligence will not be realized. *Humanities and Social Sciences Communications, 7*(1), 1–9. https://doi.org/10.1057/s41599-020-0494-4.

Gelernter, H. (1959). Realization of a geometry theorem proving machine. In *IFIP Congress.* https://doi.org/10.1007/978-3-642-81952-0_8.

Gill, K. S. (2016). Artificial super intelligence: Beyond rhetoric. *AI & Society, 31*(2), 137–143. https://doi.org/10.1007/s00146-016-0651-x.

Gödel, K. (1931). Über formal unentscheidbare Sätze der Principia Mathematica und verwandter Systeme, I. *Monatshefte Für Mathematik Und Physik, 38,* 173–198.

Goodfellow, I., Bengio, Y., & Courville, A. (2017). *Deep learning.* Mit Pr.

Gopnik, A., Meltzoff, A. N., & Kuhl, P. K. (2007). *The scientist in the crib: What early learning tells us about the mind (reprint edizione).* William Morrow & Co.

Grey Walter, W. (1950). An imitation of life. *Scientific American, 182*(5), 42–45.

Guest, D., Cranmer, K., & Whiteson, D. (2018). Deep learning and its application to LHC physics. *Annual Review of Nuclear and Particle Science, 68*(1), 161–181. https://doi.org/10.1146/annurev-nucl-101917-021019.

Hartigan, J. A. (2001). Statistical clustering. In N. J. Smelser & P. B. Baltes (Eds.), *International encyclopedia of the social & behavioral sciences* (pp. 15014–15019). Pergamon. https://doi.org/10.1016/B0-08-043076-7/00400-9.

Hastie, T., Tibshirani, R., & Friedman, J. (2013). *The elements of statistical learning: Data mining, inference, and prediction: Data mining, inference, and prediction* (second ed.). Springer Nature.

Hebb, D. O. (1949). *The organization of behavior: A neuropsychological theory* (1 edizione). Psychology Press.

Hochreiter, S., & Schmidhuber, J. (1997). Long short-term memory. *Neural Computation, 9*(8), 1735–1780. https://doi.org/10.1162/neco.1997.9.8.1735.

Hopfield, J. J. (1982). Neural networks and physical systems with emergent collective computational abilities. *Proceedings of the National Academy of Sciences, 79*(8), 2554–2558. https://doi.org/10.1073/pnas.79.8.2554.

Jean, N., Burke, M., Xie, M., Davis, W. M., Lobell, D. B., & Ermon, S. (2016). Combining satellite imagery and machine learning to predict poverty. *Science, 353*(6301), 790–794. https://doi.org/10.1126/science.aaf7894.

Johnston, A. H., & Weiss, G. M. (2017). Identifying Sunni extremist propaganda with deep learning. In *2017 IEEE Symposium Series on Computational Intelligence (SSCI),* 1–6. https://doi.org/10.1109/SSCI.2017.8280944.

Jordan, M. I. (1986). *Serial order: A parallel distributed processing approach. Technical report, June 1985–March 1986* (AD-A-173989/5/XAB; ICS-8604). California University, San Diego, La Jolla (USA). Institute for Cognitive Science. https://www.osti.gov/biblio/6910294

Jumper, J., Evans, R., Pritzel, A., Green, T., Figurnov, M., Ronneberger, O., Tunyasuvunakool, K., Bates, R., Žídek, A., Potapenko, A., Bridgland, A., Meyer, C., Kohl, S. A. A., Ballard, A. J., Cowie, A., Romera-Paredes, B., Nikolov, S., Jain, R., Adler, J., …, Hassabis, D. (2021). Highly accurate protein structure prediction with AlphaFold. *Nature, 596*(7873), 583–589. https://doi.org/10.1038/s41586-021-03819-2.

Kleinberg, J., Ludwig, J., Mullainathan, S., & Sunstein, C. R. (2018). Discrimination in the age of algorithms. *Journal of Legal Analysis, 10*, 113–174. https://doi.org/10.1093/jla/laz001.

Knight, W. (2015). Marvin Minsky reflects on a life in AI. *MIT Technology Review.* https://www.technologyreview.com/2015/10/30/165358/marvin-minsky-reflects-on-a-life-in-ai/

LeCun, Y., & Bengio, Y. (1998). Convolutional networks for images, speech, and time series. In *The handbook of brain theory and neural networks* (pp. 255–258). MIT Press.

LeCun, Y., & Misra I. (2021). Self-supervised learning: The dark matter of intelligence. Meta AI Research. https://ai.facebook.com/blog/self-supervised-learning-the-dark-matter-of-intelligence/

Luca, M., Barlacchi, G., Lepri, B., & Pappalardo, L. (2021). A survey on deep learning for human mobility. *ArXiv:2012.02825 [Cs].* http://arxiv.org/abs/2012.02825

Marcus, G., Rossi, F., & Veloso, M. (2016). Beyond the Turing test. *AI Magazine, 37*(1), 3–4. https://doi.org/10.1609/aimag.v37i1.2650.

McCarthy, J. (1960a). *Programs with common sense.* https://www.semanticscholar.org/paper/Programs-with-common-sense-McCarthy/494aedf82da4755badc1fe74e4d21cf5fc029e9d

McCarthy, J. (1960b). Recursive functions of symbolic expressions and their computation by machine, part I. *Communications of the ACM, 3*(4), 184–195. https://doi.org/10.1145/367177.367199.

McCarthy, J. (2007). *What is artificial intelligence?* http://35.238.111.86:8080/jspui/bitstream/123456789/274/1/McCarthy_John_What%20is%20artificial%20intelligence.pdf

McCarthy, J., Minsky, M. L., Rochester, N., & Shannon, C. E. (1955). *A proposal for the Dartmouth Summer Research Project on artificial intelligence.* http://jmc.stanford.edu/articles/dartmouth/dartmouth.pdf

McCulloch, W. S., & Pitts, W. (1943). A logical calculus of the ideas immanent in nervous activity. *The Bulletin of Mathematical Biophysics, 5*(4), 115–133. https://doi.org/10.1007/BF02478259.

Miller, G. A. (1956). The magical number seven, plus or minus two: Some limits on our capacity for processing information. *Psychological Review, 63*(2), 81–97. https://doi.org/10.1037/h0043158.

Miller, S., & Hughes, D. (2017). The quant crunch: How the demand for data science skills is disrupting the job market. *VOCEDplus – NCVER's International Tertiary Education Research Database.* https://www.voced.edu.au/content/ngv:76399

Mims, C. (2021, June 5). Self-driving cars could be decades away, no matter what Elon Musk said. *Wall Street Journal*. https://www.wsj.com/articles/self-driving-cars-could-be-decades-away-no-matter-what-elon-musk-said-11622865615

Minsky, M. L. (1991). Logical versus analogical or symbolic versus connectionist or neat versus scruffy. *AI Magazine*, *12*(2), 34–34. https://doi.org/10.1609/aimag. v12i2.894.

Minsky, M. (2007). *The emotion machine: Commonsense thinking, artificial intelligence, and the future of the human mind*. Simon and Schuster.

Mitchell, T. M. (1997). *Machine learning*. McGraw-Hill Science/Engineering/Math.

Miyamoto, S., & Umayahara, K. (2000). Methods in hard and fuzzy clustering. In Z.-Q. Liu & S. Miyamoto (Eds.), *Soft computing and human-centered machines* (pp. 85–129). Springer Japan. https://doi.org/10.1007/978-4-431-67907-3_5.

Monti, F., Frasca, F., Eynard, D., Mannion, D., & Bronstein, M. M. (2019). Fake news detection on social media using geometric deep learning. *ArXiv:1902.06673 [Cs, Stat]*. http://arxiv.org/abs/1902.06673

Müller, V. C. (2020). *Ethics of artificial intelligence and robotics*. https://plato.stanford.edu/entries/ethics-ai/?TB_iframe=true&width=370.8&height=658.8

Müller, V. C., & Bostrom, N. (2016). Future progress in artificial intelligence: A survey of expert opinion. In V. C. Müller (Ed.), *Fundamental issues of artificial intelligence* (pp. 555–572). Springer International Publishing. https://doi.org/10.1007/978-3-319-26485-1_33.

Newell, A., & Simon, H. (1956). The logic theory machine – A complex information processing system. *IRE Transactions on Information Theory*, *2*(3), 61–79. https://doi.org/10.1109/TIT.1956.1056797.

Newell, A., Shaw, J. C., & Simon, H. (1959). *Report on a general problem solving program*. https://exhibits.stanford.edu/feigenbaum/catalog/sy501xd1313

Nilsson, N. J. (2005). Human-level artificial intelligence? Be serious! *AI Magazine*, *26*(4), 68–68. https://doi.org/10.1609/aimag.v26i4.1850.

Pearl, J. (1988). *Probabilistic reasoning in intelligent systems*. Morgan Kaufmann.

Piaggesi, S., Gauvin, L., Tizzoni, M., Cattuto, C., Adler, N., Verhulst, S., Young, A., Price, R., Ferres, L., & Panisson, A. (2019). *Predicting city poverty using satellite imagery*, 90–96. https://openaccess.thecvf.com/content_CVPRW_2019/html/cv4gc/Piaggesi_Predicting_City_Poverty_Using_Satellite_Imagery_CVPRW_2019_paper.html

Pinar Saygin, A., Cicekli, I., & Akman, V. (2000). Turing test: 50 years later. *Minds and Machines*, *10*(4), 463–518. https://doi.org/10.1023/A:1011288000451.

Popat, K., Mukherjee, S., Yates, A., & Weikum, G. (2018). DeClarE: Debunking fake news and false claims using evidence-aware deep learning. *ArXiv:1809.06416 [Cs]*. http://arxiv.org/abs/1809.06416

Ramón y Cajal, S. (1899). *Textura del sistema nervioso del hombre y de los vertebrados*. Imprenta y Librería de Nicolás Moya: Madrid.

Rashevsky, N. (1936). Physico-mathematical aspects of excitation and conduction in nerves. *Cold Spring Harbor Symposia on Quantitative Biology*, *4*, 90–97. https://doi.org/10.1101/SQB.1936.004.01.011.

Rosenblatt, F. (1958). The perceptron: A probabilistic model for information storage and organization in the brain. *Psychological Review*, *65*(6), 386–408. https://doi.org/10.1037/h0042519.

Rudin, C. (2019). Stop explaining black box machine learning models for high stakes decisions and use interpretable models instead. *Nature Machine Intelligence*, *1*(5), 206–215. https://doi.org/10.1038/s42256-019-0048-x.

Rumelhart, D. E., Hinton, G. E., & Williams, R. J. (1986). Learning representations by back-propagating errors. *Nature*, *323*(6088), 533–536. https://doi.org/10.1038/323533a0.

Russell, S. J., & Norvig, P. (2010). *Artificial intelligence: A modern approach* (3° edizione). Pearson College Div.

Samuel, A. L. (1959). Some studies in machine learning using the game of checkers. *IBM Journal of Research and Development*, *3*(3), 210–229. https://doi.org/10.1147/rd.33.0210.

Searle, J. R. (1992). *The rediscovery of the mind*. Bradford Books.

Sejnowski, T. J. (2018). *The deep learning revolution*. MIT Press.

Shortliffe, E. H. (1977). Mycin: A knowledge-based computer program applied to infectious diseases. In *Proceedings of the annual symposium on computer application in medical care*, 66–69.

Silver, D., Huang, A., Maddison, C. J., Guez, A., Sifre, L., van den Driessche, G., Schrittwieser, J., Antonoglou, I., Panneershelvam, V., Lanctot, M., Dieleman, S., Grewe, D., Nham, J., Kalchbrenner, N., Sutskever, I., Lillicrap, T., Leach, M., Kavukcuoglu, K., Graepel, T., & Hassabis, D. (2016). Mastering the game of Go with deep neural networks and tree search. *Nature*, *529*(7587), 484–489. https://doi.org/10.1038/nature16961.

Skinner, B. F. (1948). *Verbal behavior (William James lectures)*. Harvard University.

Thomason, R. (2020). Logic and artificial intelligence. In E. N. Zalta (Ed.), *The Stanford encyclopedia of philosophy* (Summer 2020). Metaphysics Research Lab, Stanford University. https://plato.stanford.edu/archives/sum2020/entries/logic-ai/

Trabesinger, A. (2017). Quantum computing: Towards reality. *Nature*, *543*(7646), S1. https://doi.org/10.1038/543S1a.

Turing, A. M. (1937). On computable numbers, with an application to the Entscheidungs problem. *Proceedings of the London Mathematical Society*, *s2-42*(1), 230–265. https://doi.org/10.1112/plms/s2-42.1.230.

Turing, A. M. (1950). Computing machinery and intelligence. *Mind*, *LIX*(236), 433–460. https://doi.org/10.1093/mind/LIX.236.433.

Veale, M., Van Kleek, M., & Binns, R. (2018). Fairness and accountability design needs for algorithmic support in high-stakes public sector decision-making. In *Proceedings of the 2018 CHI Conference on Human Factors in Computing Systems*, 1–14. https://doi.org/10.1145/3173574.3174014.

von Neumann, J., & Burks, A. W. (1967). *Theory of self-reproducing automata*. University of Illinois Press.

Wang, B., Zhang, D., Zhang, D., Brantingham, P. J., & Bertozzi, A. L. (2017). Deep learning for real time crime forecasting. *ArXiv:1707.03340 [Cs, Math, Stat]*. http://arxiv.org/abs/1707.03340

Weischedel, R. M., Voge, W. M., & James, M. (1978). An artificial intelligence approach to language instruction. *Artificial Intelligence*, *10*(3), 225–240. https://doi.org/10.1016/S0004-3702(78)80015-0.

Widrow, B. (1960). *An adaptive 'Adaline' neuron using chemical 'memistors'* (No. 1553–2; Stanford Electronics Laboratories technical report).

Widrow, B., & Hoff, M. (1960). *Adaptive switching circuits*. https://doi.org/10.21236/ad0241531.

Wiener, N. (1961). *Cybernetics: Or control and communication in the animal and the machine* (2° edizione). MIT Press.

Wilks, Y. (1972). *An artificial intelligence approach to machine translation.* Stanford University CA Department of Computer Science. https://apps.dtic.mil/sti/citations/AD0741199

Xie, M., Jean, N., Burke, M., Lobell, D., & Ermon, S. (2016, March 5). Transfer learning from deep features for remote sensing and poverty mapping. In *Thirtieth AAAI Conference on Artificial Intelligence.* https://www.aaai.org/ocs/index.php/AAAI/AAAI16/paper/view/12196

Zhang, A., Lipton, Z. C., Li, M., & Smola, A. (2021). *Dive into deep learning.* arXiv preprint *ArXiv:2106.11342.*

3

CRIMINOLOGY AT THE CROSSROADS?

Computational Perspectives

The Increasingly Computational Nature of Criminology

Crime and Geospatial Modeling

Weisburd's Call

Almost every scientific discipline is populated by a myriad of controversial findings that commit scholars to their resolution. Criminology certainly does not represent an exception to this fact. The study of crime and criminal behaviors is, still nowadays and despite (or maybe precisely for) the increasing amount of data available, characterized by the presence of results going in opposite directions and, as a consequence, by the lack of universal or quasi-universal tendencies. Whether this is a structural problem of research originating from issues such as replicability, simply an intrinsic feature of human behavior's complexity, or both remains an open problem. Nonetheless, criminology has also produced results that hold regardless of the social, economic, and political contexts in which they are investigated. Among these, certainly lies the widely recognized role of space (or "place") in explaining crime (Johnson, 2010).

Scholarly efforts have demonstrated that many types of criminal behaviors cluster in time and across space. The definition and scale of space might vary based on several key factors, including for instance the nature of the urban landscape under scrutiny, yet the non-random distribution of crime is an undisputed truth worldwide. Research has corroborated this truth through a multitude of studies focusing on many different countries, including cities in the United States (Eck & Weisburd, 1995), United Kingdom (Malleson & Andresen, 2016), Canada (Andresen & Malleson, 2015; Law et al., 2015), Italy (Favarin, 2018), China (Liu et al., 2016; Ye et al., 2015), Brazil (de Melo et al., 2015), India (Mazeika & Kumar, 2017), Spain (Giménez-Santana et al., 2018), Nigeria (Umar et al., 2020), and South Africa (Breetzke, 2018).

This wealth of knowledge has mostly emerged in parallel with or after Weisburd's seminal work presenting the so-called "law of crime concentration"

DOI: 10.4324/9781003217732-3

(2015). The law establishes that few specific areas (e.g., communities, neighborhoods, blocks, street segments) are responsible for a disproportionate amount of crimes within the same city. The empirical evidence supporting this finding further illustrates that crime concentration holds across time and cities. The 2015 article called for a recalibration of the main criminological focus from person-based perspectives, which are mostly connected to life-course and developmental theories, to a place-based perspective. Weisburd's work sought to provoke a "turning point" in criminology by illustrating the potential for achieving "general propositions of universal validity" – an expression quoted from Sutherland (1939) – through the study of the spatial patterns that describe criminal behaviors. His call highlighted this potential from a scientific point of view and, importantly, from a policy standpoint. In his view, Weisburd anticipated the promises of this new paradigm in the definition, development, and application of crime prevention and reduction policies.

The Origins

Although the article written by Weisburd has represented a crucial moment for the recognition of place-based approaches for the study and countering of crime, the key ingredients for this recognition were already accumulated by decades, if not centuries, of scientific quest aiming at understanding the relationship between crime and space. The origins of this quest, de facto, date back to the 19th century, when European statisticians produced the first maps unfolding the geographical distribution of specific types of crime-related phenomena. In 1892, Adriano Balbi and André Michel Guerry created maps that illustrated the links between education and certain types of crime in France (Dent, 2000). A few years later, in 1831, Adolphe Quetelet generated maps focusing on the distribution of crime against property in France (Cullen & Wilcox, 2010). Similarly, Joseph Fletcher in 1849 and Henry Mayhew in 1861 crafted instead maps displaying male incarcerations rates and county-level crimes in England and Wales (Chamard, 2006).

Inquiries on the geography of crime grew over the decades in sophistication and sensibly touched also Shaw and McKay (1942): their studies on juvenile delinquency not only pertained to the individual autobiographies of juveniles involved in criminal activities but also addressed the geographical distribution of crime in Chicago. These historical trajectories testify to the longstanding fascination of social scientists with the relationship between crime and place and anticipated the growing emphasis that criminologists began to put into this area of research starting from the second half of the twentieth century.

Space has a relevant role in the definition of the Routine Activities Theory by Cohen and Felson (1979) as well as in the architecture of the environmental criminology framework, heralded by the Crime Pattern Theory developed by Paul Brantingham and Patricia Brantingham (1984).

The evolution and advancement in empirical research of these decades are intrinsically connected with the many changes occurring in the policing sphere, directly resulting from an increasing dialogue between academics and law enforcement, especially in the United States. One of the landmark transitions in this evolution is the definition of the problem-oriented policing (POP) paradigm proposed by Goldstein in 1979, which aimed at defining a new policing strategy directed toward the identification and resolution of problems directly connected to increasing crime risks, mostly in areas characterized by high levels of crime (the so-called "hot-spots") (Goldstein, 2018).

As a second landmark transition, in 1998, Sherman outlined the definition of "evidence-based policing." Building upon the intuitions of August Vollmer and the novelties introduced in police practice by POP,[1] Sherman posited the need for a new paradigm in which empirical evidence is systematically used to formalize guidelines and evaluate agencies and officers (1998).

Sherman's appeal came in a historical period in which the first crime-mapping platforms were already being engineered and used by law enforcement agencies and in which the computerized data-recording systems such as Compstat were gaining considerable popularity across the United States (Magers, 2004). Over the years, the widespread adoption of these tools has also been facilitated by the necessity for many police departments to cope with consistent budget cuts and shortages of officers, especially in the United States (Perry, 2013).

This process, a result of various causes that include institutional and organizational changes within the police and the increase of data-driven approaches to the study of crime, led to the diffusion of the predictive policing model. Predictive policing refers to a set of techniques that rely on considerable amounts of data fed into computational methods to forecast crime-exploiting information on the spatiotemporal occurrence of crime itself. Building upon the widely corroborated evidence that crime indeed clusters across space and time, predictive policing seeks to leverage these regularities to anticipate locations and timeframes in which crime will happen in a given urban context.

The consolidation of the predictive policing model is often accredited to LAPD Chief William Bratton, who in 2008 widely sponsored the benefits of predictive analytics to reduce crime. Bratton, sustained by the National Institute of Justice, was in fact defined as the man who brought predictive policing to the forefront (Rose, 2009). Following two symposia in 2009, and as a consequence of decades of interest in empirical and analytical approaches to crime reduction by academics and practitioners, the concept of predictive policing hence attracted unprecedented attention in the United States first and then in other regions of the world.

While it is highly debatable whether all predictive policing solutions are constructed using sophisticated computational methods and, most importantly, work in the first place, this new path in applied research and policing marked a new course with researchers increasingly exploring the promises offered by computing for studying, forecasting, and ultimately, reducing crime.

Current Approaches

Several geospatial modeling approaches and solutions have emerged recently, and many of them transcended the boundaries of purely academic research to strengthen their ties with law enforcement, taking advantage of business opportunities in this regard. One of the most popular and debated solutions is PredPol. The software is developed and owned by the homonymous company, launched in 2012, which recently transitioned to a new name, Geolitica, as an answer to the vast demand for reform and even dismantling of predictive policing algorithms in the United States. PredPol has been at the forefront of a vivid discussion in the last few years, with activists and academics (often outside the field of criminology) questioning its actual ability (as well as the ability of other similar approaches) to reduce crime and advancing accusations of reinforcing discrimination, bias, and systemic racism in policing practices in the United States (Heaven, 2020; Lum & Isaac, 2016; Miller, 2020; Soss & Weaver, 2017).

Its functioning is based on a machine learning algorithm that uses three data points to assess what areas (and in what hours) are at the highest risk of being targeted by crime: the crime type, the location, and the time of the crime itself.

The core algorithmic dimension of the software relies on so-called "self-exciting point process" models that were originally developed and deployed for the study the spatiotemporal distribution of earthquakes (Hawkes, 1971; Ogata, 1988; Reinhart, 2018). The intuition behind these algorithms is that crime is concentrated in space and time and, most importantly, possesses a self-excitation feature similar to aftershocks in earthquakes. Using these regularities, the authors claim that it is possible to offer insights to optimize patrolling and policing activity in general (Mohler et al., 2011).

Another approach that has become particularly popular in research and practice in the last decade is Risk Terrain Modeling (RTM) (see for instance Marchment and Gill's recent systematic review on its use across different contexts (2021)). RTM is based on the idea that space directly influences crime distribution, even in etiological terms, and that the spatial characterization of a specific area is therefore crucial to identify places at high risk. This spatial characterization is operationalized by defining distinct risk map layers, each including landscape features that correlate with crime, such as parks, abandoned facilities, and so on. Among the benefits of the approach, according to the authors of the landmark 2011 paper that first unraveled the approach, lies the lack of complex statistical modeling in favor of user-friendly data models based on raster and spatial layers (Caplan et al., 2011). The selection of spatial risk factors can be made in different ways, including meta-analysis or professional experience, and then RTM connects the presence of each factor to a certain risk value mapping its presence, absence, or intensity. Every factor is defined as a separate layer, and when all the layers are combined, a composite risk value is generated that computes an aggregated risk value signifying greater risk of crime occurrence in that specific geographical area. Similar to PredPol, RTM has also become popular across US police departments as a tool for assisting law enforcement in the definition of effective policing strategies. A third, widely diffused (and debated) software is Hunchlab, which somehow blends together components characterizing PredPol and RTM. The goal of the machine learning-empowered system is to forecast areas that will be targeted by crime, and also offers recommendations on potential tactics to tackle crime occurring in a specific area.

To accomplish this, HunchLab uses more data than PredPol and RTM, meaning that not only it uses data on offenses and the surrounding environment, but also information related to weather, major events, and contextual variables that may be correlated with crime dynamics. The software builds on two core ideas. First, different types of crime and, most importantly, different types of communities should be linked to tailored policing strategies. Second, crimes that can be more effectively addressed by direct police intervention are weighted more in the predictions compared to crimes that cannot be properly countered by police presence.

Interestingly, Ferguson (2019) states that we can trace parallelisms between the three traditional philosophies of policing, i.e., hot spot policing, problem-oriented policing, and community-based policing, and the three software here described, i.e., PredPol, RTM and HunchLab.

Future Frontiers

As new methods appear in the research landscape, place-based perspectives on crime have been assisted by a growth in the multitude of different computational approaches that go beyond the abovementioned ones. Many of these approaches never became operational in the policy domain, and many of them also came from scholars that are not originally embedded in criminology. Though all based on the intuition that crime clusters across space, the specific algorithmic mechanisms governing the different approaches, the assumption underlying data, or the type of data utilized often differ significantly.

One line of research that fostered a particular interest in scholars, for instance, aims at combining traditional criminal, spatial, and social features with information gathered from mobile usage or social media activity (Bogomolov et al., 2014; De Nadai et al., 2020; Gerber, 2014). The ubiquity of communication technologies allows research to inform computational models with information that can map the dynamic nature of human behavior to surpass the limits posed by the static nature of traditional data sources, as well as their cost in terms of money and time.

Novel sources of data do not represent, as anticipated, the only type of innovation in this sphere. Artificial intelligence (AI), and particularly machine learning, can offer new solutions too (Huang et al., 2018; Yi et al., 2019). Alternatively, they expand and advance existing theoretical approaches. As an example, recently the risk terrain approach has been tested against the use of machine learning algorithms, showing that in spite of their higher computational and theoretical complexity, Random Forests can provide more accurate crime forecasts exploiting spatially varying associations of generators of crime as well as demographic characteristics (Wheeler & Steenbeek, 2021).

Weisburd's call for a new turning point in criminology does not seem to have gone unheard, as developments in the area of place-based methods and geospatial modeling demonstrate. What surely remains now an utterly open problem is how to integrate new methodologies with existing theories and, furthermore, how to use such methodologies to ameliorate crime prevention policies with social justice, fairness, and accountability in mind.

Crime and Networks

The Networked Criminology Viewpoint

A little more than ten years ago, Papachristos wrote a passionate and lucid book chapter showcasing the missed opportunities for criminologists and, in general, crime researchers resulting from the scarce and mostly superficial diffusion of social network analysis approaches in the study of deviance and criminal behavior. Besides few notable exceptions (see Morselli, 2009). Papachristos' appeal (2011) for the adoption of a networked perspective in criminology may resemble the one made by Weisburd concerning place-based approaches for the study and prevention of crime. Despite the many similarities, one main difference has to be noted. Weisburd's call was made standing on decades of inquiry on the role of geography and space for criminal and deviant processes. Papachristos' appeal instead appeared without a backup of dozens of studies justifying, corroborating, or sponsoring such network perspective. A notable exception was the scholarship of Carlo Morselli, who was among the very first to understand and underscore the power of networks for the study of crime (see for instance, Morselli et al., 2007, Morselli & Roy, 2008, Morselli, 2009). In fact, among the several points Papachristos made, one particularly highlighted the low-intensity, flat trend of the number of publications in criminology measuring or utilizing networks, further reinforcing the finding by comparing the same type of trend with sociology and public health, two disciplines in which the scientific production showed consistent growth over the years. In this regard, Papachristos' starting point is radically different from Weisburd's and precisely calls out the almost complete indifference of criminologists for the application of network science as a fruitful methodological and theoretical framework of inquiry.

Ten years in research have a very relative value. There are disciplines and historical moments in which these seem to last like a month, as major breakthroughs struggle to be made and theories remain mostly unchanged or undisputed. Conversely, there exist cases in which 10 years seem more similar to a century, as almost every piece of knowledge is torn apart by new findings or new methodological approaches that revolutionize the way in which scientists were used to address old and new problems. The feelings about research on crime and networks are somehow mixed.

There is no doubt that, in the last decade, the trend in publications that adopt, describe, measure, or theorize networks in relation to crime has grown tremendously. This trend has diffused across criminology journals and beyond, spreading over various other outlets transcending the boundaries set by the categorization of venues by disciplines. It may have taken a while, but in the end, criminologists got fascinated by the power, flexibility, and promises of graphs (Bouchard & Malm, 2016; Kertész & Wachs, 2021; Malm et al., 2017). At the same time, however, there are still several lingering issues, curbing the full potential that networks can have in advancing our knowledge in relation to a myriad of dimensions in research on crime.

Recently, Faust and Tita (2019) aptly examined the main patterns in the state of the art of networks in criminology, focusing particularly on perspectives in co-offending networks, illicit networks, gang-rivalry networks, and neighborhoods and crime. By all means, the selected list of topics covered in their review article does not encompass all the multifaceted areas of applications that have been investigated in the past years, testifying to the heterogeneous tentacles emerging from the increasing adoption of the "networked criminology" viewpoint. Yet, these four are probably those areas in which most scholarly attention has been allocated and, consequently, most technical and theoretical progresses have been made. In surveying these areas of research, Faust and Tita take score of the accumulated knowledge and unfold the pitfalls associated with network approaches in each of the areas, further proposing paths forward to either fix these pitfalls or in general move into new unexplored research directions.

It is beyond the scope of this section to comprehensively review the state of the art of the literature intersecting crime and networks. Yet, without specifically targeting the "banana skins" outline by Faust and Tita, some reflections can be made on a number of general issues that still affect the sophistication and possibilities posed by network crime research.

The Limits in Contemporary Network Crime Research

A first problematic tendency in "network criminology" is an overreliance on descriptive research design as the dominant rationale. Though description is critical as it gathers the first fundamental layer of empirical knowledge on the criminal processes under investigation, it does not provide sufficient adherence to the complexity of human behavior in the criminal and deviant sphere. Papachristos and similarly Faust and Tita already warned about the problematic consequences of using description as the only lens through which to extract findings from networks, calling for more careful attention to topics such as generative processes of network formation, among others. Node-level measures of centrality, network-level accounts of centralization as well as more localized perspectives on network motifs such as triads and dyads have been, and still are, decisive in providing scholars with a new range of information for characterizing influence, importance, or vulnerability of individuals (or locations) in criminal settings. Yet, there is a need to go beyond this paradigm and move toward deeper forms of investigation in the network crime research realm.

As anticipated, generative processes are one of the most propitious directions, as they inform us on the mechanisms through which connections emerge and networks are formed. In fact, scholars have consistently started to delve into this line of inquiry, as the literature on Exponential Random Graph Modeling (ERGM) applied to crime networks demonstrates (Duxbury & Haynie, 2018; Papachristos & Bastomski, 2018; Schaefer, 2012; Smith & Papachristos, 2016). Yet, generative processes alone do not solve the underlying issues curbing the potential of the network paradigm in criminology and crime research.

A second problematic tendency that is deeply connected to the first one as it constitutes an obstacle to inference is the disproportionate use of cross-sectional networks. The remarkable difficulties associated with sampling and gathering of data on illicit networks, as well as the infamous issues related to information completeness and the definition of boundaries in crime networks, play a significant role in the sedimentation of this second tendency (Berlusconi, 2013; Bright et al., 2021; Campana & Varese, 2020).

Albeit the literature contains works that introduce a dynamic or temporal component in the analysis of networks (Bright & Delaney, 2013; Bright et al., 2019; Davies & Marchione, 2015; Iwanski & Frank, 2013), still most research is bounded to use networks that only represent static snapshots of a given phenomenon at a certain point in time or, alternatively, networks that represent a cumulative result of preceding interactions and dynamics that, however, are not sequentially ordered. Trivially, this constitutes a major obstacle in the quest for understanding how criminal networks change, evolve, and respond to exogenous shocks, such as police interventions. Unfortunately, criminologists and crime researchers are not as lucky as other social scientists who can far more easily obtain network data or measure network interactions over time. In this sense, the massive explosion of network research relying on social media data for investigating a wide spectrum of topics, from polarization to dating dynamics, reflects the increasing salience of these topics from both research and policy perspectives as well as a cheap and fast opportunity for researchers to acquire rich information on complex social phenomena. It is unreasonable to think about a similar revolutionizing process for research on crime. With the tiny exception of scholars focusing on crime behaviors in the cyberspace, the rest of the literature is still dependent upon more traditional, costly, slow data construction and gathering mechanisms.

Even those studies designed with a dynamic or temporal component are subjected to many issues, such as the lack of fine-grained temporal scales and the source of the data which often come from police or criminal justice records and thus do not guarantee full completeness. I see this problem as the most difficult to overcome. It is the most difficult because it is naturally linked to the structural problems that characterize police and criminal justice data, as well as open-source information from reports and newspapers, and the one for which even creative methodological solutions may not suffice. Especially for wide networks, computational approaches that seek to go beyond cross-sectionality through simulation face combinatorial issues that are impossible to ignore. Even being able to simulate network dynamics starting from a single ground-truth snapshot, which is again theoretically doable if the network has a reasonably limited size, poses validation problems that become dramatically pressing, especially in the transition from research to policy. There is probably no silver lining for solving the problem of cross-sectionality in criminal network research. Efforts instead would perhaps require a mix of new strategies. These would include a strengthened partnership with those institutions that primarily "create" the data. These partnership might be centered on training activities to emphasize the importance of reliable and consistent data imputation practices as well as the definition of time-saving practices that allow law enforcement, intelligence analysts, or army members not to invest excessive time in data gathering practices, allowing them instead to concentrate on their core activities, while preserving information accuracy.

The third and fourth problems, which are structurally connected, instead refer to the lack of multi-modal and multi-layer approaches for studying and characterizing interdependency in criminal behaviors. While the formal concepts of "graph" and "network" are assumed to be known to the readers of this book, it is worth explaining what a multi-modal and a multi-layer network represent, given the very marginal use of these two concepts in the criminological literature.

A multi-modal network is a heterogeneous network in which each node belongs to a particular mode, and corresponding edges belong to a given cross-network, which is a specific interaction between two nodes (Heath & Sioson, 2009). To further exemplify, it is helpful to think about a crime dataset in which affiliates, weapons, and skills are the three modes. Then, affiliate-affiliate interactions, affiliate-weapon interactions, and affiliate-skill interactions map the three cross-networks in our multi-modal case.

A multi-layer network is instead a network that is composed of a set of nodes, as occurs in traditional networks, and a set of layers that map different types of relationships between the same nodes in the dataset (Kivela et al., 2014). Connections among nodes might be both intra- and inter-layers. A good example of a multi-layer network is the case of an illicit network in which the relations among the agents are formally different: one layer might consist of operational connections mapping whether two people act together in the preparation of a crime, one other layer might consist of familiar links between associates, a third instead might map communication interactions, and so on.

Two main factors can explain why crime network research has substantially overlooked multi-modal and multi-layer graph representations over the years. The first is related to the paucity of information embedded in criminal justice, police, and intelligence data. When law enforcement or other bodies gather and store data that can be used to derive criminal networks, these data generally contain only one type of information that can be used for network creation, for example, phone calls and co-arrest. For researchers, it is thus impossible to go beyond traditional unimodal, single-layer representations. The second factor concerns the delay of criminologists and crime researchers to keep up with methodological advances in graph theory and complex networks that are often more swiftly absorbed in other disciplines.

Although the first factor is, as also mentioned above, very difficult to overcome and will definitely require efforts that go beyond the mere academic sphere of crime network research, the second one is far more easily solvable through innovation pertaining to academic research directly. Beyond transdisciplinary collaboration – a critical topic that will be discussed in Chapter 4 – crime researchers and criminologists need to be more creative and proactive in receiving and incorporating methodological innovations from other fields, them being adjoining to criminology (e.g., sociology, economics, political sciences) or not (e.g., computer science, mathematics, physics, statistics). Especially in the cases in which data that can be structured in multi-modal or multi-layer forms are available, research on crime networks needs to test, apply, and even develop ad hoc solutions to better understand how crime and criminal behavior function in terms of their interdependence.

Networks are central in the current study of crime, as many things changed from Papachristos' article in 2011. However, the major tendency toward the use of cross-sectional, unimodal, single-layer networks prevents us all from gathering fundamental knowledge about temporal evolutions, correlates of interdependence, generative processes, and even causal mechanisms behind essential themes such as crime commission and co-offending, crime concentration, complex criminal like organized crime, and many others.

Crime research and foremost criminology have been areas of inquiry dominated by regression (Abbott, 1999; Papachristos, 2011), and every single student enrolled in a criminology program worldwide is instructed to be very cautious in trusting description and analysis of a single variable to explain a phenomenon, regardless of its factual or perceived complexity. Regression, broadly intended, serves to test, find, and interpret associations between covariates and a variable of interest. If the research design is appropriate, assumptions are met, and data are of acceptable quality, then we can have much more confidence in the explanation of a phenomenon compared to the description – and even the most sophisticated computational modeling – of a single variable of interest. Network crime research faces the same inherent problem: though with significant improvements in the last decade, we are most often trusting studies addressing single variables with the sole difference that in the network framework these are not vectors but, instead, take the form of matrices. It is of interest for the entire discipline – and for the policy community itself – to move forward and find solutions to take advantage of the continuously increasing methodological resources at our disposal.

Several other challenges stand in front of crime network research, like the use of heterogeneous data sources, including alternative ones, and the integration between online and offline behaviors. Nonetheless, I believe that the greatest benefits for this field of research can be achieved with systemic efforts to move from the current dominant paradigm based on unidimensional single-layer snapshots to novel dynamic, multidimensional perspectives. The pathways to put this into practice may be demanding and multi-fold, but as previously noted by Papachristos and Faust and Tita, the promises of a truly comprehensive "networked criminology" are tremendous.

Simulating Crime

Emergence and Promises of Agent-based Models in Research on Crime

The third trend that testifies to the increasing computational nature of research on crime concerns the diffusion of agent-based models (ABM) for studying crime. Agent-based modeling refers to the simulation of specific behaviors or dynamics through the computational generation of artificial agents (Epstein, 1999). This definition is far from being exhaustive: it is, in fact, overly general and its generality reflects the massive number of nuances, approaches, techniques, frameworks, and paradigms that characterize the development and application of ABM. Agent-based modeling has emerged due to achievements and progress in several fields, including computer science, physics, cognitive science, and applied mathematics. Bonabeau (2002) identified three main benefits of agent-based modeling (which he defines as a "mindset rather than a technology"): its ability to capture emergent phenomena, its potential for providing a natural description of a system, and finally, its flexibility.

These, and potentially other, benefits explain the great success that ABM have obtained in many scientific disciplines and fields, including the social sciences and criminology (Bankes, 2002; Gerritsen, 2015; Macy & Willer, 2002). ABM allow to formally model complex systems at the micro-level, with explicit mechanisms marked by different underlying principles or computational approaches, tracking interactions between agents and observing the emergence of macro-phenomena. This feature makes them particularly suitable for targeting complex systems, such as human societies, subjected to heterogeneity, nonstationarity, non-normality, and other quantitative characteristics that are most often extremely challenging to model effectively through traditional statistical models. Trivially, crime is a purely human and social phenomenon, and all such features are intrinsically connected to its complexity. Albeit decades of empirical research have unraveled the existence of clear macro-level patterns across many domains, these patterns are often abstractions of micro-level dynamics and quantitative synthesis among individuals or individual units, such as street segments in the crime and place literature. Agent-based modeling, on the contrary, provides an exciting paradigm that enable researchers to capture these macro-level patterns without discarding the micro and meso-mechanisms that generate them.

ABM possess an additional crucial feature that makes them particularly palatable to criminologists and crime researchers: they enable designing, conducting, and evaluating artificial experiments. Criminology scholars are often limited in the possibility of setting up and assessing experiments because of an array of issues, including economic costs and ethical concerns. ABM, on the contrary, are most often very cheap in terms of economic burden and bypass many of the ethical concerns connected with experiments in the real world (Groff & Mazerolle, 2008). The fact that artificial agents populate ABM guarantees scholars the freedom to explore and test virtually infinite possibilities without causing harm or leading to unintended societal consequences at scale.

Programs that Hit Limits: Two Issues

Nonetheless, it is worth highlighting that while virtual experiments by means of computer simulations, particularly ABM, are a precious alternative to real-world experiments, they come with limitations that prevent them from fully achieving the optimal standards of answers gathered through well-designed randomized controlled trials. Two main interrelated limitations are particularly important in this sense. The first regards the necessary stylization of reality and the second refers to the need for high-quality data.

Regardless of the sophistication of a simulation in terms of formalized mechanisms, a modeler will necessarily need to synthesize reality, explicitly (or implicitly) excluding phenomena occurring in the real world. Computational efficiency is, in this sense, critical. Researchers and people interested in ABM of crime and criminal behaviors are interested in flexible computational frameworks that do not require overly expensive resources or prohibitive amounts of time to be run. And yet, even assuming to have an infinite amount of computational power at disposal, it remains very challenging to try to accurately model a virtual society in all its facets and dimensions. In this sense, oversimplification is a likely threat to ABM reliability.

Concerning the second limitation, informing a model with accurate and realistic data is fundamental to ensure that, regardless of its formal correctness, it also functions based on information that resembles reality as much as possible. Empirical calibration serves precisely this purpose. Data are not always available, especially when aiming at simulating a society at large. A recent review by Groff et al. (2019) dedicated to ABM applications in urban crime found that only 37.8% of the publications in their sample of 45 articles used empirical distributions to validate model outcomes, highlighting how often researchers fail to embed real-world information in their ABM, posing a consistent challenge for future use in criminology and crime research. The review aptly points out that ABM are often used exactly because data are unreliable or not available. Nonetheless, it is of paramount importance that efforts in the community will be devoted to the increasing integration of empirical data in agent-based modeling approaches. Alternatively, when data are problematic, guidelines ensuring that researchers explicitly motivate their choices and clarify the limitations of their data infrastructures and the reliability of their models – which should be assessed through sensitivity analysis – are crucial.

One of the tools to encourage researchers to describe their assumptions, data sources, and theoretical foundations is the ODD+D protocol, which expands upon the original ODD (Müller et al., 2013). Founded in the context of ecology studies, its inclusion in studies involving the use of ABM for research on crime can significantly help the entire community in being better informed about the usability, portability, and applicability of simulation approaches for studying crime. This suggestion was one of the several ones advanced by Groff and colleagues in their review paper. The question of the use of this protocol or, more in general, the inclusion of detailed information about how ABM are designed, developed, and informed yet remains open. Potential strategies to foster changes in this regard may also involve journals through a set of incentives or friendly policies that reward authors for their diligence in this context, similarly to what has happened in many disciplines with preregistration (Nosek et al., 2018).

The Present and Future of ABM in research on crime

In spite of these issues that still affect the diffusion and impact of ABM in research on crime this approach (or, again, "mindset") has been demonstrated to be a powerful tool for criminological research. So far, scholars have addressed research questions and problems from the perspective of agent-based modeling in a variety of domains. Besides urban crime and policing (Malleson et al., 2010; Weisburd et al., 2017), studies have been published focusing on illicit network resilience (Duxbury & Haynie, 2019), interpersonal victimization (Birks et al., 2014), organized crime (Calderoni et al., 2021; Nardin et al., 2016; Pint et al., 2010), drug trafficking (Magliocca et al., 2019), and terrorism (Elliott & Kiel, 2004; Keller et al., 2010; Moon & Carley, 2007).

This variety of application domains is coupled with the variety of computational procedures through which ABM have been designed in the literature.

In general, agent-based modeling can be structured through manifold different techniques and philosophies regardless of the discipline. While works on ABMs and crime have not yet reached the level of sophistication of other fields, in which for instance the link between simulations and intelligent agents is stronger (e.g., reinforcement learning), scholars are increasingly demonstrating higher creativity in the ways in which such simulations are engineered. Moving from simple "if-then" approaches (Bosse et al., 2009), which become highly inefficient when the number of agents and the number of possible actions (and combinations of actions) grow, more recent scholarship has provided a set of new interesting methodological solutions that testify to the advances in this area of research. Among these are probabilistic approaches that combine individual and relational factors in flexible and adaptable ways (Calderoni et al., 2021) and applications integrating mobility data which are increasingly available to inform statistical investigations of crime patterns (Rosés et al., 2020).

A final aspect worth outlining concerns the interesting possibilities put in place by agent-based modeling as a bridge between geospatial modeling and crime network research. ABM offer a promising opportunity – that some have already explored – to approach the study of crime or the assessment of strategies for reducing crime from a multidimensional perspective that puts equal attention to the spatial dynamics of crime concentration and the interconnectedness and interdependence of criminal behaviors. Trivially, the future pathways of ABM in research on crime will not be confined to research on crime and place and scientific enterprise on crime networks; nevertheless, it is relevant to note how for these two strands of research – which are increasingly getting closer – ABM represent a possible game-changer in the definition of more comprehensive analytical strategies.

There may be – to be honest, there are – disciplines in which computing has diffused more rapidly, rigorously, and effectively: yet, research on crime is evolving. The open point is now to understand whether machine learning will become the fourth important methodological turning point of contemporary research on crime.

Assessing the State of the Art in Research Intersecting Artificial Intelligence and Criminology

Background

The previous subsections have delineated the emergence, limits, and promises of three main trends that define the increasingly computational nature of research on crime. Interestingly, one key aspect is that as methodological (and theoretical) progress are made, the horizon becomes much less compartmentalized and much more homogeneous because the three become closer and closer. Integration and contamination among approaches, techniques, or "mindsets" is a fundamental force to push forward the boundaries of scientific discovery. It requires time, a certain degree of maturity, and a sufficient level of creativity in imagining new ways to tackle old unsolved problems as well as unanswered questions.

There are reasons to think that machine learning and AI approaches in general will represent the next significant disruption in methodological trends in research on crime. The future is difficult to predict, and I do not want to venture into speculative forecasts. What I can do, however, is trying to empirically assess the state of the art of machine learning and AI in criminology and draw some conclusions about the point in which we are all standing now.

In a recent article, I scanned the literature at the intersection of AI and research on crime using Scopus, a database containing over 69 million abstracts of peer-reviewed literature (Campedelli, 2021). The analysis of 692 relevant works highlighted several patterns related to this evolving area of scientific inquiry. The article first showed that researchers working at the intersection of AI and research on crime mainly focused on cyber-related topics, such as malware detection, cyber frauds, phishing, and other similar issues. Contrarily, studies addressing themes related to algorithmic discrimination, fairness, and ethics were found to be highly peripheral. Concerning the structure of the authorship network, the analysis revealed a highly disconnected structure. I argued that this fragmentation represents a substantial obstacle to the development of a more solid and diverse scientific community.

Finally, the paper also looked at the country-level patterns of collaboration. Findings showed that international collaboration was mostly a signature of countries that are less central in the co-authorship network and that, conversely, scientists in more productive countries (e.g., the United States and China) tend to mainly collaborate domestically. I hypothesized that this pattern might be the effect of two distinct causes. First, more peripheral countries might seek international collaboration to overcome the burden of the unequal distribution of resources affecting research at the global level. Second, most central countries might be less prone to share their knowledge with other potentially competing countries given this particularly critical area of inquiry that intersects domains of public and national security in many different ways.

My article has been the first to quantitatively analyze this area of research and offer some insights on some of the directions and most relevant trends emerging from the rapidly evolving literature exploring the potential of machine and deep learning to predict, forecast, and study criminal phenomena.

Taking inspiration from that approach, in this chapter I will analyze the trends and patterns of scientific production at the intersection between AI and research on crime by focusing on a restricted sample of relevant sources in the AI and criminology domains, respectively. The rationale is to further shed light on this area of research and, foremost, do so by considering the top 20 venues in each discipline. While in my previous article (Campedelli, 2021) I used all the relevant Scopus entries, here I will specifically concentrate on those outlets that generally attract the manuscripts that may potentially become the most influential articles in each of the two disciplines. The literature has documented and discussed the fact that journals in many fields, especially top-tier ones, are often more resistant to publish papers that contain innovative methodological approaches or interdisciplinary perspectives (Mingers & Willmott, 2013; Rafols et al., 2012; Richiardi et al., 2006). The result of my search in the top-tier venues in criminology and AI will then give us a measure of how well research at the intersection of the two has been able to "infiltrate" outlets that might be traditionally more prone to value well-established methodologies and approaches or traditional topics.

Although this strategy excludes articles published in other journals (like interdisciplinary ones) and the analysis here presented should not be considered a systematic review, it will notwithstanding offer a new significant perspective to understand whether crime-related applications have become popular in the most impactful AI venues. At the same time, it will help us explore whether AI approaches have started to gain momentum also in those criminology journals that generally produce more citations. The methodology and search strategy are detailed below.

Methodology

Search Strategy

The openly accessible data provided by Google Scholar Metrics have been used to identify the 20 most impactful venues in AI and criminology. At the time of writing, the accessed data were based on the Google index as it was in June 2020. Specifically, criminology journals are listed in the "Criminology, Criminal Law & Policing" subcategory within the broader "Social Sciences" category. AI journals and proceedings instead are listed in the "Artificial Intelligence" subcategory that is part of the "Engineering and Computer Science" primary field.

Tables 3.1 and 3.2 report the 20 venues per each field along with Google data on each outlet's h5-index and h5-median. The h5-index is defined as the largest number h such that h articles published from 2015 to 2019 have at least h citations each. The h5-median for a given journal or conference is instead the median number of citations for the articles making up the venues' h5-index.

For all the total 40 venues, I have manually performed dedicated searches in each journal or conference proceeding archive, restricting the timeframe to works that were published after 2009 (2010–2021). Trivially, searches have been different based on the type of venue. For criminology journals, where possible I have performed the query:

"machine learning" OR "artificial intelligence"

in abstracts, titles, or article keywords. Where detailing the field to be searched was not allowed, I have searched these words in the entire text

Table 3.1 Top 20 journals in criminology according to data from Google Scholar Metrics

Rank	Journal	h5-index	h5-median
1	British Journal of Criminology	42	60
2	Journal of Criminal Justice	40	58
3	Criminal Justice & Behavior	39	60
4	Crime & Delinquency	38	49
5	Law and Human Behavior	38	48
6	Justice Quarterly	36	58
7	Criminology & Public Policy	36	54
8	Journal of Quantitative Criminology	35	53
9	Criminology	35	51
10	Journal of Experimental Criminology	32	52
11	Journal of Research in Crime and Delinquency	31	50
12	Sexual Abuse	31	45
13	European Journal of Criminology	31	42
14	International Journal of Offender Therapy and Comparative Criminology	30	45
15	Policing and Society	30	41
16	Theoretical Criminology	28	44
17	Criminology and Criminal Justice	28	42
18	Criminal Justice Policy Review	27	34
19	Youth Violence and Juvenile Justice	26	37
20	American Journal of Criminal Justice	26	36

and then included or excluded the retrieved items based on relevance (e.g., if an article included the expression "machine learning" only in the background section as a reference to another work using a particular classification approach to predict recidivism, that article would not be deemed relevant and would then be excluded).

Concerning AI venues, which include both journals and conferences, I have instead relied on the following query:

"crime" OR criminal* OR "police" OR "policing"

As done for the criminology outlets this query was directed toward abstract, titles, or article keywords when possible. Given that this was not always feasible due to the particular functioning schemes of most journal or conference websites, I first retrieved records based on the presence of one of the keywords in the text and then included and excluded each work based on the relevance for the purposes of the current analysis.

Description of the Sample

A total of 132 articles have been gathered from the search across the 40 different venues. Out of 132, 43 originated from journals belonging to the field of criminology, and the remaining 89 have been published in AI

Table 3.2 Top 20 journals and conferences in artificial intelligence according to data from Google Scholar Metrics

Rank	Journal/Conference	h5-index	h5-median
1	International Conference on Learning Representations	203	359
2	Neural Information Processing Systems	198	377
3	International Conference on Machine Learning (ICML)	171	309
4	AAAI Conference on Artificial Intelligence	126	183
5	Expert Systems with Applications	111	152
6	IEEE Transactions on Systems, Man and Cybernetics Part B, Cybernetics	111	150
7	IEEE Transactions on Neural Networks and Learning Systems	107	146
8	Neurocomputing	100	143
9	Applied Soft Computing	96	123
10	International Joint Conference on Artificial Intelligence (IJCAI)	95	140
11	IEEE Transactions on Fuzzy Systems	87	117
12	Knowledge-based Systems	85	121
13	The Journal of Machine Learning Research	82	153
14	Neural Computing and Applications	67	98
15	Neural Networks	64	92
16	International Conference on Artificial Intelligence and Statistics	57	89
17	Engineering Applications of Artificial Intelligence	57	78
18	Robotics and Autonomous Systems	56	87
19	Conference on Learning Theory (COLT)	54	80
20	Journal of Intelligent & Fuzzy Systems	50	79

journals or conferences. Concerning criminology, the *Journal of Quantitative Criminology* is the venue that accounted for the majority of the works in the sample, with a total of 15 records obtained. The second most represented journal is *Criminology & Public Policy*, with a total of 6 articles, and the third ones are ex-aequ Policing and Society and the Journal of Experimental Criminology with 4 articles each.

In AI-related outlets, the *Journal of Intelligent & Fuzzy System* is ranked first with a total of 20 papers addressing or focusing on crime-related applications, followed by the *Journal of Machine Learning Research* (15) and *Neural Computing and Applications* (13). The distribution for both criminology and AI venues is provided in Figures 3.1 and 3.2. Besides the title and journal of each paper, I have compiled a dataset containing the name of the authors of each record, along with the associated country in relation to each affiliation (e.g., if an author publishes a paper while at Harvard University, their associated country will be the United States) and the author-specified keywords.

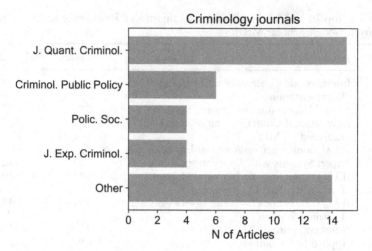

Figure 3.1 Distribution of articles across journals in the criminology sample.

From a temporal standpoint, publication patterns are similar in both criminology and AI. Figures 3.3 and 3.4 report the raw temporal trend in the number of publications disaggregated by field and overall, along with the cumulative share per each of the three categories, respectively.

As anticipated, the trends appear similar in both criminology and AI. In the first years considered in the analysis, the interest in the application of AI methods for research on crime measured by the number of recorded publications remained particularly low. The trends considerably grew from 2018 onward, reaching the peaks in 2020. In criminology and AI, around

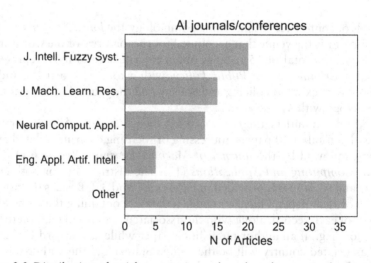

Figure 3.2 Distribution of articles across journals and conferences in the AI sample.

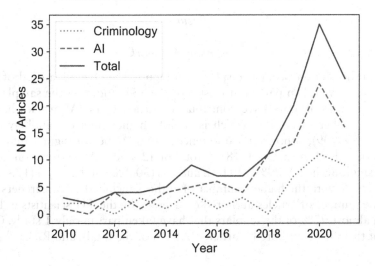

Figure 3.3 Raw temporal trends of publications in the sample for criminology, AI, and overall.

63% and 61% of the articles have been published in 2019, 2020, and 2021 alone. The cumulative plot documents that, although slightly, criminology has been more proactive in exploring machine learning for the study of crime from 2010 to 2017 given the higher cumulative share compared to AI works. After 2017, however, papers addressing crime-related problems or experimenting with crime-related data in AI journals have grown slightly more steeply than the criminological counterpart.

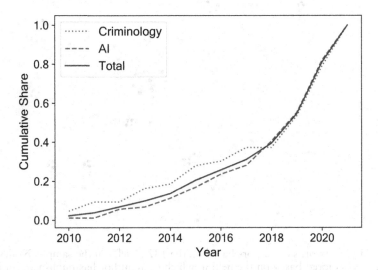

Figure 3.4 Cumulative share of works in the sample in criminology, AI, and overall.

Results

Authorship Network

The authorship network is displayed in Figure 3.5. Overall, a total of 441 scholars have taken part in at least 1 of the 132 studies in the sample. On average, 3.45 authors have contributed to each work: AI articles have a mean number of authors which is slightly higher than criminology ones (3.62 and 3.09), although the difference is found to be non-significant (*t*-test statistic = 1.34, *p*-value = 0.18). A total of 12 studies have been conducted by a single author (9.09%), 40 by 2 authors (30.3%), and 23 by 3 (17.42%). The article with the highest number of authors included 17 researchers.

The number of articles authored on average by the 441 scientists is 1.04, with almost 97% of the scholars that have taken part in only 1 study. Only 13 of them have authored 2 articles (2.94% of the total), and Richard Berk

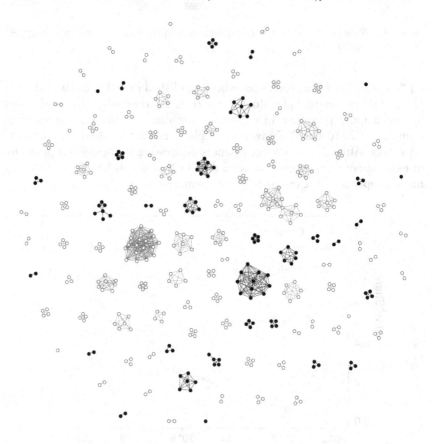

Figure 3.5 Networks of authors based on the 132 articles in the sample. Nodes are colored based on the field in which each author has published. Authors in criminology are black, authors in AI are white.

Table 3.3 Descriptive statistics of the authorship network

Network Feature	Value
No. of nodes (authors)	441
Density	0.009
Total No. of edges	1,766
No. of isolates	9
No. of dyads	31
No. of triads	24
No. of larger components (>3)	54
Nodes in the largest component	18
Avg. nodes in components with >3 nodes	5.51
St. dev. of nodes in components with >3 nodes	2.51
Avg. number of publications per author	1.04
St. dev. of number of publications per author	0.37

from the University of Pennsylvania is the most prolific author ($n = 8$), and the only one to have published more than 2 studies.[2] These figures clearly emphasize the immaturity of this area of research, at least from the mere perspective of scientific collaboration. Although it is possible that some of the authors here represented have participated in other works intersecting AI and research on crime published elsewhere, the fact that more than 10 years of data in the most influential venues in the two fields report such a low degree of average contribution plays a major obstacle in the construction of frameworks, lines of inquiry, and theories and limits the cumulative construction of knowledge. Data on the authorship graph are summarized in Table 3.3.

This low degree of mean contribution should be read in conjunction with scientists' low degree of collaboration. The low degree of collaboration is empirically signaled by two results. First, the network is, in reality, a collection of many disconnected components.

Second, beyond this atomized structure, Figure 3.5 documents the complete absence of cross-collaboration between disciplines. Authors that published in criminology journals only collaborated with authors that also published in criminology journals, and the same applies to AI researchers. Data report that none of the 441 authors could co-author works in at least one venue in each discipline. This result sheds clear light on the current compartmentalized nature of research at the intersection of AI and crime, especially concerning publication patterns in the most influential venues.

Country-wide Collaboration Network

Besides the author-level collaboration network, the graph of country collaboration provides insights on macro-level patterns of co-authorship focusing on the affiliation of all the scholars in the sample. The dataset has been compiled to include the affiliation of each of them and particularly the country in which the associated institutions are located.[3] Such information allow to

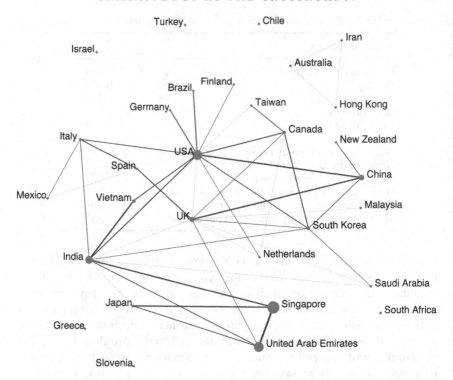

Figure 3.6 Country collaboration network based on all the 132 articles in the sample. Nodes are scaled based on their degree centrality and edges are log-scaled based on the weight of each connection.

understand the degree to which the gathered works are characterized by a degree of internationalization. Figure 3.6 displays the resultant network, with node size scaled based on each country's centrality and edges log-scaled based on the weight of each country-to-country connection.

Overall, scientists in the sample come from a total of 30 countries and the network counts a total of 86 edges – not taking into account self-loops which map domestic collaboration between scientists affiliated to institutions in the same country – meaning that on average each country collaborates with 2.86 other countries. Without considering self-loops, the total density of the network is 0.098, with the graph including six isolates (Chile, Greece, Israel, Slovenia, South Africa, and Turkey) and one triad, composed by Australia, Hong Kong, and Iran. The remaining 21 countries are all part of the same main component (Table 3.4).

To investigate country-level statistics I have relied on the binarized version (with no self-loops) of the country collaboration network. Data reveal that the five most central countries, based on their total degree centrality, are the United States of America (12 connections, density equal to 0.414), the United Kingdom (10, 0.345), India (9, 0.310), South Korea (6, 0.207), and Canada (5, 0.172).

Table 3.4 Description of the country collaboration network

Network Feature	Value
No. of nodes (countries)	30
Density (without self-loops)	0.098
Total No. of edges	86
No. of isolates	6
No. of dyads	0
No. of triads	1
No. of larger components (>3)	1
Nodes in the largest component	21

In terms of betweenness centrality, which maps the brokerage role of countries in the network, the United States (0.212), the United Kingdom (0.133), and India (0.107) remain the most central ones, followed by China (0.047) and Italy (0.041).

The third selected indicator of centrality, namely, eigenvector centrality, measures the centrality of a given country as a function of the centrality of the connections of that same country. Put differently, according to eigenvector centrality, a country is central if the other countries to which it is connected are also central. With this regard, the ranking remains identical to the one obtained after the computation of degree centrality (Table 3.5).

More generally, a wider analysis of a total of 15 centrality measures[4] reports that the United States are among the top 3 countries in 80% of the selected measures, followed by India and the United Kingdom (both among the top 3 in the 73.33% of the measures). This further confirms the critical role of these three countries for research in this evolving area of inquiry. Notably, although researchers based at Chinese institutions are

Table 3.5 Ranking of 10 most central countries in the country collaboration network, based on total-degree centrality, betweenness centrality, and eigenvector centrality

	Total-Degree Centrality		Betweenness Centrality		Eigenvector Centrality	
Rank	Country	Value	Country	Value	Country	Value
1	The United States	0.414 (12)	The United States	0.212	The United States	0.435
2	The United Kingdom	0.345 (10)	The United Kingdom	0.133	The United Kingdom	0.421
3	India	0.310 (9)	India	0.107	India	0.373
4	South Korea	0.207 (6)	China	0.047	South Korea	0.336
5	Canada	0.172 (5)	Italy	0.041	Canada	0.266

Note: For total-degree centrality, the number of raw connections is reported between parentheses.

widely present in the sample, China is not among the most central countries in the network due to the predominant tendency to domestic collaboration.

In terms of degree of scientific collaboration between scientists based in different countries in criminology and AI, the two fields reveal similar trends. Excluding from the computation the publications with one single author ($n = 12$), the mean of countries involved in each publication in criminology-based studies is 1.26, while it is 1.36 for AI (t-test statistic = 0.8, p-value = 0.41): this signals an overall tendency toward domestic collaboration rather than internationalization of research.

Overall, 90 non-solo publications (68.18% of the total) have been authored by authors based at institutions in the same given country. Out of 90, 33 articles have been written and published by at least two US-based researchers (36.66%). The second country with the highest number of publications authored by researchers based in the same country is India (12, 13.33% out of 90 articles), and the third is China (8, 8.88%). These numbers should not be interpreted without also considering the other side of the coin, namely, the international attitude of each country and, foremost, the overall amount of research activity produced by each country. The United States is ranked as the country with the highest number of domestically produced articles, but they are at the same time the country with the highest number of international connections in the country collaboration network: these two findings are not mutually exclusive but, rather, testify to the overall very high prevalence of US-based scholars in the sample.

Topics

To assess the heterogeneity of the topics investigated at the intersection of AI and criminology, I have focused on the author-generated keyword assigned to each article and constructed a co-occurrence weighted network, as done for the co-authorship and country collaboration networks. Out of the 132 total articles, 13 did not report any keyword (9.84%). Furthermore, I have performed a preliminary data processing step to ensure consistency across keywords by re-labeling keywords associated with very similar concepts or keywords written using different acronyms or stop words. To exemplify, "convolutional neural networks" were labeled in four different ways, including "CONVNets" and "CNNs." I have only kept the most common or general label through the pre-processing step to avoid noisy labels and reduce the risk of double-counting very similar concepts. The result of the data extraction and processing steps led to a total of 437 unique keywords. The associated co-occurrence network is visualized in Figure 3.7.

The generated network has a density equal to 0.012 and, as visualized in Figure 3.7, its structure consists of a major component covering the majority of the keywords (310, accounting for 70.93% of the total) and a considerable number of other minor components ($n = 28$). Besides the major component, the network comprises 5 triads and 23 components that range

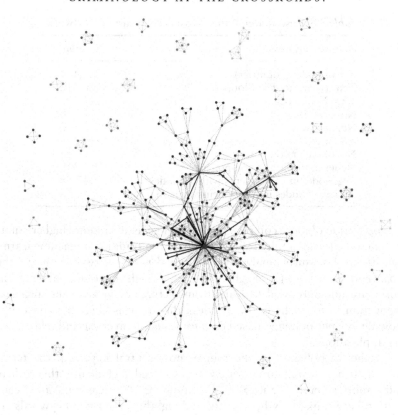

Figure 3.7 Keyword network. Nodes are colored based on the component they belong to and sized according to their degree centrality value. Edges are log-scaled based on the weight of each connection.

from 4 to 9 nodes. With the exception of the major component and the second largest one including nine keywords, which have densities equal to 0.019 and 0.556, respectively, all the other ones have density equal to 1, meaning that they are fully connected subgraphs. This points in the direction of a core set of keywords that are used to label most of the studies and highlights a number of topics, applications, algorithms, and problems that remain marginal and mostly connected to single studies. These network measures are synthesized in Table 3.6.

Analyzing keyword-level patterns, that is node-level information in the current network, allows gaining insights on the trends of the literature at the intersection of AI and research on crime. In terms of degree centrality, "machine learning" and "neural networks" are – not really surprisingly – ranked first and second, respectively. "Machine learning" is connected to a total of other 129 keywords, while "neural networks" shares edges with 44. Interestingly, "deep learning" is ranked third, testifying to a certain interest in

Table 3.6 Description of the keyword co-occurrence network

Network Feature	Value
No. of nodes (countries)	437
Density (without self-loops)	0.012
Total No. of edges	2,296
No. of isolates	0
No. of dyads	0
No. of triads	5
No. of larger components (>3)	24
Nodes in the largest component	310
Avg. nodes in components with >3 nodes	17.58
St. dev. of nodes in components with >3 nodes	60.98

the application of more complex models that generally require higher amount of data to be meaningfully trained compared to traditional machine learning algorithms. Also surprisingly, "convolutional neural networks" is the third most central keyword (29 neighbors). Even though convolutional neural networks are not only used to learn from pictures or videos (one alternative application is, for instance, time series), this result is likely the effect of the growing salience of image-based data for research on crime and related security applications.

"Predictive policing" is the fourth most central keyword: the term is related to a research area widely investigated technically, theoretically, and – more recently – critically. "Data mining," "forecasting," and "classification" are ranked sixth, seventh, and eighth: these three keywords concern rather broad areas, tasks, and approaches that are generally common also across other disciplines in which AI is employed. The ninth keyword in terms of centrality is "recidivism," which mostly refers to the development and deployment of risk assessment models for estimating the probability of re-offending, another area that in the past years has attracted critiques from scholars, and activists, mostly in the United States. Finally, the tenth most central keyword is "malware," demonstrating the considerable amount of research that addresses cyber-related crimes employing AI methods.

In terms of brokerage roles, proxied through betweenness centrality, "machine learning," "neural networks," and "deep learning" remain the three most important keywords. "Predictive policing" is ranked fourth and is followed by "artificial intelligence" which, while not being remarkably central in terms of overall number of connections, acts as an important bridge between different keywords and, in principle, between different studies and lines of inquiry. "Data mining" confirms to be central (ranked sixth), and the seventh term with the highest brokerage value is "randomized experiments." This finding positively suggests that there is a growing tendency to explore possible ways to integrate tools from machine learning and approaches from causal inference to investigate crime-related research problems (see Chapter 5). "Classification" – especially in comparison with "regression" – keeps a critical role in connecting keywords in the sample (ranked ninth), while "fraud detection" and "decision trees" are the last 2 terms in the top 10 ranking related to betweenness centrality.

In line with the approach seen with the country collaboration network, eigenvector centrality has been selected as the third indicator of centrality, to inspect what are the keywords that are most central because they are connected to other significantly central terms. "Machine learning" confirms its central role. "Forecasting" is ranked second, hinting to the diffused interest in this particular task. "Recidivism" is ranked third, followed by "cybersecurity" and "phishing attack," two other terms testifying to the salience of cyber-related topics. "Risk assessment," which broadly refers to a number of application problems, including recidivism prediction as noted before, is ranked sixth. "Soft computing," a term describing the wide area of formal and probabilistic reasoning that has strong links with machine learning and modern computational approaches, is ranked seventh. Following are "data mining," "random forest" – a very common algorithm used both for regression and classification tasks – and "malicious URL," another signal of the relevance of research addressing cyber-related topics. The full data for the three rankings are provided in Table 3.7.

Table 3.7 Ranking of 10 most central countries in the keyword co-occurrence network, based on total-degree centrality, betweenness centrality, and eigenvector centrality

	Total-Degree Centrality		Betweenness Centrality		Eigenvector Centrality	
Rank	Keyword	Value	Keyword	Value	Keyword	Value
1	Machine learning	0.059 (129)	Machine learning	0.332	Machine learning	0.614
2	Neural networks	0.020 (44)	Neural networks	0.127	Forecasting	0.272
3	Deep learning	0.019 (42)	Deep learning	0.119	Recidivism	0.234
4	Convolutional neural networks	0.013 (28)	Predictive policing	0.068	Cybersecurity	0.157
5	Predictive policing	0.012 (27)	Artificial intelligence	0.059	Phishing attack	0.150
6	Data mining	0.011 (23)	Data mining	0.053	Risk assessment	0.137
7	Forecasting	0.011 (23)	Randomized experiments	0.038	Soft computing	0.134
8	Classification	0.009 (20)	Classification	0.034	Data mining	0.120
9	Recidivism	0.009 (19)	Fraud detection	0.029	Random forest	0.112
10	Malware	0.008 (18)	Decision trees	0.028	Malicious URL	0.104

Note: For total-degree centrality, the number of raw connections is reported between parentheses.

A further investigation in network dynamics at the node level reveals the peripheral role of keywords addressing the ethical dimensions of learning algorithms applied to crime-related research problems. The only keywords that can be matched to such dimensions are "discrimination," "fairness," "predictive discrimination," and "transparency." Among these, "fairness" is overall the most central one, although when put in the context of the entire sample of keywords, its centrality significantly fades, as it is ranked 44th in terms of total degree centrality (0.0036), 30th in terms of betweenness (0.0099), and 32nd in terms of eigenvector centrality (0.0709).

Discrimination is the 54th most central keyword in the degree centrality ranking (0.0032), the 54th also in the betweenness centrality one (0.0013), and is ranked 134th in terms of eigenvector centrality (0.0159). "Predictive discrimination" instead is 174th concerning total degree centrality (0.0018), 45th regarding its brokerage role (0.0612), and 71st in relation to eigenvector centrality (0.0007).

Among the four, "transparency" is on average the least most central keyword, as it is only ranked 95th in terms of degree centrality overall (0.0022), has betweenness centrality equal to 0, and its eigenvector centrality places it 433rd in the corresponding ranking (0.00001).

However, centrality should not only be taken as the only measure for assessing the popularity of a given topic. In principle, it can lead to an overestimation by the presence of few studies with many connections or, contrarily, to an underestimation if there are many similar studies that only use the same set of keywords disconnected from the core component of keywords emerging from a certain set of studies. I hence looked at the raw frequency of these keywords compared to the rest of the remaining 434 ones. The distribution of the frequency of the used keywords is extremely skewed, with only less than 5% of the keywords being used by more than two articles.

Within this distribution, "discrimination" and "fairness" have been used by two studies, while "transparency" and "predictive discrimination" by one only. This means that not only keywords mapping ethical aspects of research at the intersection of AI and crime are peripheral in terms of centrality, but they are also rarely part of research designs, questions, and problems of the studies in the analyzed sample.

Besides the indications that can be drawn from the various measures of centrality and salience with specific reference to these four terms, the skewness of the keyword distribution also provides another important indication. The fact that most of the 438 keywords have been only used once points in the direction of a very low level of consistency in this area of research. The heterogeneity of topics, read in conjunction with their sparsity, manifests the impossibility to build consistent knowledge and the tendency of scholars to concentrate independently and autonomously on distinct subareas of research avoiding advancements in specific areas of applications.

To conclude the analysis of the keyword dynamics here presented, it is worth mentioning that ethics-related topics are not the only ones currently overlooked, at least from what emerges from the sample. In fact, the sample documents an almost complete absence of references to theory-related keywords, foremost from the criminological point of view, and also, in general, from the standpoint of other social sciences that are often helpful to complement explanations and descriptions of criminal phenomena, such as sociology and economics. The only keywords that are connected to theories overall are "criminological theory and research" and "routine activities," which have been used in only one study each.

The former is 174th in terms of degree centrality (0.0018), 116th in terms of betweenness (0.0004), and 84th concerning eigenvector centrality (0.0462), and the latter, which can be easily assumed to be referred to routine activity theory (Cohen & Felson, 1979), is ranked 174th concerning degree centrality (0.0018), has betweenness equal to 0, and is 157th in the eigenvector centrality ranking (0.0088).

These results offer additional hints for discussing the current state of scientific inquiry intersecting AI and research on crime which will be outlined in the next section.

Discussion and Conclusions

The methodological landscape in criminology and crime research has evolved considerably in the last decades. Concerning quantitative approaches specifically, the computational wave that has diffused across many disciplines and fields has also influenced how research on crime is developed, conducted, and communicated. In this chapter, I have specifically described three trends that contributed to this "computational wave," along with a discussion on their current issues and promises. These trends refer to the geospatial modeling of crime, the connection between crime and networks, and the application of simulation paradigms (mostly agent-based modeling) to crime modeling.

The discussion on geospatial modeling of crime has started from the long-standing origins of crime-mapping efforts in the nineteenth century, going through the strong connection between research and practice explained by the "place-based" revolutions in policing, up to the most recent advances made possible by the application of computational methods relying on a diverse set of methodological approaches. As the backbone of this process, I identified the "law of crime concentration" defined by Weisburd (2015) as the symbolic landmark point in which decades of empirical evidence have finally converged and symbolically opened up new possibilities for scientific inquiry and policy in research on crime. Besides the chronological unfolding of this strand of research, I also reported the recent inflamed debate concerning the use of predictive policing algorithms by law enforcement as tools for reinforcing disparities and systemic racism.

Concerning the use of network approaches to study crime, I used Papachristos' appeal published in 2011 as well as Faust and Tita's review in 2019 to take stock of what has changed over the course of a decade of research and what are the most pressing issues that scholars are continuing to face to date. Compared to the state of the art of crime network research in 2011, the diffusion of network approaches – measured by the amount of published works – has certainly increased with great pace. Not only has the quantity increased, but also the quality, depth, and sophistication of the specific techniques have sensibly grown. Nonetheless, practices that linger the potential of network paradigms in criminology and crime research continue to exist. In particular, I discuss the overreliance on cross-sectional data and the lack of multi-modal and multi-layer approaches to network design and analysis. I argued that while researchers have little control over the quality of official data they often use in their work, there is an urgent need for more creativity in how networks are conceptualized and used. Similar to what has been done in recent years, moving from simple network description to inference, scholars working in this area need to move beyond the dominant tendency toward using single-snapshot networks characterized by unidimensional and unimodal representations. The challenging goals are then to form stronger partnerships with institutions to obtain richer data and, at the same time, explore and exploit advances made in other fields to fully achieve the potential of the so-called "networked criminology" through new comprehensive perspectives on crime network research embracing the multidimensional complexity of crime and criminal behaviors.

The use of simulation approaches, and particularly ABM, constitutes the third trend in this computational transition in research on crime. Agent-based modeling, as also reported by Groff and colleagues (2019), has increasingly been employed as a tool – or "mindset" to borrow again the expression used by Bonabeau (2002) – to study crime dynamics. This trend has touched a variety of problems, phenomena, and areas within criminology and crime research. Along with the increasing use of ABM, I also examine two main limitations affecting their use and effectiveness, namely, the necessary stylization of facts and the need for empirical data to inform models and validate them in order to obtain plausible results that both academics and practitioners can trust. Furthermore, I also highlighted the interesting brokering property of ABM as a connector between geospatial modeling and crime network research: their flexibility enable to comprehensive explore the promising venues deriving from the integration of place-based perspectives with complex network science.

After the first section, this chapter has provided an empirical account of the current state of the art at the intersection of criminology and AI. Expanding the approach I previously used in a paper published in 2021, I gathered a total of 132 relevant studies published from 2010 to May 2021 in the top 40 venues – according to Google Scholar rankings – in the 2 disciplines (20 outlets each). Although I previously used a larger (and perhaps noisier) sample with data covering a more extended period (from 1980 to the very beginning of 2020), most results of this chapter are in line with those of my earlier article.

Through the lenses of network science, and after having offered descriptive statistics on the temporal nature of the diffusion of studies intersecting crime and AI research, I have specifically examined patterns in individual co-authorship, country collaboration, and trends in research topics.

Regarding the trends, data document a steady increase in scientific production, for both disciplines and overall, with articles appearing in AI venues representing the majority of the studies in the sample. For what concerns individual co-authorship dynamics, the analysis reveals several things. Among the most relevant first is the very low average of studies per scientist (1.04), with almost 97% of the authors that have worked on a single article. The problem of "one-timers" has been reported also in other fields and disciplines, and it has been generally considered as a major obstacle to an effective creation and accumulation of knowledge (González-Alcaide et al., 2016; Gordon, 2007). Second, the resulting co-authorship network including 441 scholars is extremely disconnected. The absence of a giant component connecting the majority of authors in the sample resonates with the findings presented in my previous article using Scopus data and indicates the immaturity and incohesive nature of the research community (Newman, 2004). Other works analyzing co-authorship networks in other disciplines always detected the presence of a giant component (Franceschet, 2011; Moody, 2016), whereas here the structure appears remarkably atomized.[5] Curiously, no research as co-authored at least one study in each of the disciplines, reinforcing the evidence regarding the atomization not only at the author-level but also at the discipline level.

In terms of country-level macro patterns, a total of 30 countries have been represented in the sample, with a network counting a total of 86 edges. Six countries are isolates (meaning that researchers based at a given country's institutions only collaborated with scholars based in institutions located in their same country), and 3 form a triad, while all the other 21 countries are all part of the same nucleus. By using a set of 15 centrality measures, the United States, India, and the United Kingdom have demonstrated to be the most relevant and central hubs for research in this area. Interestingly, however, the United States – as a demonstration of their disproportionate contribution – are also the country that produced the highest number of articles without international collaborators (33 out of 90 non-solo publications in the sample).

Finally, the analysis of 437 author-generated keywords sought to shed light on the most trending and central topics investigated or associated with the studies in the sample. At the structural level, the resulting keyword network documented the presence of a major component that maps the core set of topics that attracted the interest of researchers, with the presence of a considerable number of minor components including marginal keywords that, in most cases, have been used only in a single study. Total degree-centrality, betweenness centrality, and eigenvector centrality have been utilized to assess the relevance of the keywords from different perspectives. Machine learning is the dominant "approach," followed by the use of neural networks and deep learning. Fairly central application-linked keywords refer to cybercrime-related topics, recidivism, and predictive policing.

Notably, in line again with my previous article, this chapter also reports the marginality of scholarship dedicated to investigating the ethical implications and dimensions of machine intelligence approaches in research on crime. This marginality has been detected in terms of network centrality as well as in terms of prevalence of ethics-related keywords in the sample. Being rarely investigated or discussed by research, and at the same time being outside the core set of topics that constitute the bulk of this evolving area, sensibly impairs the chances that works on discrimination, fairness, bias, and accountability, among others, will easily increase their prevalence and role. Things may swiftly change if exogenous mechanisms intervene, such as real-world events, top-down calls for action from scientific organizations, or the establishment of dedicated funding programs from public and private institutions. Concerning the first of the three real-world events such as activism campaigns or the vivid debate around the need for police reform in the United States have undoubtedly increased research production around the technical, practical, political, and moral problems caused by the use of algorithmic decision-making in criminal justice and policing. Such trend is demonstrated by the many works published in recent years in conferences that are explicitly dedicated to fairness and accountability in AI applications, such as the ACM Conference on Fairness, Accountability, and Transparency (FAccT), and the AAAI/ACM Artificial Intelligence, Ethics, and Society (AIES) conferences (see for instance Abebe et al., 2020; Akpinar et al., 2021; Bates et al., 2020; Green & Chen, 2019; Matthews et al., 2020). Yet, when analyzing the most influential outlets in criminology and AI, these lines of inquiry are substantially marginal.

Finally, the ethical dimension is not the only one that has been almost completely discarded in the studies under scrutiny: the role of theory, and particularly of criminological theory, is completely neglected and may represent a major issue for the development of plausible, responsible, and interpretable studies at the intersection between research on crime and AI.

The current chapter, and particularly the empirical analysis presented, should not be taken as a systematic, comprehensive review of the state of the art of research concerning AI approaches to study crime and criminal behavior. This was not the intent. There are many journals in the two fields that have been excluded from the search strategy simply because they were not ranked among the top 20 according to Google Scholar. Additionally, there are a lot of journals or conferences that are not part of AI or criminology which publish or accept studies blending the two (e.g., interdisciplinary and mega journals, security studies, sociology, and economics journals). All that literature has been excluded from the analysis, although it contributes nonetheless to the scientific enterprise that seeks to exploit statistical learning algorithms for research on crime.

Instead, the precise goal was to assess the state of the art of such research by looking at a very specific, peculiar, and restricted set of publication venues.

These venues should – keeping in mind all the issues related to journals rankings – represent the most influential outlets in each of the two related disciplines, therefore mostly giving a measure of how much AI has become part of the establishment in criminology and crime-related applications have become more common in journals that traditionally dealt with different perspectives.

Several conclusions can be drawn from the results presented here along with those described in Campedelli (2021), without falling into the trap of mere speculation. Notable trends have been detected, revealing issues that can significantly impair the growth of the area in this space. The next chapter will try to propose pathways to solve some of these issues. Only time will tell whether the nature and patterns of scientific inquiry involving AI and crime research will evolve and move toward a more transdisciplinary, collaborative, inclusive, and cohesive model. The sensation is that it will require years and considerable efforts (or at least one of the two). Machine learning and machine intelligence in general have the potential of becoming the next key turning point in the profound modification of the quantitative methodological landscape in criminology and crime research, but the immaturity and disconnectedness of this landscape unfolded by empirical data underscore the inherent problems that obstruct a swift process in this direction.

Notes

1 August Vollmer was the first police chief of Berkeley, California. An advocate for the existence of racial types, heredity, and racial degeneration in explaining crime and by many regarded as the father of modern policing (Go, 2020; Newitz, 2021).
2 These are: Berk (2010, 2011, 2017), Berk and Bleich (2013, 2014), Berk and Elzarka (2020), Berk and Sorenson (2020), and Berk et al. (2021).
3 When an author was affiliated with more than one institution, only the primary one was recorded.
4 These include: total degree centrality, betweenness centrality, ego-betweenness centrality, betweenness centrality with links inverted, closeness centrality, closeness centrality with links inverted, eigenvector centrality, contribution centrality, hub centrality, authority centrality, structural holes, PageRank centrality, and clustering coefficient.
5 Interestingly, however, a research paper from González-Alcaide and colleagues (2013) reported that in their quantitative analysis of a sample of criminology articles, most of the co-authorship groups were composed by two or three researchers. The authors argued then that criminology sees a predominant tendency towards work organized around reduced nuclei of scholars.

References

Abbott, A. (1999). *Department and discipline: Chicago sociology at one hundred.* University of Chicago Press.
Abebe, R., Barocas, S., Kleinberg, J., Levy, K., Raghavan, M., & Robinson, D. G. (2020). Roles for computing in social change. In *Proceedings of the 2020 conference on fairness, accountability, and transparency*, 252–260. https://doi.org/10.1145/3351095.3372871.

Akpinar, N.-J., De-Arteaga, M., & Chouldechova, A. (2021). The effect of differential victim crime reporting on predictive policing systems. In *Proceedings of the 2021 ACM conference on fairness, accountability, and transparency*, 838–849. https://doi.org/10.1145/3442188.3445877.

Andresen, M. A., & Malleson, N. (2015). Intra-week spatial-temporal patterns of crime. *Crime Science*, 4(1), 12. https://doi.org/10.1186/s40163-015-0024-7.

Bankes, S. C. (2002). Agent-based modeling: A revolution? *Proceedings of the National Academy of Sciences*, 99(Supplement 3), 7199–7200. https://doi.org/10.1073/pnas.072081299.

Bates, J., Cameron, D., Checco, A., Clough, P., Hopfgartner, F., Mazumdar, S., Sbaffi, L., Stordy, P., & de la Vega de León, A. (2020). Integrating FATE/critical data studies into data science curricula: Where are we going and how do we get there? In *Proceedings of the 2020 conference on fairness, accountability, and transparency*, 425–435. https://doi.org/10.1145/3351095.3372832.

Berk, R. (2010). What you can and can't properly do with regression. *Journal of Quantitative Criminology*, 26(4), 481–487. https://doi.org/10.1007/s10940-010-9116-4.

Berk, R. (2011). Asymmetric loss functions for forecasting in criminal justice settings. *Journal of Quantitative Criminology*, 27(1), 107–123. https://doi.org/10.1007/s10940-010-9098-2.

Berk, R. (2017). An impact assessment of machine learning risk forecasts on parole board decisions and recidivism. *Journal of Experimental Criminology*, 13(2), 193–216. https://doi.org/10.1007/s11292-017-9286-2.

Berk, R. A., & Bleich, J. (2013). Statistical procedures for forecasting criminal behavior. *Criminology & Public Policy*, 12(3), 513–544. https://doi.org/10.1111/1745-9133.12047.

Berk, R., & Bleich, J. (2014). Forecasts of violence to inform sentencing decisions. *Journal of Quantitative Criminology*, 30(1), 79–96. https://doi.org/10.1007/s10940-013-9195-0.

Berk, R., & Elzarka, A. A. (2020). Almost politically acceptable criminal justice risk assessment. *Criminology & Public Policy*, 19(4), 1231–1257. https://doi.org/10.1111/1745-9133.12500.

Berk, R. A., & Sorenson, S. B. (2020). Algorithmic approach to forecasting rare violent events. *Criminology & Public Policy*, 19(1), 213–233. https://doi.org/10.1111/1745-9133.12476.

Berk, R., Olson, M., Buja, A., & Ouss, A. (2021). Using recursive partitioning to find and estimate heterogenous treatment effects in randomized clinical trials. *Journal of Experimental Criminology*, 17(3), 519–538. https://doi.org/10.1007/s11292-019-09410-0.

Berlusconi, G. (2013). Do all the pieces matter? Assessing the reliability of law enforcement data sources for the network analysis of wire taps. *Global Crime*, 14(1), 61–81. https://doi.org/10.1080/17440572.2012.746940.

Birks, D., Townsley, M., & Stewart, A. (2014). Emergent regularities of interpersonal victimization: An agent-based investigation. *Journal of Research in Crime and Delinquency*, 51(1), 119–140. https://doi.org/10.1177/0022427813487353.

Bogomolov, A., Lepri, B., Staiano, J., Oliver, N., Pianesi, F., & Pentland, A. (2014). Once upon a crime: Towards crime prediction from demographics and mobile data. In *Proceedings of the 16th international conference on multimodal interaction*, 427–434. https://doi.org/10.1145/2663204.2663254.

Bonabeau, E. (2002). Agent-based modeling: Methods and techniques for simulating human systems. *Proceedings of the National Academy of Sciences*, *99*(Supplement 3), 7280–7287. https://doi.org/10.1073/pnas.082080899.

Bosse, T., Gerritsen, C., & Klein, M. C. A. (2009). Agent-based simulation of social learning in criminology. In *Proceedings of the international conference on agents and artificial intelligence*, 5–13. https://doi.org/10.5220/0001512000050013.

Bouchard, M., & Malm, A. (2016). *Social network analysis and its contribution to research on crime and criminal justice* (Vol. 1). Oxford University Press. https://doi.org/10.1093/oxfordhb/9780199935383.013.21.

Brantingham, P. J., & Brantingham, P. L. (1984). *Patterns in crime*. Macmillan.

Breetzke, G. D. (2018). The concentration of urban crime in space by race: Evidence from South Africa. *Urban Geography*, *39*(8), 1195–1220. https://doi.org/10.1080/02723638.2018.1440127.

Bright, D., & Delaney, J. J. (2013). Evolution of a drug trafficking network: Mapping changes in network structure and function across time. *Global Crime*, *14*(2–3), 238–260. https://doi.org/10.1080/17440572.2013.787927.

Bright, D., Koskinen, J., & Malm, A. (2019). Illicit network dynamics: The formation and evolution of a drug trafficking network. *Journal of Quantitative Criminology*, *35*(2), 237–258. https://doi.org/10.1007/s10940-018-9379-8.

Bright, D., Brewer, R., & Morselli, C. (2021). Using social network analysis to study crime: Navigating the challenges of criminal justice records. *Social Networks*, *66*, 50–64. https://doi.org/10.1016/j.socnet.2021.01.006.

Calderoni, F., Campedelli, G. M., Szekely, A., Paolucci, M., & Andrighetto, G. (2021). Recruitment into organized crime: An agent-based approach testing the impact of different policies. *Journal of Quantitative Criminology*. https://doi.org/10.1007/s10940-020-09489-z.

Campana, P., & Varese, F. (2020). Studying organized crime networks: Data sources, boundaries and the limits of structural measures. *Social Networks*. https://doi.org/10.1016/j.socnet.2020.03.002.

Campedelli, G. M. (2020). Where are we? Using Scopus to map the literature at the intersection between artificial intelligence and research on crime. *Journal of Computational Social Science*, *4*(2), 503–530. https://doi.org/10.1007/s42001-020-00082-9.

Caplan, J. M., Kennedy, L. W., & Miller, J. (2011). Risk terrain modeling: Brokering criminological theory and GIS methods for crime forecasting. *Justice Quarterly*, *28*(2), 360–381. https://doi.org/10.1080/07418825.2010.486037.

Chamard, S. (2006). The history of crime mapping and its use by American police departments. *Alaska Justice Forum*, *23*(3), 4–8.

Cohen, L. E., & Felson, M. (1979). Social change and crime rate trends: A routine activity approach. *American Sociological Review*, *44*(4), 588–608. https://doi.org/10.2307/2094589.

Cullen, F. T., & Wilcox, P. (2010). Quetelet, Adolphe: Explaining crime through statistical and cartographic techniques. In *Encyclopedia of criminological theory*. SAGE Publications.

Davies, T., & Marchione, E. (2015). Event networks and the identification of crime pattern motifs. *PLoS One*, *10*(11), e0143638. https://doi.org/10.1371/journal.pone.0143638.

de Melo, S. N., Matias, L. F., & Andresen, M. A. (2015). Crime concentrations and similarities in spatial crime patterns in a Brazilian context. *Applied Geography*, *62*, 314–324. https://doi.org/10.1016/j.apgeog.2015.05.012.

De Nadai, M., Xu, Y., Letouzé, E., González, M. C., & Lepri, B. (2020). Socio-economic, built environment, and mobility conditions associated with crime: A study of multiple cities. *Scientific Reports, 10*(1), 13871. https://doi.org/10.1038/s41598-020-70808-2.

Dent, B. D. (2000). Brief history of crime mapping. In L. S. Turnbull, E. H. Hendrix, & B. D. Dent (Eds.), *Atlas of crime: Mapping the criminal landscape.* Oryz Press.

Duxbury, S. W., & Haynie, D. L. (2018). The network structure of opioid distribution on a Darknet Cryptomarket. *Journal of Quantitative Criminology, 34*(4), 921–941. https://doi.org/10.1007/s10940-017-9359-4.

Duxbury, S. W., & Haynie, D. L. (2019). Criminal network security: An agent-based approach to evaluating network resilience. *Criminology, 57*(2), 314–342. https://doi.org/10.1111/1745-9125.12203.

Eck, J. E., & Weisburd, D. (Eds.). (1995). *Crime and place: Crime prevention studies.* Willow Tree Pr.

Elliott, E., & Kiel, L. D. (2004). A complex systems approach for developing public policy toward terrorism: An agent-based approach. *Chaos, Solitons & Fractals, 20*(1), 63–68. https://doi.org/10.1016/S0960-0779(03)00428-4.

Epstein, J. M. (1999). Agent-based computational models and generative social science. *Complexity, 4*(5), 41–60. https://doi.org/10.1002/(SICI)1099-0526(199905/06)4:5<41::AID-CPLX9>3.0.CO;2-F.

Faust, K., & Tita, G. E. (2019). Social networks and crime: Pitfalls and promises for advancing the field. *Annual Review of Criminology, 2*(1), 99–122. https://doi.org/10.1146/annurev-criminol-011518-024701.

Favarin, S. (2018). This must be the place (to commit a crime): Testing the law of crime concentration in Milan, Italy. *European Journal of Criminology, 15*(6), 702–729. https://doi.org/10.1177/1477370818757700.

Ferguson, A. (2019). Predictive Policing Theory. In T. Lave & E. Miller (Eds.), The Cambridge Handbook of Policing in the United States (Cambridge Law Handbooks, pp. 491–510). Cambridge: Cambridge University Press. doi:10.1017/9781108354721.025

Franceschet, M. (2011). Collaboration in computer science: A network science approach. *Journal of the American Society for Information Science and Technology, 62*(10), 1992–2012. https://doi.org/10.1002/asi.21614.

Gerber, M. S. (2014). Predicting crime using Twitter and kernel density estimation. *Decision Support Systems, 61*, 115–125. https://doi.org/10.1016/j.dss.2014.02.003.

Gerritsen, C. (2015). Agent-based modelling as a research tool for criminological research. *Crime Science, 4*(1), 2. https://doi.org/10.1186/s40163-014-0014-1.

Giménez-Santana, A., Medina-Sarmiento, J. E., & Miró-Llinares, F. (2018). Risk terrain modeling for road safety: Identifying crash-related environmental factors in the province of Cádiz, Spain. *European Journal on Criminal Policy and Research, 24*(4), 451–467. https://doi.org/10.1007/s10610-018-9398-x.

Go, J. (2020). The imperial origins of American policing: Militarization and imperial feedback in the early 20th century. *American Journal of Sociology, 125*(5), 1193–1254. https://doi.org/10.1086/708464.

Goldstein, H. (2018). On problem-oriented policing: The Stockholm lecture. *Crime Science, 7*(1), 13. https://doi.org/10.1186/s40163-018-0087-3.

González-Alcaide, G., Melero-Fuentes, D., Aleixandre-Benavent, R., & Valderrama-Zurián, J.-C. (2013). Productivity and collaboration in scientific publications on criminology. *Journal of Criminal Justice Education, 24*(1), 15–37. https://doi.org/10.1080/10511253.2012.664153.

González-Alcaide, G., Llorente, P., & Ramos, J. M. (2016). Bibliometric indicators to identify emerging research fields: Publications on mass gatherings. *Scientometrics*, *109*(2), 1283–1298. https://doi.org/10.1007/s11192-016-2083-2.

Gordon, A. (2007). Transient and continuant authors in a research field: The case of terrorism. *Scientometrics*, *72*(2), 213–224. https://doi.org/10.1007/s11192-007-1714-z.

Green, B., & Chen, Y. (2019). Disparate interactions: An algorithm-in-the-loop analysis of fairness in risk assessments. In *Proceedings of the conference on fairness, accountability, and transparency*, 90–99. https://doi.org/10.1145/3287560.3287563.

Groff, E., Johnson, S. D., & Thornton, A. (2019). State of the art in agent-based modeling of urban crime: An overview. *Journal of Quantitative Criminology*, *35*(1), 155–193. https://doi.org/10.1007/s10940-018-9376-y.

Groff, E., & Mazerolle, L. (2008). Simulated experiments and their potential role in criminology and criminal justice. *Journal of Experimental Criminology*, *4*(3), 187. https://doi.org/10.1007/s11292-008-9058-0.

Hawkes, A. G. (1971). Spectra of some self-exciting and mutually exciting point processes. *Biometrika*, *58*(1), 83. https://doi.org/10.2307/2334319.

Heath, L. S., & Sioson, A. A. (2009). Multimodal networks: Structure and operations. *IEEE/ACM Transactions on Computational Biology and Bioinformatics*, *6*(2), 321–332. https://doi.org/10.1109/TCBB.2007.70243.

Heaven, W. D. (2020, July). *Predictive policing algorithms are racist. They need to be dismantled. MIT Technology Review*.

Huang, C., Zhang, J., Zheng, Y., & Chawla, N. V. (2018). DeepCrime: attentive hierarchical recurrent networks for crime prediction. In *Proceedings of the 27th ACM international conference on information and knowledge management*, 1423–1432. https://doi.org/10.1145/3269206.3271793.

Iwanski, N., & Frank, R. (2013). The evolution of a drug co-arrest network. In *Crime and networks*. Routledge.

Johnson, S. D. (2010). A brief history of the analysis of crime concentration. *European Journal of Applied Mathematics*, *21*(4–5), 349–370. https://doi.org/10.1017/S0956792510000082.

Keller, J. P., Desouza, K. C., & Lin, Y. (2010). Dismantling terrorist networks: Evaluating strategic options using agent-based modeling. *Technological Forecasting and Social Change*, *77*(7), 1014–1036. https://doi.org/10.1016/j.techfore.2010.02.007.

Kertész, J., & Wachs, J. (2021). Complexity science approach to economic crime. *Nature Reviews Physics*, *3*(2), 70–71. https://doi.org/10.1038/s42254-020-0238-9.

Kivela, M., Arenas, A., Barthelemy, M., Gleeson, J. P., Moreno, Y., & Porter, M. A. (2014). Multilayer networks. *Journal of Complex Networks*, *2*(3), 203–271. https://doi.org/10.1093/comnet/cnu016.

Law, J., Quick, M., & Chan, P. W. (2015). Analyzing hotspots of crime using a Bayesian spatiotemporal modeling approach: A case study of violent crime in the Greater Toronto area. *Geographical Analysis*, *47*(1), 1–19. https://doi.org/10.1111/gean.12047.

Liu, D., Song, W., & Xiu, C. (2016). Spatial patterns of violent crimes and neighborhood characteristics in Changchun. China. *Australian & New Zealand Journal of Criminology*, *49*(1), 53–72. https://doi.org/10.1177/0004865814547133.

Lum, K., & Isaac, W. (2016). To predict and serve? *Significance*, *13*(5), 14–19. https://doi.org/10.1111/j.1740-9713.2016.00960.x.

Macy, M. W., & Willer, and R. (2002). From factors to factors: Computational sociology and agent-based modeling. *Annual Review of Sociology*, 28(1), 143–166. https://doi.org/10.1146/annurev.soc.28.110601.141117.

Magers, J. S. (2004). Compstat: A new paradigm for policing or a repudiation of community policing. *Journal of Contemporary Criminal Justice*, 20(1), 70–79. https://doi.org/10.1177/1043986203262312.

Magliocca, N. R., McSweeney, K., Sesnie, S. E., Tellman, E., Devine, J. A., Nielsen, E. A., Pearson, Z., & Wrathall, D. J. (2019). Modeling cocaine traffickers and counterdrug interdiction forces as a complex adaptive system. *Proceedings of the National Academy of Sciences*, 116(16), 7784–7792. https://doi.org/10.1073/pnas.1812459116.

Malleson, N., & Andresen, M. A. (2016). Exploring the impact of ambient population measures on London crime hotspots. *Journal of Criminal Justice*, 46, 52–63. https://doi.org/10.1016/j.jcrimjus.2016.03.002.

Malleson, N., Heppenstall, A., & See, L. (2010). Crime reduction through simulation: An agent-based model of burglary. *Computers, Environment and Urban Systems*, 34(3), 236–250. https://doi.org/10.1016/j.compenvurbsys.2009.10.005.

Malm, A., Nash, R., & Moghadam, R. (2017). Social network analysis and terrorism. In G. LaFree & J. D. Freilich (Eds.), *The handbook of the criminology of terrorism* (pp. 221–231). John Wiley & Sons, Inc. https://doi.org/10.1002/9781118923986.ch14.

Marchment, Z., & Gill, P. (2021). Systematic review and meta-analysis of risk terrain modelling (RTM) as a spatial forecasting method. *Crime Science*, 10(1), 12. https://doi.org/10.1186/s40163-021-00149-6.

Matthews, J. N., Northup, G., Grasso, I., Lorenz, S., Babaeianjelodar, M., Bashaw, H., Mondal, S., Matthews, A., Njie, M., & Goldthwaite, J. (2020). When trusted black boxes don't agree: Incentivizing iterative improvement and accountability in critical software systems. In *Proceedings of the AAAI/ACM conference on AI, ethics, and society*, 102–108. https://doi.org/10.1145/3375627.3375807.

Mazeika, D. M., & Kumar, S. (2017). Do crime hot spots exist in developing countries? Evidence from India. *Journal of Quantitative Criminology*, 33(1), 45–61. https://doi.org/10.1007/s10940-016-9280-2.

Miller, L. (2020). LAPD will end controversial program that aimed to predict where crimes would occur. *Los Angeles Times*. https://www.latimes.com/california/story/2020-04-21/lapd-ends-predictive-policing-program

Mingers, J., & Willmott, H. (2013). Taylorizing business school research: On the 'one best way' performative effects of journal ranking lists. *Human Relations*, 66(8), 1051–1073. https://doi.org/10.1177/0018726712467048.

Morselli, C., Giguère, C., & Petit, K. (2007). The efficiency/security trade-off in criminal networks. Social networks, 29(1), 143–153.

Morselli, C., & Roy, J. (2008). Brokerage qualifications in ringing operations. Criminology, 46(1), 71–98.

Morselli, C. (2009). Inside criminal networks (Vol. 8). New York: Springer.

Mohler, G. O., Short, M. B., Brantingham, P. J., Schoenberg, F. P., & Tita, G. E. (2011). Self-exciting point process modeling of crime. *Journal of the American Statistical Association*, 106(493), 100–108. https://doi.org/10.1198/jasa.2011.ap09546.

Moody, J. (2016). The structure of a social science collaboration network: Disciplinary cohesion from 1963 to 1999. *American Sociological Review*. https://doi.org/10.1177/000312240406900204.

Moon, I.-C., & Carley, K. M. (2007). Modeling and simulating terrorist networks in social and geospatial dimensions. *IEEE Intelligent Systems, 22*(5), 40–49. https://doi.org/10.1109/MIS.2007.4338493.

Müller, B., Bohn, F., Dreßler, G., Groeneveld, J., Klassert, C., Martin, R., Schlüter, M., Schulze, J., Weise, H., & Schwarz, N. (2013). Describing human decisions in agent-based models – ODD + D, an extension of the ODD protocol. *Environmental Modelling & Software, 48*, 37–48. https://doi.org/10.1016/j.envsoft.2013.06.003.

Nardin, L. G., Andrighetto, G., Conte, R., Székely, Á, Anzola, D., Elsenbroich, C., Lotzmann, U., Neumann, M., Punzo, V., & Troitzsch, K. G. (2016). Simulating protection rackets: A case study of the Sicilian mafia. *Autonomous Agents and Multi-Agent Systems, 30*(6), 1117–1147. https://doi.org/10.1007/s10458-016-9330-z.

Newitz, A. (2021, June 3). How the father of modern policing 'abolished' the police. *The New York Times.* https://www.nytimes.com/2021/06/03/opinion/august-vollmer-abolish-police.html

Newman, M. E. J. (2004). Coauthorship networks and patterns of scientific collaboration. *Proceedings of the National Academy of Sciences, 101*(Suppl. 1), 5200–5205. https://doi.org/10.1073/pnas.0307545100.

Nosek, B. A., Ebersole, C. R., DeHaven, A. C., & Mellor, D. T. (2018). The preregistration revolution. *Proceedings of the National Academy of Sciences, 115*(11), 2600–2606. https://doi.org/10.1073/pnas.1708274114.

Ogata, Y. (1988). Statistical models for earthquake occurrences and residual analysis for point processes. *Journal of the American Statistical Association, 83*(401), 9–27. https://doi.org/10.2307/2288914.

Papachristos, A. V. (2011). The coming of a networked criminology? In J. MacDonald (Ed.), *Advances in criminological theory, vol. 17* (pp. 101–140). Routledge.

Papachristos, A. V., & Bastomski, S. (2018). Connected in crime: The enduring effect of neighborhood networks on the spatial patterning of violence. *American Journal of Sociology, 124*(2), 517–568. https://doi.org/10.1086/699217.

Perry, W. L. (2013). *Predictive policing: The role of crime forecasting in law enforcement operations.* Rand Corporation.

Pint, B., Crooks, A., & Geller, A. (2010). Exploring the emergence of organized crime in Rio de Janeiro: An agent-based modeling approach. In *2010 second Brazilian workshop on social simulation*, 7–14. https://doi.org/10.1109/BWSS.2010.24.

Rafols, I., Leydesdorff, L., O'Hare, A., Nightingale, P., & Stirling, A. (2012). How journal rankings can suppress interdisciplinary research: A comparison between innovation studies and business & management. *Research Policy, 41*(7), 1262–1282. https://doi.org/10.1016/j.respol.2012.03.015.

Reinhart, A. (2018). A review of self-exciting spatio-temporal point processes and their applications. *Statistical Science, 33*(3), 299–318. https://doi.org/10.1214/17-STS629.

Richiardi, M. G., Leombruni, R., Saam, N. J., & Sonnessa, M. (2006). A common protocol for agent-based social simulation. *Journal of Artificial Societies and Social Simulation, 9*, 15.

Rose, K. (2009). *Predictive policing symposium: Opening remarks [predictive policing symposium: Opening remarks].* National Institute of Justice.

Rosés, R., Kadar, C., Gerritsen, C., & Rouly, C. (2020). Simulating offender mobility: Modeling activity nodes from large-scale human activity data. *Journal of Artificial Intelligence Research, 68*, 541–570. https://doi.org/10.1613/jair.1.11831.

Schaefer, D. R. (2012). Youth co-offending networks: An investigation of social and spatial effects. *Social Networks, 34*(1), 141–149. https://doi.org/10.1016/j.socnet.2011.02.001.

Shaw, C. R., & McKay, H. D. (1942). *Juvenile delinquency and urban areas* (pp. xxxii, 451). University of Chicago Press.

Sherman, L. W. (1998). *Evidence-based policing (ideas in American policing)*. The Police Foundation.

Smith, C. M., & Papachristos, A. V. (2016). Trust thy crooked neighbor: Multiplexity in Chicago organized crime networks. *American Sociological Review, 81*(4), 644–667. https://doi.org/10.1177/0003122416650149.

Soss, J., & Weaver, V. (2017). Police are our government: Politics, political science, and the policing of Race–Class subjugated communities. *Annual Review of Political Science, 20*(1), 565–591. https://doi.org/10.1146/annurev-polisci-060415-093825.

Sutherland, E. H. (1939). *Principles of criminology*. J. B. Lippincott Company.

Umar, F., Johnson, S. D., & Cheshire, J. A. (2020). Assessing the spatial concentration of urban crime: An insight from Nigeria. *Journal of Quantitative Criminology*. https://doi.org/10.1007/s10940-019-09448-3.

Weisburd, D. (2015). The law of crime concentration and the criminology of place. *Criminology, 53*(2), 133–157. https://doi.org/10.1111/1745-9125.12070.

Weisburd, D., Braga, A. A., Groff, E. R., & Wooditch, A. (2017). Can hot spots policing reduce crime in urban areas? An agent-based simulation. *Criminology, 55*(1), 137–173. https://doi.org/10.1111/1745-9125.12131.

Wheeler, A. P., & Steenbeek, W. (2021). Mapping the risk terrain for crime using machine learning. *Journal of Quantitative Criminology, 37*(2), 445–480. https://doi.org/10.1007/s10940-020-09457-7.

Ye, X., Xu, X., Lee, J., Zhu, X., & Wu, L. (2015). Space–time interaction of residential burglaries in Wuhan, China. *Applied Geography, 60*, 210–216. https://doi.org/10.1016/j.apgeog.2014.11.022.

Yi, F., Yu, Z., Zhuang, F., & Guo, B. (2019). Neural network based continuous conditional random field for fine-grained crime prediction. In *Proceedings of the twenty-eighth international joint conference on artificial intelligence*, 4157–4163. https://doi.org/10.24963/ijcai,2019/577.

4

TO REFRAME AND REFORM

Increasing the Positive Social Impact of Algorithmic Applications in Research on Crime

Introduction

In the last decade, the growing availability of data, the popularity and accessibility of algorithms, and the increase in funding opportunities contributed to the pervasive deployment of algorithmic systems using (or claiming to use) computational techniques and artificial intelligence (AI) to predict future crimes and offenders. Criminal justice and policing are not the only real-world contexts in which algorithms have massively influenced people's lives: inter alia, health care (Eubanks, 2018; Obermeyer et al., 2019), education (Hao, 2020b; Loukina et al., 2019), the internet (Bozdag, 2013; Noble, 2018), and political propaganda (Bolsover & Howard, 2019; Howard et al., 2018; Woolley & Howard, 2018) all share the widespread diffusion of automatized data-driven tools having massive impacts on society.

Although actuarial and risk assessment tools have been used in the American criminal justice system since the 1920s, their deployment has touched almost every angle of the system, informing judges and prosecutors on a large number of decisions, including pretrial release, release on parole, and sentencing (including probation) (Berk, 2019).

The popularity of these tools has been accompanied by the widespread diffusion of predictive policing software. As anticipated in Chapter 3, predictive policing relies on the use of historical spatiotemporal data and the application of statistical methods to forecast locations and time windows that are at high risk of crime occurrence, and is theoretically founded on the principles of the so-called "Law of Crime Concentration" and in the context of the criminology of place (Sherman et al., 1989; Weisburd, 2015).

A third line of research and application tested the use of facial recognition tools in the attempt to forecast likely offenders (Wu & Zhang, 2016), reinstantiating worrisome and dangerous recalls to nephrology and physiognomy (Fussell, 2020; Venkataramakrishnan, 2020).

Despite the hype associated with the claimed promises of algorithms in these three areas, systematic evaluation of the benefits of such systems is controversial (Fitzpatrick et al., 2019; Gerstner, 2018; Meijer & Wessels, 2019; Saunders et al., 2016; Taylor & Ratcliffe, 2020). Furthermore, several

DOI: 10.4324/9781003217732-4

scandals and activism campaigns, nurtured by debunking scholarly works, have put into question the accountability of these algorithms, highlighting actual issues in terms of discrimination and transparency (Carlson, 2017; Fogliato et al., 2021; Land & Aronson, 2020; Lum & Isaac, 2016; Selbst, 2017).

The contemporary social, political, and historical context, marked by police brutality, violence, and racism, has consequently contributed to further raising awareness in the research community, leading to the emergence of petitions and public announces to stop funding and research that applies AI to predict likely criminals or forecast crime locations (Heaven, 2020).

Following empirical demonstrations of gender and racial bias and advocacy by many organizations, activists, and scholars, several major tech companies (i.e., Amazon, IBM, and Microsoft) responded to various appeals by (temporarily or permanently) halting the sale of facial recognition tools created for law enforcement policing and intelligence purposes (Heilweil, 2020). Police agencies, especially in the United States, have started to turn down predictive policing software following public concerns (Miller, 2020; Murray & Giammarise, 2020; Nilsson, 2018; Thomas, 2016). Furthermore, a recent letter signed by more than 2,000 scholars working in different disciplines (Coalition for Critical Technology, 2020) led to the decision of Springer to retract a publishing offer for an article championing facial recognition to predict criminality (Hao, 2020a).

Systemic and wide change in the research and policy communities that goes well beyond the technical and legal borders of predictive policing, risk assessment tools, and facial recognition in the United States is critical and required. While advocating for the abolition of technology solutions that lead to high-stakes decisions and that have been proved to reinforce discrimination, racism, and inequality, I proffer that there exist ways to unfold the beneficial potential of AI in this field. This chapter is constructed around two long-terms strategies: the reframing and the reforming of computational methods in research on crime.

Concerning the reframe side, I will elaborate on two goals for social good that should govern research practices, namely, the halting and elimination of algorithmic systems that have been found to perpetrate discrimination at various levels and the recalibration of scholarly focus on areas in which computational methods have been overlooked but may guarantee less controversies and more benefits to society.

Regarding the reform dimension, instead, this chapter aims to highlight four possible pathways that can help reduce the harmful consequences of research in AI and computational sciences while concurrently increasing the positive social impact of such applications. These four pathways entail (a) working to create more integration between the different scientific communities working in this domain, (b) improving the educational offer to students and practitioners, (c) widening the scope of research (both theoretical and applied) outside the United States and the Western world, and (d) investigating human knowledge and perceptions regarding the application of AI and computational methods to study crime at the global level, also concerning existing deployed solutions.

Although these represent complex pathways that involve a large variety of players and stakeholders and a vast amount of commitment and resources, they must not be seen as mutually exclusive. Instead, the only way to efficaciously pursue a more equitable, fair, and just use of AI for research on crime is to invest efforts on each of them, to guarantee a change for the present generation and for the future ones that is not only confined to the United States or Europe but also encompasses the rest of the world.

The entire work will mainly reflect upon the role of academic research because academia is often the most relevant bridge in the pipeline that goes from pure scientific research to proper real-world deployment. Academia is where first ideas are generated and then consolidated through publications or wider projects, academia often gives birth to entrepreneurial spin-offs and private companies, academia educates and trains generations of students that will become relevant actors in tomorrow's society, and finally, academia is also a privileged interlocutor of the policy-making arena in many countries. The centrality of academia imposes thus to reflect on its responsibilities and its potential in changing the future.

This chapter will first briefly describe the use of AI algorithms to study crime and review the current debates around their practical pitfalls. Second, it will elaborate on the "reframe" of the area by focusing on the two goals for social good previously states. In the third section, the four abovementioned pathways for "reform" are outlined. Finally, summarizing conclusions are provided.

To Reframe: Recasting Computational Crime Research

Algorithmic Systems in Policing and Criminal Justice

Criminology and criminal justice research have undergone a paradigmatic shift in the last decades, toward an increasingly predominant use of data and quantitative methods (Woodward et al., 2016). As anticipated, contextual factors boosted the popularity and use of quantitative techniques for studying crime, leading to a massive amount of literature that relies on methods imported from applied mathematics, statistics, and computer science. Increasing data accessibility and the rapid availability of software and programming languages designed for statistical analyses and data science both contributed to this process.

Whilst this structural change in the discipline is relatively recent, the use of quantitative data for studying crime dates has a long history, as we previously saw. Far from being confined only to the ivory tower of basic academic research, this revolution has been reinforced by the interest of institutions in evidence-based policy solutions, especially in the areas of policing and criminal justice. During the 1920s, the United States was already deploying actuarial risk assessment tools to aid decision-makers in making criminal justice forecasts (Berk, 2019). The oscillating fortune of risk assessment in criminal justice is explained by the switch from a retributive approach to a punishment one (Garrett & Monahan, 2020). The desirable aim to reduce mass incarceration and jail overburden has turned into the exploding diffusion of statistical risk assessment for pre-trial detection. Over the decades, these tools have evolved from basic clinical judgments to machine learning-based real-time approaches that exploit both static and dynamic features associated with individuals that entered in contact with the criminal justice system. Different ranges of applications include the use of these tools for sentencing, both concerning adults and juveniles. Dozens of risk assessment tools are now deployed in the United States and many others are used in other countries, and not only directly in courts but also in adjoining sectors as clinical and psychiatric settings (Singh et al., 2014), in line with the actuarial revolution that marked many far-reaching aspects of public decision-making.

As anticipated in Chapter 3, the emergence of predictive policing dates back to the late 2000s and is the result of decades of academic and policy interests in empirical methods to study and predict the spatial and temporal distribution of crime.

As a multifaceted discipline, criminology has been impacted by these major changes and, in turn, contributed to reinforcing the idea that data, the scientific method, and the power of statistical techniques can explain, predict, and forecast crime.

On the one hand, developmental and life-course criminology (Farrington, 2003), interested in offending careers' dynamic nature, indirectly provided the scientific basis for empowering risk assessment tools. On the other hand, research in urban crime activity, supported by main criminological theories such as routine activity theory (L. E. Cohen & Felson, 1979), rational choice theory (Cornish & Clarke, 1987), and crime pattern theory (P. J. Brantingham & Brantingham, 1984), led to empirically demonstrate that crime is spatiotemporally clustered (Johnson, 2010). During the 2000s, the growing body of research corroborating the patterned nature of offending trends reinvigorated the promises of predictive policing.

A Breaking Point? Moving beyond Predictive Policing and Criminal Justice Risk Assessments

The explosive diffusion of predictive policing software and modern machine learning risk assessment tools in criminal justice and policing has stirred vivid discussions inside and outside academia (Angwing et al., 2016; Brayne, 2017; Eubanks, 2018; Prins & Reich, 2018; Shapiro, 2017). In the last years, concerns involving theoretical debates on penal approaches (Slobogin,

2018; Werth, 2019), data collection (Richardson et al., 2019), formal limits of predictive accuracy (Dressel & Farid, 2018; Green, 2020b), racial and social discrimination (Eubanks, 2018; Huq, 2019; Lum & Isaac, 2016), and disparate impact (Chouldechova, 2016; Selbst, 2017), along with pleas for more transparency, have deeply questioned their utility and the ethics behind these instruments. Activism and demand for reform in the name of social justice have been encouraged by empirical studies that illustrated the presence of racial bias and discrimination against disadvantaged minorities in technological applications intended to predict crime and likely offenders. In terms of public outreach, one of the most influential works has been the 2016 ProPublica report that unmasked the racial bias against Blacks present in COMPAS,[1] a risk assessment software used by US courts to determine the likelihood of defendants' future recidivism (Angwing et al., 2016). The shock provoked by the article's contents further fueled the efforts already in place to reform or disband algorithmic decision-making in criminal justice.

The dramatic events of 2020, and especially the murder of George Floyd in Minneapolis, sparked wide demand for radical police changes in the United States. Academics, activists, and policy-makers called, among the others, for police defunding and even for the abolition of certain agencies. This climate has reinforced the already existing requests to abolish the use of technology for policing and sentencing purposes, which primarily appeared in public media outlets (Ongweso, 2020; Sassaman, 2020; Stop LAPD Spying Coalition, 2018).

In June 2020, a letter signed by more than 2,000 scholars and scientists from many different backgrounds and countries asked the international published Springer to stop the publication of a study that claimed to predict future criminals using facial recognition tools (Coalition for Critical Technology, 2020). The paper, unfortunately, was not the first one to create a scandal in these terms (Hashemi & Hall, 2020; Wu & Zhang, 2017). In one of the most crucial points of the letter, the authors write that data that are generated by the criminal justice system cannot be used to identify offenders and predict criminal behaviors, due to the inherently biased nature of the information that the criminal justice system itself records and produces.

Relying upon abundant literature that indeed indicates how arrest and court data reflect prejudice, racism, and far-from-being-fair practices against minorities and disadvantaged communities, the authors and the signatories of the letter harshly oppose the use of these sources to train machine and deep learning algorithms. Among the other issues, they specifically underline the alarming connections between Lombrosianism and technology deployment in reference to facial recognition tools.

Most of the demand for transparency and reform of these tools has come from fields outside of criminology, such as computer science and law. Although a dense criminological literature has been produced that addresses the need for police and policing reforms (for recent scholarship on the topic, see Koper and Lum (2020)), the mainstream quantitative side of the community has only mildly reckoned with the ethical issues arising from the real-world deployment of algorithmic systems (Ugwudike, 2020).

Facing two incumbent important discipline wide-issues represented by the replication and transparency crisis (Lösel, 2018; Pridemore et al., 2018) and the low degree of diversity in the community (Chesney-Lind & Chagnon, 2016), criminology has not yet responded with the same strength demonstrated by the computer science counterpart in relation to the third big challenge that the discipline has to face: the one dealing with the ethics of machine-aided tools for studying, predicting, and reducing crime.

The legitimate and rightful actions taken against the structural issues that revolve around the use of criminal justice and policing data for high stakes decisions involving arrests, detention, and sentencing, however, shall not let the entire debate derail in the direction of an indiscriminate process toward halting research at the intersection of AI, computational sciences and crime.

The complexity of this contamination goes well beyond the boundaries set by predictive policing and criminal justice risk assessment which, although being for clear reasons the two most common areas of applications, are by no means the only ones in which computational modeling and AI have been or may be applied in the future. A landscape of alternative practices, areas of study and applications, and real-world impact are possible, as already pointed out by recent scholarship (Barabas et al., 2018; Raghavan et al., 2020; Sunstein, 2018).

An epistemological, ethical, and political discontinuity is necessary to achieve two results that are now more than ever intertwined: serving social good and advancing our understanding of crime by exploiting the strengths that novel research methodologies provide to the research and policy communities.

A recasting approach that will work toward the factual modification of how and for what purposes algorithms function may represent a driving force (not the only one) for a political change. By comprehending and reshaping the epistemological core of these instruments, the research community (along with the wider human society) can restructure how they are developed and be incisive in substantially improving the condition of human beings, especially those who are disadvantaged and marginalized. The improvement of this condition necessarily comes from two directions: the elimination of the discrimination and disparate impact caused by the current algorithmic decision-making systems and, jointly, a renovated inclusive use of technology as a result of a new deal in the creation and governance of algorithmic decision-making systems.

Interrelated processes such as the policy demand for technology-aided solutions to crime prevention and the higher availability of data led to the disproportionate use of such instruments to address a relatively small number of problems, which can be roughly traced back to the applications in policing and criminal justice discussed above. Yet, this disproportionate focus has somehow shadowed many other questions, issues, and perspectives that algorithmic tools may – or, say, should – consider. Barabas and co-authors (2018), for instance, proposed to move from regression-based paradigms to approaches that directly target the etiology of crime commission to fully exploit the positive power that modern technology may have on this social problem (a more detailed discussion of causal inference and algorithms in research on crime is provided in Chapter 5). However, the shift from correlational to causal evidence is not the only alternative direction that should be taken to reform this evolving strand of research and practice.

Two Goals for Social Good

A naïvely optimistic appeal about algorithmic approaches to the study and contrast of crime is not the point of this discussion. On this matter, there should be no role for naiveness and acritical optimism, which are two treacherous enemies of complexity, especially when dealing with societal problems. Nonetheless, I believe there is room for social good in this sphere, and – as long as it may take, and as hard as it may get – I do believe there are ways to unlock it. The core of this chapter lies in this rational hope, and the four pathways that will be later introduced have the precise role of producing a discussion on how to enhance this positive societal change. Concerning the destination of such process, as anticipated in the previous subsection, this positive societal change can be translated into two goals: the eradication of discrimination and disparate impact caused by current algorithmic decision-making systems and a renovated and inclusive use of technology encompassing both the engineering and the governance steps.

Toward the Elimination of Discrimination and Disparate Impact of Algorithmic Systems

The former goal should be straightforwardly clear at this point. The extant evidence points out that current algorithmic systems deployed do not work sufficiently well and, even most importantly, damage categories of people disproportionately targeted by law enforcement and the criminal justice system. This aspect can be framed and better understood through the lenses of critical algorithmic studies and social constructivism.

As profusely mentioned in this chapter, critical approaches to algorithmic decision-making in many contexts have unveiled extensive issues of data discrimination (Eubanks, 2018; Noble, 2018; Ugwudike, 2020). Such data discrimination targets specific identities and communities, reinforcing, among other things, racism, and – mostly in other contexts – sexism. In parallel, social constructivism argues that the definition of crime is inherently produced by a process of social construction, and that the status of a certain behavior (e.g., its legal acceptability) is the effect of public responses toward that behavior, rather than the behavior *per se* (Rafter, 1990; Rosenfeld,

2009). Social constructions can be positive forces for advancing civil, political, and human rights in the context of progressist, advanced societies. Yet, social construction can also lead to the politicization of certain behaviors, posing the risk of unjust or disproportionate criminalization. Such mechanism, in turn, results in the disproportionate targeting of specific groups and communities (Brewer & Heitzeg, 2008). These two theoretical lenses facilitate a comprehensive view of the perils and poorly addressed issues that current algorithmic systems imply in policing and criminal justice.

Nevertheless, beyond macro-level theoretical explanations that we have to take into account when we consider the deployment of these systems at the global level, often also coupled with aggressive surveillance systems, there are also related practical aspects that deserve attention. These particularly relate to the inherent nature of data used to feed these algorithmic systems and to the type of actions and effects that they imply.

Concerning predictive policing, for instance, the very first source of problems is the type of data that are generally exploited, namely, crime reports and arrest data. Predictive policing software generates predictions or recommendations to allocate policing resources in those areas where more crimes are discovered or the risk of victimization is higher, namely, those areas in which more crimes are reported. One could argue that there should be no problems in this sense: it is logical that police will be sent to those neighborhoods, blocks, streets, and segments where crime is high.

However, there is a two-fold loophole in this reasoning, a very well-known one by criminologists and crime researchers – hopefully. First, it is demonstrated that the probability that an individual will report a crime is not homogenous across groups in a society, and that differences are particularly stark across ethnic or racial groups (Hart & Rennison, 2003; Morgan & Thompson, 2021). This non-homogeneity in the probability of reporting leads to greater numbers of crime reports in areas where certain communities are concentrated, which in countries with a high level of spatial segregation as the United States implies strong feedback loops. Second, in cases where the true distribution of crime is not clustered (which may happen for some crime categories), but police forces are allocated to certain areas, only a spatially concentrated portion of crime will be targeted, as a result of the reinforcement of dispoportionate law enforcement attention. This disproportion will hence be reflected in the historical data used for predictive purposes. These feedback loops simply reinforce the "problematic" or "risky" status of certain neighborhoods or communities, hence strengthening police presence in those areas. This disproportionate targeting of areas where minorities live trivially increases the probability that delinquency, crimes, and deviance are detected and, more importantly, raises the perception of harassment, persecution, preventive criminalization in such groups. One again may argue that, although crime reports and arrest data are biased, contrasting "half" of the crime in a city is better than contrasting none: non-homogeneity of crime reports arrest data is not that problematic if in the end law enforcement is able to stop crime in those disadvantaged areas. Again, however, there is an important loophole in this line of thinking: in countries where the use of force by police and the law enforcement is significantly higher against minorities (Curtis et al., 2021; Edwards et al., 2019; Harris et al., 2021; Palmater, 2016; Peeples, 2019; Pierson et al., 2020; Sollund, 2006), the fact that police is allocated with much higher frequency to areas where those minorities reside does not automatically imply that those communities will be safer. Contrarily, this could lead to the erosion of trust and various forms of harms and negative consequences, both individual and collective, in turn also fueling social unrest (Curtis et al., 2021; Toro et al., 2019).

This chain of problems goes all the way to the other main application mentioned above, namely, criminal justice risk assessment tools. If those data upon which high-stake decisions are made are naturally mirroring or embedding information that originate from partial police data and discriminatory police practices, those decisions are intrinsically driven by different layers of bias. Then, what could be the solutions to eradicate these discriminatory practices, and the disparate impact of algorithmic systems deployed in policing and criminal justice?

There is no simple answer to this, and a complete discussion on this topic would barely fit into a dedicated book. However, I dare to make some suggestions that I hope can help the discussion on this topic.

In the first place, considerable attention should be devoted to the first problematic ingredient at the basis of such systems: data. If calls for service and arrest data mirror disparities linked to different attitudes toward crime reporting and policing, then debiasing mechanisms and statistical corrections through additional sources (e.g., victimization surveys) might be a reasonable starting point for improving these tools. Yet, victimization surveys are costly in terms of time and economic resources and cannot guarantee fast-pace injection into calls for service information, which are collected much quicker and in much cheaper ways. Therefore, other strategies should be added to this menu of adjustments. Among these are the construction of better relationships with communities in which police operate, and stronger connections with them through initiatives that go beyond the often-punitive role of law enforcement, entailing instead strategies designed to protect communities through better social policy programs. Members of the law enforcement would not be the only subjects involved in such programs: they should involve community leaders, social workers, and all those institutions (e.g., schools) that have a role in shaping the health, safety, and cohesion of a given community. By recalibrating the role of police within a broader framework of social policy, we can target the problem of biased data collection at its core. Critics of this view may see my position as naïve, but I am genuinely convinced that better policing necessarily comes from better relationships between institutions and citizens.

Second, such systems should be open to scrutiny. Accountability in this sense is fundamental to ensure that citizens and institutions alike are able to test, inspect, and evaluate their functioning to make sure that awareness is raised and that technical, legal, and political issues affecting the way in which they are constructed can be solved. To make this possible, it would be advisable – if not necessary – to open source the codebase of these systems, so that every detail, even the most marginal ones, can be evaluated. The call for open science and replicability has forced scholars to improve the transparency of their works in the last years. Though commercial and business interests are at play when considering most of these algorithmic systems, I argue that companies active in this area should follow their steps. Even more radically, such systems should be designed through cooperative efforts with all the stakeholders involved, including members of the institutions, civil and human rights organizations, community leaders, and representatives of the civil society in general. Instead, the secretive nature of these systems, mostly motivated by commercial reasons, makes it virtually impossible to really capture all their facets, from the engineering components to the effects they can lead to. It is reasonable to expect that predictive and algorithmic systems will be part of decision-making in public institutions for the foreseeable future, and therefore, it should be imperative to give the chance to all the people that are going to be affected by them to take part to their definition. Avoiding such dialogue will have considerable impacts on the attitudes of people on policing, criminal justice, institutions, and politics in general, even in the presence of the fairest tool. A "double-black box" approach to algorithmic systems should be defined as both ethically unacceptable as well as damaging for institutional credibility and perceived legitimacy.

Third, and mostly concerning predictive policing tools, strict recommendations or even regulatory efforts should be issued to make sure that a clear perimeter is set up for these tools, and that its boundaries are respected by those who use them. Specifically, each tool should clearly state the purpose for which it has been designed and the range of criminal phenomena that it targets. Indiscriminately adopting these systems for all types of crime without distinguishing between offense categories can be problematic for a variety of reasons, as crime clusters in time and space in different ways when different crimes are considered – and some crimes do not even cluster at all. Furthermore, clearly defining how predictions or recommendations are utilized is also critical, enabling easier evidence reconstruction in malpractice cases or misspecifications. Regulating or, at least, defining these boundaries then is important to make these tools more accountable and transparent, allowing citizens the right to know what these systems do and how they are employed.

We should continue to evaluate and audit present tools and possibly dismiss them or strictly regulate their functioning as a consequence of the negative effects they have on society. Yet other solutions should then be investigated, scrutinized in depth and explored to reconnect technology with research and practice. This directly involves the second goal, which is inherently linked to the idea that computational approaches should not be labeled as "bad" right away.

A Renovated Use of Algorithmic Systems
in Alternative Contexts

Beyond predictive policing and criminal justice risk assessment applications, there exist areas in which the deployment of algorithms and similar technologies can be far less controversial and far more beneficial to the greater good of society. Although it is imperative to continue working toward technical and nontechnical fixing of said tools in the traditional arenas of policing and criminal justice (first goal), the academic community – which encompass much many actors than those merely affiliated to criminology departments – should work toward the exploration of AI and related approaches to criminal problems that are less at risk of dragging behind major issues of discrimination and bias against certain groups within society.

As not all crimes are equally prone to be politicized or used to disproportionately criminalize certain strata of the population, then not all crimes can be reduced to the terms of social constructivism or radical theories on crime. Proponents of radical views in critical criminology theory claim that crime is the result of conscious or unconscious reactions to exploitation (Quinney, 1973). In addition, champions of this school of thought argue that crime control and the legal system act as tools for the dominant classes to maintain the power accumulated by targeting the rest of the population (Chambliss, 1975; Quinney, 1977; Vold, 1958). These positions view crime and criminal justice solely in the context of a conflict between social groups, fundamentally missing the multifaceted complexity of these phenomena, which are multidimensional and involve too many aspects of human nature and society to be reduced to flat abstractions. There exists no field or use cases in which algorithms do not require to be scrutinized, audited, and evaluated but certainly exist areas or problems that escape the characterization of mere outcomes of unjust institutional treatments and in which computational solutions may in fact work better, in theory and possibly also in practice.

Examples of such alternative and less controversial problems include, for instance, environmental crime, sexual violence, cybercrime, financial crimes, political corruption, human trafficking, and illegal waste trafficking. These are all areas that are disproportionately less considered by researchers, compared to policing and criminal justice risk assessment applications. More importantly, these are all areas that saw far less translation from research to practice, from peer-reviewed articles to deployed products used by institutions or companies. A few years ago, Lynch and colleagues (2017) warned against the neglect of quantitative research in Green criminology, the area of criminology which is concerned about crimes against the environment. In the article, the authors particularly signaled that such a process contributed to marginalizing Green criminology compared to other areas of research. This also reduced the influence that Green criminologists could have on policy-makers and policy decisions, among other effects. Quantitative modeling only partially overlaps with computational modeling, but the core

103

underlying message of the article holds anyways. It would be inaccurate to say that researchers focusing on the criminal and deviant phenomena mentioned above neglect quantitative modeling. Yet, the efforts toward using computational systems for producing evidence-based findings that may turn useful to the policy debates are often tiny or marginal, with most attention attracted by predictive policing studies and products and criminal justice risk assessment tools.

Being able to recognize that crime is made of hundreds of different phenomena and shades, and that definitions of crime vary across countries and cultures, is fundamental to capture the potential of computational modeling, AI, and data science for playing a positive role for change in society, leaving behind ideologically fueled positions which are detrimental to the debate.

The importance of reframing and continuing research in computational criminology also lies in an additional fact that is often ignored or forgotten, testifying the hardly reducible complexity of crime, a social phenomenon with myriads of ramifications and implications for individuals and communities. It is in fact irrefutable that minorities and other disadvantaged strata of the population have been significantly targeted by the criminal justice system in the United States (and elsewhere). Then minimizing or, possibly, eliminating the additional discrimination and disparate impact posed by algorithmic solutions is fundamental (goal 1). However, empirical evidence has also revealed that these same groups are also disproportionately damaged by crime, and especially violent crime (Friedman et al., 2011; Lauritsen & Heimer, 2010; Peterson & Krivo, 1999). Ignoring this aspect largely oversimplifies the interdependencies and overlap between victims and offenders (Jennings et al., 2010, 2012; Muftić et al., 2015) and would underestimate the role that many times victimization plays in triggering offending behaviors (Turanovic & Pratt, 2013; Turanovic et al., 2015).

Recasting computational crime research is hence fundamental to avoid that who those have been previously penalized by unfair systems are penalized again. By missing the chance to direct resources and efforts toward alternative pressing issues, researchers would miss the possibility to benefit those communities which already pay a higher cost for deviance, crime, violence, and insecurity.

A significant shift toward new objects of inquiry would involve new partnerships with institutions, new data, and especially new collection strategies – three factors that clash with the need for researchers to produce results with a certain frequency, and the urge of policy-makers to exploit new tools to tackle ancient problems. Yet, reforming how algorithmic systems are deployed in this sphere requires thinking about long-term horizons, rather than tenure-track trajectories or electoral mandates. Most importantly, a redistribution of intellectual resources toward unexplored or underexplored topics is one of the very few ways to reconnect the intellectual journey of criminology to the mission of reaching a safer and more just society.

To Reform: Four Pathways

These two goals – the eradication of discrimination and disparate impact caused by current algorithmic systems and a reframed and inclusive use of technology – are in line with the fourfold structure of computing as a force for (positive) social change proposed by Abebe and co-authors (2020), who outlined computing as *diagnostic, formalizer, rebuttal,* and *synecdoche*. The efforts to recalibrate the use of algorithms in criminal justice and policing is first motivated by the role of computing as rebuttal, since the community has demonstrated how current technologies have inherent limits and lead to inextricable negative ramifications at scale. However, as also warned by the proponents of this formalization, seeing computing in the sole form of a rebuttal force can overshadow promising applications or policy, causing a new form of harm. In fact, computing here can first act as a diagnostic tool, unmasking the salience of discrimination and bias produced by current predictive policing software and risk assessment tools. In addition, by adopting a reformative approach, computing can also play the critical role of a formalizer, redesigning systems based on the necessity to ask new questions (e.g., "what is the causal pathway that leads subject i to crime commission and how can we prevent it?" rather than "who will commit a crime?"). Finally, in this context computing also fits the synecdochal role: the technological lens on crime may highlight new perspectives on crime as a longstanding social problem which is intrinsically shaped by an array of other phenomena, including political and economic ones.

Yet, this call for epistemological and practical reform implies that the research and policy communities already have the tools and sufficient coordination and organization to convert them into real-world practices. Unfortunately, this is not true at this point. Paradigmatic changes require time. As one of the collective driving forces having the chance to influence the political and public debate, the research community is currently characterized by several structural flaws in how these topics are addressed. At the same time, the research community has a privileged role in this context: scholars and scientists are those that create and engineer algorithms and computational techniques that then become real-world products, and they are also those who educate the next generations of scholars, entrepreneurs, decision-makers, and voters. This three-folded nature (i.e., the lobbying, the technical and the educational one) testifies to a delicate equilibrium that characterizes the role of academia in this context.

I hence set forth four pathways that should be conjointly traveled to address as many critical aspects concerning how scholars and faculty deal with algorithms in criminology and crime research in general. These critical aspects severely limit the possibility of working toward new paradigms, frameworks, and policies worldwide to successfully improve the outcomes that automatized systems have on society. The suggested pathways are far from being exhaustive in capturing the entire complexity of the underlying topics (and necessary solutions) but hopefully offer a stimulus to think about the role of AI in relation to crime more broadly in terms of disciplines, education, geography, and stakeholders.

Increasing Integration between Communities Working in the Area

The convergence of objectives regarding the use of AI and akin technologies to predict or forecast crime in criminology, computer science, applied mathematics, and statistics did not result in the development of a community and the emergence of a dedicated subfield. On the criminological side, in spite of calls highlighting the benefit of computational and algorithmic criminology (Berk, 2013; P. L. Brantingham, 2011), scholarly production is still scarce and clustered around a very limited number of influential authors (see Chapter 3).

Overall, criminologists tend to prefer classical quantitative methods, dominated by regression modeling. Three exceptions are represented by the increasing diffusion of geospatial modeling simulation frameworks, such as agent-based models, and network science (Faust & Tita, 2019; Groff et al., 2019).[2] Both, however, do not necessarily conform with the principles, tools, and approaches of statistical learning.

On the other hand, the main alternative disciplines of interest in the current framing, i.e., computer science and applied mathematics, are offering many new techniques, methods, and frameworks to study crime. However, paradoxically, the main contributions have not been strictly technical but rather ethical. Scholars from such fields have deeply engaged in the scientific discourse pertaining to the issues discussed in the previous sections, moving from the purely formal criticalities of the concepts of accuracy and fairness to a more comprehensive discussion that goes beyond the mere metrics utilized to evaluate the performance of an algorithm (Barabas et al., 2020; Green & Viljoen, 2020; Selbst et al., 2019).

A bridge between these two intellectual traditions, however, is missing. With the exceptions of sparse and occasional collaborations, no consistent connection has been created to instantiate a constructive dialogue between disciplines. The low level of integration in this area of research transcends the blurred definition of academic disciplines and, instead, holds also for individual research groups. As recently documented by Chapter 3 and Campedelli (2020), the network structure of author-level collaborations in research at the intersection between AI and research on crime is highly fragmented, characterized by the absence of a core giant component of scientists working on these topics. Additionally, at least in the specific sample analyzed in this book, this field lacks individuals acting as bridges between the communities, as no scholar was recorded as author of at least one study in both subsamples (i.e., the criminology and the AI ones).

Such disconnectedness implies three orders of issues. First, it impedes the emergence of a community and a rapid exchange of ideas, techniques, and models, as already warned by Newman in his seminal studies on scientific networks (Newman, 2001, 2004). Second, it prevents the different communities working in the area from learning from each other's histories of achievement and failures. Third, the fragmentation of scholarly collaboration and the absence of a strong community only leave much more freedom of action to scholars (and entrepreneurs) that are less aware or interested in the risks and harm produced by technologies in research (and practice) concerned with crime.

All the three orders of issues inevitably contribute to weaker responses to the injustice perpetrated by currently deployed technologies in criminal justice and policing and, further, make it very difficult to approach complex practical problems in a meaningful way. A strong and yet diverse community (that should also engage with the larger society, including public organizations, and activists) would be far more constructive than sparse groups of scholars in performing political pressure to promote systemic change and reforms in policy and practice.

The background of criminologists could be useful to focus more meaningfully on relevant theoretical and conceptual aspects of criminal activity that scholars with other backgrounds may overlook or misunderstand. This does not only applies to criminologists that possess computing knowledge: instead, great (maybe even greater) benefits can also come from those scholars working in the qualitative and critical realms, who have demonstrated to be particularly sensible to the issues of discrimination, race, and inequality. Contrarily, the expertise and education of computer scientists and applied mathematicians could help to scoop technical pitfalls and maximize the exploitation of state of the art models that might be hardly accessible for social scientists. In general, again, the four roles of computing for social change outlined by Abebe and co-authors (2020) fit also in this context. Far from being exhaustive, these are only two examples of the possible positive out-turns of creating a cohesive community.

Additionally, with an increasing dialogue between disciplines, new research agendas that seek long-term changes may be formulated, instead of only relying on small project-wise changes that can have a low impact on the society. Further steps in this roadmap would lead to the creation of annual meetings, workshops, and dedicated venues in which projects, ideas, promises, and perils are openly and broadly discussed without being limited to the perimeter of each individual's background. The 2021 Annual Meeting of the American Society of Criminology held in Chicago has, in this sense, showed some developments. These developments entailed ad hoc workshops, panels, and sessions dedicated to the role of AI and computational modeling in criminology, as well as discussions on the delicate issues pertaining ethics, racism, and fairness in algorithmic systems related to policing and criminal justice.

Yet, to date, we are very far from the emergence and construction of a proper transcdisciplinary community. Resistance on both sides does not help in moving things forward in this direction. For this reason, the second pathway becomes crucial.

Improving Educational Portfolios

Guaranteeing continuity in scholarship and vigilance against injustice in applying AI and computational technologies in policing and criminal justice is crucial to lead to reforms and policy changes. At the same, it is critical to make sure that future generations of scholars will not perpetuate the same errors that have been committed before by the research community. Enthusiastic views of technology applications, market opportunities, and the absence of a diverse but cohesive community all played a role in facilitating the diffusion of biased predictive policing software and discriminatory criminal justice risk assessment tools, among others. For this reason, concomitantly with the efforts to create such a community, it is fundamental to design educational curricula and portfolios that are able to equip the future generations of scholars, practitioners, policy-makers, and (more in general) citizens with the tools to handle the complexity posed by computing in research on crime.

This does not only mean that students must be trained on the practical side of algorithms alone, but that specific courses embracing the topics of AI ethics, race theory, critical criminology, philosophy of law, and punishment and inequality studies must become a salient ingredient of these curricula.

The process is partially already in place. In the last years, many universities around the world have integrated their educational portfolios in computer science with courses and seminars on the use of computational models for social good and, in general, on the ethics of AI and computing (Quinn, 2006; B. R. Shapiro et al., 2020; Urman & Blumenthal, 2018). The recommendation is to make them more central: the trajectory of the desired change for a more just society inevitably intersects with the education of those that tomorrow will have the chance to change or modify the social, political, and economic structure of the world.

This call does not only pertain to students coming from computer science and applied mathematics. Instead, it applies also to social scientists, and criminologists especially. In the last years, several programs in criminology and criminal justice have increased the offer in terms of courses dealing with advanced statistics and computational models (see for instance Valentine et al., 2013). Besides the technical amount of knowledge distilled to students, however, the education offered should also contemplate the presence of courses that specifically address the themes of discrimination, bias, accountability of algorithmic decision-making processes in criminology, policing, and criminal justice. An offer that only focuses on the mere algorithmic and computational side fails to educate students to critically understand the manifold reverberations that technology is having on society.

Green (2020a) warns about the risks of including politically-neutral ethics in computing, indicating that data and computational scientists must recognize themselves as political actors to work toward social justice. I concur with this view, suggesting that ethics – being often vague and opaquely regulated – must be accompanied by parallel courses, workshops, or activities that inform students about the political impact that seemingly technical-only decisions can have on humanity.

One of the benefits generated by the renovation of educational portfolios will be the facilitation of communication and exchange between disciplines in the future, in contrast with extant siloed approaches. Transdisciplinary research is often complicated to implement because of communication barriers among scholars with very different backgrounds. If such obstacles are removed, this will eventually contribute to creating a stronger and less disconnected research community.

Improving educational portfolios should not be seen as a preliminary step leading to a progressive abolition of boundaries between disciplines and fields. The strength of transdisciplinary research and education, in fact, is the mixture of distinct perspectives, competencies, and expertise. Each experience and background should play a complementary and necessary role within the process of scientific inquiry. What is currently lacking is the common set of tools that enables different fields, communities, and stakeholders to join forces effectively.

Widening the Scope Outside the United States (and the Western World)

The United States has been central in both the scandals that led to fully reappraising the benefits of predictive policing and criminal justice risk assessment tools, and the scientific production tightly connected to these topics. However, technologies in policing and criminal justice are by no means confined to the United States. In 2018, a meeting held in Singapore organized by the INTERPOL and the United Nations Interregional Crime and Justice Research Institute (UNICRI) brought together 50 participants belonging to law enforcement, public institutions, academia, and the private sector. Participants came from more than 20 countries to discuss the implications of AI and robotics in policing (UNICRI & INTERPOL, 2019). Around the world, many countries have reported using predictive policing tools, including the United Kingdom, the Netherlands, Italy, Denmark, Switzerland, Germany, but also China and India (Egbert, 2018; Hardyns & Rummens, 2018; Leese, 2018; Oosterloo & van Schie, 2018; Sommerer, 2017).

Following the release of a white paper by the European Commission on AI regulation in Europe (European Commission, 2020), in February 2020 a European Parliament hearing focused on the use of AI technologies in criminal justice. The hearing resulted in a request for stronger legal frameworks for law enforcement use of facial and recognition techniques, issued by the Civil Liberties, Justice and Home Affairs Committee, highlighting the limits of the current adopted General Data Protection Regulation (GDPR) (European Parliament, 2020). In April 2021, the EU Commission also published a first proposal for the regulation of AI.[3] The aim of the proposal was to lay out a legislative framework designed to achieve the responsible and equitable use of AI and algorithmic systems. Similarly to the GDPR, also the draft AI Regulation is be characterized by extraterritoriality, meaning that it will apply to members of the European Union as well as organizations outside it, including providers or companies selling AI products in the EU market. Although with perplexities and critics on a number of aspects including the risk of over-regulation or the difficult implementation of certain provisions,[4] this first attempt to regulate AI shows how the topic (and its broad and specific consequences on society) is considered a serious one in European policy-making.

On the other side of the spectrum of democratic guarantees and open scrutiny over such technologies, China has recently set a powerful information infrastructure to strengthen and increase the surveillance role of the state on society. Reports have purported how AI is being used to persecute the Uighur minority (Yang, 2019). Leaks showing the role of algorithms in violating human rights are abundant. Other accounts highlight how China is preparing a massively funded national laboratory for advanced policing, including a spectrum of technological endeavors such as emotion recognition (Yang & Murgia, 2020).

In India, after the Delhi's Police implementation of the Crime Mapping, Analytics and Predictive System (CMAPS) in 2015, evidence has shown the presence of biases in various forms: historical, representational, and measurement ones (Marda & Narayan, 2020). The authors outline how the CMAPS opacity is a deliberate choice rather than an unintended bug, and in their review of the adopted instruments, they highlight the existence of peculiar algorithmic issues that are associated with the specific context of application. They recommend, in fact, that the study of any algorithmic decision-making system in predictive policing should be developed through the lenses of the institutional culture in which it is embedded.

Italy as well represents another interesting case. In the last years, many police departments around the country have started to use predictive policing software. Nonetheless, besides a recently published study that evaluates the postintervention effect of one of these software deployed in Milan (Mastrobuoni, 2020), to this date, no empirical and nonpartisan analysis of the possible biases in these software has been provided. This is especially worrisome given that one of the two most frequently media-covered predictive software does not focus on geographical hotspots but, instead, seeks to find alleged patterns in serial actions, concentrating on suspects. The source code of this software is private and nonaccessible. Furthermore, from a methodological point of view, overly general descriptions are openly provided. While this secrecy is reasonable and legit for commercial purposes, it leaves nonetheless doubts regarding the consequences of potential wrongful predictions or recommendations. Additionally, the debate around the topic inside and outside academia is absent, with the exception of few journalistic pieces that tried to showcase the risks in the use of these technologies (Coluccini, 2018; Signorelli, 2016).

Notwithstanding the numerous countries that have tested or adopted the algorithmic decision-making systems in criminal justice and policing, scientific inquiry and the resulting public debate mostly revolve around the United States. This is problematic for two reasons.

First, it limits the promises of computing as a diagnostic tool in social change (Abebe et al., 2020). Second, it exacerbates asymmetries between regions of the world.

Concerning the first point, studying algorithmic bias and discrimination by solely concentrating on a peculiar political, social, and economic system, characterized by very specific criticalities in policing and criminal justice, means that we will continue to ignore the effects of algorithmic systems in the rest of the world. This, trivially, sensibly reduces the possibility for computing to influence society as a whole positively, as framed by Abebe and colleagues (2020). Each country is characterized by a gigantic multitude of social, economic, and political features. Around the world, discrimination occurs in many forms against very different social groups or communities, crime is heterogeneously patterned at the geographical level, and the criminal justice system is organized in many distinct ways. Data themselves are collected in very different ways, at very distinct temporal and geographical scales. The discrimination problems occurring in the United States, the violence and brutality of the police, and the marginalization of certain communities are not problems that we can find in every other country. They are specifically tied to the history, society, and political context of the United States. Other countries, however, may have many other different issues in terms of human and civil rights, racism, and equal opportunities. If we do not comprehensively study what is happening outside the United States, we will never be able to comprehensively understand the multifaceted harmful consequences of algorithmic decision-making in criminal justice and policing – as well as their possible benefits. And by doing so, we will refrain to contributing to the creation of a society in which technology is meant to protect rather than harm.

Concerning the second point, an overwhelming focus on the United States (and on very few other Western countries) can be instrumental in reinvigorating the asymmetries across countries and areas of the world. This process, in turn, leads to two negative effects. On the one hand, it hardens the chance of scholars from the Global South and many developing countries to be part of the scientific arena in which algorithmic decision-making is discussed and scrutinized, impacting diversity, representativeness, and equality at the global scale. On the other hand, this intellectual schism between areas of the world reduces the possibility of providing people, communities, and scholars with the necessary tools to act against the unfair, unaccountable, and harmful use of technology in criminal justice and policing. Cooperation and inclusiveness across countries and regions are not only ways for widening and deepening scientific knowledge but also to facilitate positive social impact by raising awareness and consciousness through science and its communication.

Scientists and scholars in the United States and several Western countries have accumulated a vast amount of knowledge and solid experience on the issues of AI ethics: the impact that such widespread shared knowledge would have on the entire planet could be enormous and help in contrasting the increasing diffusion of technologies that, in a way or another, cause harm to different strata of the world population.

To spread the benefits of years of research in this domain, however, it is critical to go beyond the physical borders of the Western world.

Investigating Human Knowledge and Perceptions

What do we know about what people worldwide know regarding algorithmic decision-making in criminal justice and policing? Almost nothing. On the one side, studies that investigate people's preferences, reliance, and attitudes about algorithms exist, but they focus on other application domains (Dietvorst et al., 2016; Jung et al., 2017; Lee, 2018; Logg, 2017; Logg et al., 2019). On the other side, scholars have contributed to a now longstanding literature examining people's perceptions and opinions about police, law enforcement, and judicial systems in general (Ashworth & Feldman-Summers, 1978; Brunson, 2007; Flanagan et al., 1985; Mazerolle et al., 2013; Miles-Johnson, 2015; Overby et al., 2004; Reichman, 2007; Tankebe, 2013; Weitzer & Tuch, 2004). Nonetheless, besides a few isolated examples (Binns et al., 2018; Grgic-Hlaca et al., 2018, Kennedy et al., 2022), a line of research that comprehensively explores people's positions regarding algorithms used to predict crime or assist judges is lacking. Aside from the United States and few other countries, the coverage of such topics in media and institutional communication is almost absent, hence leaving many doubts regarding the fact that citizens around the world are at least informed about the existence (and actual deployment) of risk assessment tools, predictive policing or facial recognition software.

Yet, exploring human knowledge and perceptions in this area should be a priority of the scientific community. There are two main reasons behind the necessity of addressing this point. First, connected to the third pathway described above, inquiring into human knowledge is a worthwhile way to increase and strengthen awareness, especially for people living in nondemocratic countries. Second, gathering people's perceptions represents a crucial viaticum to assess the complexity of AI ethics in this domain.

Nowadays, in a digital world, scholars have the tools to reach people all around the globe: using these instruments to measure the different levels of awareness and consciousness about the role that computing has in high stakes public decisions will contribute to better understanding the shape of

112

the trajectories of these technologies in the future. In a recent article published by the MIT Technology Review, Heaven reported how even lawyers and defense attorneys are often unaware that risk assessment tools are used to judge their clients (2020). This finding already substantiates the gray area in which these systems operate. Discovering that the vast majority of people around the world do not know about the existence of such tools would tell us much about the level of opacity of such systems, especially concerning their governance and deployment beyond technical functioning. Citizens must be central stakeholders in the political process of technology adoption in critical domains: this centrality cannot be consolidated if basic information about algorithmic systems is neglected. The scientific community, in this sense, has the responsibility to facilitate this process.

Furthermore, as anticipated, gathering information on human perceptions represents an opportunity to formulate questions about delineating universal AI ethics principles.

Human society is characterized by a high heterogeneity of values, moral principles, and priorities: this heterogeneity is linked to a manifold of factors encompassing historical, cultural, political, and religious dimensions. In 2018, the results of the massive Moral Machine experiment documented how, across the world, responses to moral dilemmas on the behavior of autonomous vehicles are far from being homogeneous and reflect both the influence of contemporary institutions and deep cultural traits (Awad et al., 2018). The outcomes of the experiments fostered the discussion on how to use such information to inform the design of ethical principles that should regulate the autonomous vehicles market.

Similar exploratory experiments that gauge people's public opinions in terms of algorithmic decision-making in criminal justice and policing report heterogeneity in attitudes (Grgic-Hlaca et al., 2018). We can only speculate on the possible magnitude of heterogeneity in outcomes when wider samples and broader experimental designs are involved. If, worldwide, people's opinions are not homogeneous in the Moral Machine experiment where the consequences of the decisions are very clear (i.e., who should die?), there is no reason to think that things would be less complex and heterogeneous in scenarios where decisions lead to less permanent effects (in most countries, a man, once served his time in prison, will return free, in principle) and where themes that can very much stimulate the irrational side of each of us are addressed.

The relevance of human perception about ethics in this sphere is multifaceted. Debating algorithmic ethics without contemplating the different inclinations and tendencies toward moral values worldwide is an oversimplification that only delays a comprehensive discussion about the broader societal implications of AI. It is of primary importance, thus, to gather sufficient information to understand how wide the spectrum of acceptability is worldwide. If investigating human knowledge is crucial to mature advocacy and information strategies and campaigns, gathering human perception is critical to understanding what people around the world consider acceptable, fair, and *ethical*. How restricted should the scope of actions of algorithms in criminal justice and policing be? How should model forecasts be treated? What crimes are to be weighted more in risk assessment decisions? Where should we set the threshold between freedom and security? These questions – among dozens of other questions – if posed to a sample of people coming from the same city would likely lead to a certain degree of variation: no shared agreement exists with our neighbors, how can it exist with people embedded in completely different cultures, political contexts, and social communities?

Scanning the intricate horizon of human perception would also help to realistically discuss the future of these technologies. Furthermore, aligned with the philosophical tradition on moral relativism, it would also dispute whether we can ever expect to develop universally shared ethical principles for algorithmic systems. In addressing this last point, we can start to reason about the political repercussions of the widespread diffusion of these tools in a global scenario where no basic agreements on technology governance exist. Where no formal regulation applies, these systems will likely continue to diffuse, potentially playing the role of a weaponized tool for empowering the surveillance state, overtaking human, political, and civil rights.

These are only speculations, and however accurate, they will remain as such until the scientific community decides to step out from the oversimplified belief that worldwide good and bad are clearly distinct entities in a binarized state.

Discussion and Conclusions

Algorithmic systems deployed in criminal justice and policing to predict, prevent, and reduce crime have been widely criticized by scholars, activists, and community leaders (Angwing et al., 2016; Chinoy, 2019; Hao, 2020b; Heaven, 2020; Horowitz, 2020). The episodes of violence and brutality perpetrated by the police in the United States in the last years have reinvigorated the appeals to reduce, reform, and even abolish the use of criminal justice risk assessment tools, predictive policing systems, and facial recognition software to finally halt some of the instruments used by institutions and law enforcement to disproportionately target and harm racial minorities, marginalized group, and disadvantaged strata of the population. The appeals concerned not only the United States but many other countries as well.

While concurring with the need to finally resolve the structural and systemic issues that many countries are facing anent crime control, punishment, and segregation, I advise against an abolitionist position concerning the use of novel (or claimed to be so) technologies to study (and contrast) crime.

An abolitionist position would lead to negative consequences for those already damaged by crime, police misconduct, and unfair algorithms. Furthermore, abolitionism would massively reduce the possibility of scanning alternative approaches to blend algorithmic processes and research on crime to deliver the social good. In this sense, I advocate for a reframing approach encompassing the eradication of discrimination and disparate impact reinvigorated through current algorithmic systems. Furthermore, I advocate for the investment of resources and efforts on the use of machine learning and computational approaches to study and counter phenomena that are less controversial and yet equally important to craft a better society. Yet, I also argue that, in the current state, the research (and the policy) communities are not sufficiently equipped to successfully espouse these new paradigms.

To facilitate this reframing strategy, I hence proposed four reformist pathways that can help in solving the issues faced by scholars working at the intersection between computational sciences and research on crime in the bold attempt to also anticipate the likely future risks that a rapidly changing world will pose to all the stakeholders included in this era of needed changes. These stakeholders include researchers, faculty, students, policymakers, and, at a higher level, citizens themselves.

The first outlined pathway regards the need for increased integration and exchange between scientific disciplines and communities working in the area. There is a critical lack of cohesiveness between communities and perspectives in this expanding area of research, as highlighted in Chapter 3 and by a previous article I published in 2021 (Campedelli, 2021). A disconnected structure of scientific collaboration impedes the construction solid knowledge and generating effective debates where all expertise and backgrounds are valued and weighted to find solutions to complex problems (Newman, 2001, 2004), as the one of algorithms in criminal justice and policing. Furthermore, this disconnectedness critically reduces the possibility of reasoning about long-term research and policy agendas. Instead, it makes it far more difficult to exercise a functional science-based pressure on policymakers, decision-makers, and institutional representatives to favor positive change.

The second pathway pertains to the necessity to improve educational offers, both for students enrolled in computer science and applied mathematics schools and to those enrolled in criminology and social science programs. This pathway warrants the need to prepare and equip future generations of scholars, decision-makers, and citizens with the necessary knowledge and attitudes to tackle the challenges posed by an increasing prevalence of automatized systems in public and private spheres. On the one hand, computer science curricula need a stronger focus on the ethics of computing and to better frame the sociopolitical out-turns of their only apparently neutral decisions. On the other hand, criminology and social science curricula should go beyond the mere delivery of courses that only emphasize the technical component of algorithms and computational methods. These curricula should also incorporate courses designed to educate about discrimination, bias, and accountability of algorithms in policing, and criminal justice.

The third pathway demands to widen the focus beyond the United States and the Western world. The United States has been central in the emergence of a line of transdisciplinary research focusing on the accountability, fairness, and reliability of algorithms in criminal justice and policing. Some other countries have followed the impetus of the United States in addressing these problems. However, there is an overwhelming unbalance between the knowledge gathered about these few countries and the rest of the world, despite what is, by now, a global diffusion of these technologies. This US-centric (or, at most, Western-centric) focus represents a major limitation for harvesting positive scientific and social progress for countries that are marginal in the international political and scientific debates. This marginalization will likely lead to an increase in the asymmetry across countries, eventually leading to causing harm to groups and people that the scientific community has overlooked. I am not certainly establishing a causal narrative here: people will not be harmed or disproportionately targeted because scholars ignored nontraditional contexts. Yet, research will miss a substantial chance to engage with themes that matter in the real world, although they might deviate from focuses that are much more attractive in mainstream research circles.

Finally, the fourth pathway proposes to investigate human knowledge and perceptions about algorithmic systems applied to crime prevention and control around the world. Except for very few works (Binns et al., 2018; Grgic-Hlaca et al., 2018; Kennedy et al., 2022), we currently lack information about the degree to which people are informed about these technologies and the degree to which they are willing to accept such systems in highly sensible public spheres such as criminal justice and policing. Besides the ignorance of the research community on these issues, it is crucial to support this path to help to raise awareness on a global scale and stimulate forces for social progress. Furthermore, exploring perceptions will help scholars to fully delve into the heterogeneity and complexity of human values, political attitudes, cultural traits, and social backgrounds in shaping beliefs and moral positions about algorithms. This analysis will eventually facilitate more meaningful discussions about the limitations (or possibilities) to design universally acceptable ethical principles that should govern the next generation of automatized decision-making systems.

To conclude, this chapter aimed at fostering a new direction in the discussion regarding algorithms in research on crime by promoting a "reframe and reforme" horizon. I advocate for a renovated phase of the debate that should bring together different traditions and disciplines. In this new phase, criminologists should no more abjure the responsibility that they hold as representatives of a field that, in the last years, has responded mildly to the calls for addressing the ethical problems imposed by the real-world deployment of algorithms mostly developed in its own community. Besides the role of criminologists here emphasized, this new phase should promote a multipolar and transdisciplinary perspective to overcome the risk of over-simplifying the depth of the topic and to structurally rethink how algorithms should assist public institutions in preventing crime.

Notes

1 Acronym for Correctional Offender Management Profiling for Alternative Sanctions.
2 See also Chapter 3 for a more detailed overview of these areas of research.
3 The full name of the document is "Proposal for a Regulation of The European Parliament And Of The Council Laying Down Harmonised Rules On Artificial Intelligence (Artificial Intelligence Act) And Amending Certain Union Legislative Acts."
4 For critical views on the draft regulation, see, for instance, Cohen et al. (2020), Veale and Borgesius (2021), and Glauner (2021). For a more positive overview, see instead Floridi (2021).

References

Abebe, R., Barocas, S., Kleinberg, J., Levy, K., Raghavan, M., & Robinson, D. G. (2020). Roles for computing in social change. *ArXiv:1912.04883 [Cs]*. https://doi.org/10.1145/3351095.3372871.

Angwing, J., Larson, J., Mattu, S., & Kirchner, L. (2016). Machine bias. There's software used across the country to predict future criminals. And it's biased against blacks. *ProPublica*. https://www.propublica.org/article/machine-bias-risk-assessments-in-criminal-sentencing

Ashworth, C. D., & Feldman-Summers, S. (1978). Perceptions of the effectiveness of the criminal justice system: The female victim's perspective. *Correctional Psychologist*, 5(3), 227–240. https://doi.org/10.1177/009385487800500303.

Awad, E., Dsouza, S., Kim, R., Schulz, J., Henrich, J., Shariff, A., Bonnefon, J.-F., & Rahwan, I. (2018). The moral machine experiment. *Nature*, 563(7729), 59–64. https://doi.org/10.1038/s41586-018-0637-6.

Barabas, C., Virza, M., Dinakar, K., Ito, J., & Zittrain, J. (2018). Interventions over predictions: Reframing the ethical debate for actuarial risk assessment. In *Conference on fairness, accountability and transparency*, 62–76. http://proceedings.mlr.press/v81/barabas18a.html

Barabas, C., Doyle, C., Rubinovitz, J., & Dinakar, K. (2020). Studying up: Reorienting the study of algorithmic fairness around issues of power. In *Proceedings of the 2020 conference on fairness, accountability, and transparency*, 167–176. https://doi.org/10.1145/3351095.3372859.

Berk, R. (2013). Algorithmic criminology. *Security Informatics*, 2(1), 5. https://doi.org/10.1186/2190-8532-2-5.

Berk, R. (2019). *Machine learning risk assessments in criminal justice settings*. Springer International Publishing: Imprint: Springer. https://link.springer.com/10.1007/978-3-030-02272-3

Binns, R., Van Kleek, M., Veale, M., Lyngs, U., Zhao, J., & Shadbolt, N. (2018). "It's reducing a human being to a percentage": Perceptions of justice in algorithmic decisions. In *Proceedings of the 2018 CHI conference on human factors in computing systems*, 1–14. https://doi.org/10.1145/3173574.3173951.

Bolsover, G., & Howard, P. (2019). Chinese computational propaganda: Automation, algorithms and the manipulation of information about Chinese politics on Twitter and Weibo. *Information, Communication & Society*, 22(14), 2063–2080. https://doi.org/10.1080/1369118X.2018.1476576.

Bozdag, E. (2013). Bias in algorithmic filtering and personalization. *Ethics and Information Technology*, 15(3), 209–227. https://doi.org/10.1007/s10676-013-9321-6.

Brantingham, P. L. (2011). Computational criminology. In *2011 European intelligence and security informatics conference*, 3. https://doi.org/10.1109/EISIC.2011.79.

Brantingham, P. J., & Brantingham, P. L. (1984). *Patterns in crime*. Macmillan.

Brayne, S. (2017). Big data surveillance: The case of policing. *American Sociological Review*. https://doi.org/10.1177/0003122417725865.

Brewer, R. M., & Heitzeg, N. A. (2008). The racialization of crime and punishment: Criminal justice, color-blind racism, and the political economy of the prison industrial complex. *American Behavioral Scientist*, 51(5), 625–644. https://doi.org/10.1177/0002764207307745.

Brunson, R. K. (2007). "Police don't like Black people": African-American young men's accumulated police experiences. *Criminology & Public Policy*, 6(1), 71–101. https://doi.org/10.1111/j.1745-9133.2007.00423.x.

Campedelli, G. M. (2020). Where are we? Using scopus to map the literature at the intersection between artificial intelligence and research on crime. *Journal of Computational Social Science*, 4(2), 503–530. https://doi.org/10.1007/s42001-020-00082-9.

Carlson, A. (2017). The need for transparency in the age of predictive sentencing algorithms. *Iowa Law Review*, 303, 303–329.

Chambliss, W. J. (1975). Toward a political economy of crime. *Theory and Society*, 2(1), 149–170. https://doi.org/10.1007/BF00212732.

Chesney-Lind, M., & Chagnon, N. (2016). Criminology, gender, and race: A case study of privilege in the academy. *Feminist Criminology*. https://doi.org/10.1177/1557085116633749.

Chinoy, S. (2019, July 10). Opinion | The racist history behind facial recognition. *The New York Times*. https://www.nytimes.com/2019/07/10/opinion/facial-recognition-race.html

Chouldechova, A. (2016). Fair prediction with disparate impact: A study of bias in recidivism prediction instruments. *ArXiv:1610.07524 [Cs, Stat]*. http://arxiv.org/abs/1610.07524

Coalition for Critical Technology. (2020). *Abolish the #TechToPrisonPipeline*. https://medium.com/@CoalitionForCriticalTechnology/abolish-the-techtoprisonpipeline-9b5b14366b16

Cohen, L. E., & Felson, M. (1979). Social change and crime rate trends: A routine activity approach. *American Sociological Review*, 44(4), 588–608. https://doi.org/10.2307/2094589.

Cohen, I. G., Evgeniou, T., Gerke, S., & Minssen, T. (2020). The European artificial intelligence strategy: Implications and challenges for digital health. *The Lancet Digital Health*, 2(7), e376–e379. https://doi.org/10.1016/S2589-7500(20)30112-6.

Coluccini, R. (2018). La polizia predittiva è diventata realtà in Italia e non ce ne siamo accorti. *Vice*. https://www.vice.com/it/article/pa5apm/polizia-predittiva-italia-lombardi-xlaw-prevedere-crimini-algoritmi

Cornish, D. B., & Clarke, R. V. (1987). Understanding crime displacement: An application of rational choice theory. *Criminology, 25*(4), 933–948. https://doi. org/10.1111/j.1745-9125.1987.tb00826.x.

Curtis, D. S., Washburn, T., Lee, H., Smith, K. R., Kim, J., Martz, C. D., Kramer, M. R., & Chae, D. H. (2021). Highly public anti-Black violence is associated with poor mental health days for Black Americans. *Proceedings of the National Academy of Sciences, 118*(17). https://doi.org/10.1073/pnas.2019624118.

Dietvorst, B. J., Simmons, J. P., & Massey, C. (2016). Overcoming algorithm aversion: People will use imperfect algorithms if they can (Even slightly) modify them. *Management Science, 64*(3), 1155–1170. https://doi.org/10.1287/mnsc. 2016.2643.

Dressel, J., & Farid, H. (2018). The accuracy, fairness, and limits of predicting recidivism. *Science Advances, 4*(1), eaao5580. https://doi.org/10.1126/sciadv. aao5580.

Edwards, F., Lee, H., & Esposito, M. (2019). Risk of being killed by police use of force in the United States by age, race–ethnicity, and sex. *Proceedings of the National Academy of Sciences, 116*(34), 16793–16798. https://doi.org/10.1073/ pnas.1821204116.

Egbert, S. (2018). About discursive storylines and techno-fixes: The political framing of the implementation of predictive policing in Germany. *European Journal for Security Research, 3*(2), 95–114. https://doi.org/10.1007/s41125-017-0027-3.

Eubanks, V. (2018). *Automating inequality: How high-tech tools profile, police, and punish the poor.* St Martins Pr.

European Commission. (2020). *White paper: On artificial intelligence – A European approach to excellence and trust.* https://ec.europa.eu/info/sites/info/files/commission-white-paper-artificial-intelligence-feb2020_en.pdf

European Parliament. (2020). *Hearing on artificial intelligence in criminal law.* European Parliament. https://www.europarl.europa.eu/committees/en/product-details/ 20200211CHE07061

Farrington, D. P. (2003). Developmental and life-course criminology: Key theoretical and empirical issues-the 2002 Sutherland Award Address. *Criminology, 41*(2), 221–225. https://doi.org/10.1111/j.1745-9125.2003.tb00987.x.

Faust, K., & Tita, G. E. (2019). Social networks and crime: Pitfalls and promises for advancing the field. *Annual Review of Criminology, 2*(1), 99–122. https://doi. org/10.1146/annurev-criminol-011518-024701.

Fitzpatrick, D. J., Gorr, W. L., & Neill, D. B. (2019). Keeping score: Predictive analytics in policing. *Annual Review of Criminology, 2*(1), 473–491. https://doi. org/10.1146/annurev-criminol-011518-024534.

Flanagan, T. J., McGarrell, E. F., & Brown, E. J. (1985). Public perceptions of the criminal courts: The role of demographic and related attitudinal variables. *Journal of Research in Crime and Delinquency, 22*(1), 66–82. https://doi.org/10.1177/00 22427885022001004.

Floridi, L. (2021). The European legislation on AI: A brief analysis of its philosophical approach. *Philosophy & Technology, 34*(2), 215–222. https://doi.org/10.1007/ s13347-021-00460-9.

Fogliato, R., Xiang, A., Lipton, Z., Nagin, D., & Chouldechova, A. (2021). On the validity of arrest as a proxy for offense: Race and the likelihood of arrest for violent crimes. *ArXiv:2105.04953 [Stat].* http://arxiv.org/abs/2105.04953

Friedman, M. S., Marshal, M. P., Guadamuz, T. E., Wei, C., Wong, C. F., Saewyc, E. M., & Stall, R. (2011). A meta-analysis of disparities in childhood sexual abuse, parental physical abuse, and Peer victimization among sexual minority and sexual nonminority individuals. *American Journal of Public Health*, *101*(8), 1481–1494. https://doi.org/10.2105/AJPH.2009.190009.

Fussell, S. (2020). An algorithm that "predicts" criminality based on a face sparks a furor. *Wired*. https://www.wired.com/story/algorithm-predicts-criminality-based-face-sparks-furor/

Garrett, B. R., & Monahan, J. (2020). Judging risk. *California Law Review*, *108*(2), 439–493.

Gerstner, D. (2018). Predictive policing in the context of residential burglary: An empirical illustration on the basis of a pilot project in Baden-Württemberg, Germany. *European Journal for Security Research*, *3*(2), 115–138. https://doi.org/10.1007/s41125-018-0033-0.

Glauner, P. (2021). An assessment of the AI regulation proposed by the European Commission. *ArXiv:2105.15133 [Cs]*. http://arxiv.org/abs/2105.15133

Green, B. (2020a). *Data science as political action: Grounding data science in a politics of justice* (SSRN Scholarly Paper ID 3658431). Social Science Research Network. https://doi.org/10.2139/ssrn.3658431.

Green, B. (2020b). The false promise of risk assessments: Epistemic reform and the limits of fairness. In *Proceedings of the 2020 conference on fairness, accountability, and transparency*, 594–606. https://doi.org/10.1145/3351095.3372869.

Green, B., & Viljoen, S. (2020). Algorithmic realism: Expanding the boundaries of algorithmic thought. In *Proceedings of the 2020 conference on fairness, accountability, and transparency*, 19–31. https://doi.org/10.1145/3351095.3372840.

Grgic-Hlaca, N., Redmiles, E. M., Gummadi, K. P., & Weller, A. (2018). Human perceptions of fairness in algorithmic decision making: A case study of criminal risk prediction. In *Proceedings of the 2018 World Wide Web conference*, 903–912. https://doi.org/10.1145/3178876.3186138.

Groff, E. R., Johnson, S. D., & Thornton, A. (2019). State of the art in agent-based modeling of urban crime: An overview. *Journal of Quantitative Criminology*, *35*(1), 155–193. https://doi.org/10.1007/s10940-018-9376-y.

Hao, K. (2020a, June). *AI researchers say scientific publishers help perpetuate racist algorithms*. https://www.technologyreview.com/2020/06/23/1004333/ai-science-publishers-perpetuate-racist-face-recognition/

Hao, K. (2020b, August). The UK exam debacle reminds us that algorithms can't fix broken systems. *MIT Technology Review*. https://www.technologyreview.com/2020/08/20/1007502/uk-exam-algorithm-cant-fix-broken-system/

Hardyns, W., & Rummens, A. (2018). Predictive policing as a new tool for law enforcement? Recent developments and challenges. *European Journal on Criminal Policy and Research*, *24*(3), 201–218. https://doi.org/10.1007/s10610-017-9361-2.

Harris, S., Joseph-Salisbury, R., Williams, P., & White, L. (2021). *Collision of crises: Racism, policing, and the COVID-19 pandemic*. CODE – Centre on the Dynamics of Ethnicity and Runnymede Trust. https://www.research.manchester.ac.uk/portal/files/200466775/Runnymede_CoDE_A_Collision_of_Crises_policing_briefing_FINAL.pdf

Hart, T. C., & Rennison, C. (2003). *Reporting crime to the police, 1992–2000* (Special Report NCJ 195710; Bureau of Justice Statistics Bulletin). United States Department of Justice, Bureau of Justice Statistics.

Hashemi, M., & Hall, M. (2020). Retraction note: Criminal tendency detection from facial images and the gender bias effect. *Journal of Big Data*, 7(1), 40. https://doi.org/10.1186/s40537-020-00323-8.

Heaven, W. D. (2020, July). Predictive policing algorithms are racist. They need to be dismantled. *MIT Technology Review.* https://www.technologyreview.com/2020/07/17/1005396/predictive-policing-algorithms-racist-dismantled-machine-learning-bias-criminal-justice/

Heilweil, R. (2020, June 11). Big tech companies back away from selling facial recognition to police. That's progress. *Vox.* https://www.vox.com/recode/2020/6/10/21287194/amazon-microsoft-ibm-facial-recognition-moratorium-police

Horowitz, J. (2020, July). Tech companies are still helping police scan your face. *CNN Business.* https://edition.cnn.com/2020/07/03/tech/facial-recognition-police/index.html

Howard, P. N., Woolley, S., & Calo, R. (2018). Algorithms, bots, and political communication in the US 2016 election: The challenge of automated political communication for election law and administration. *Journal of Information Technology & Politics*, 15(2), 81–93. https://doi.org/10.1080/19331681.2018.1448735.

Huq, A. (2019). Racial equity in algorithmic criminal justice. *Duke Law Journal*, 68(6), 1043–1134.

Jennings, W. G., Higgins, G. E., Tewksbury, R., Gover, A. R., & Piquero, A. R. (2010). A longitudinal assessment of the victim-offender overlap. *Journal of Interpersonal Violence*, 25(12), 2147–2174. https://doi.org/10.1177/0886260509354888.

Jennings, W. G., Piquero, A. R., & Reingle, J. M. (2012). On the overlap between victimization and offending: A review of the literature. *Aggression and Violent Behavior*, 17(1), 16–26. https://doi.org/10.1016/j.avb.2011.09.003.

Johnson, S. D. (2010). A brief history of the analysis of crime concentration. *European Journal of Applied Mathematics*, 21(4–5), 349–370. https://doi.org/10.1017/S0956792510000082.

Jung, J., Song, H., Kim, Y., Im, H., & Oh, S. (2017). Intrusion of software robots into journalism: The public's and journalists' perceptions of news written by algorithms and human journalists. *Computers in Human Behavior*, 71, 291–298. https://doi.org/10.1016/j.chb.2017.02.022.

Kennedy, R. P., Waggoner, P. D., & Ward, M. (2022). Trust in public policy algorithms. Journal of Politics, Ahead of print. https://doi.org/10.1086/716283.

Koper, C. S., & Lum, C. (2020). Editorial introduction to the special issue on policing. *Criminology & Public Policy*, 19(3), 691–692. https://doi.org/10.1111/1745-9133.12515.

Land, M. K., & Aronson, J. D. (2020). Human rights and technology: New challenges for justice and accountability. *Annual Review of Law and Social Science*, 16(1), null. https://doi.org/10.1146/annurev-lawsocsci-060220-081955.

Lauritsen, J. L., & Heimer, K. (2010). Violent victimization among males and economic conditions. *Criminology & Public Policy*, 9(4), 665–692. https://doi.org/10.1111/j.1745-9133.2010.00660.x.

Lee, M. K. (2018). Understanding perception of algorithmic decisions: Fairness, trust, and emotion in response to algorithmic management. *Big Data & Society*, 5(1), 2053951718756684. https://doi.org/10.1177/2053951718756684.

Leese, M. (2018). Predictive Policing in der Schweiz: Chancen, Herausforderungen, Risiken. In *Bulletin 2018 zur schweizerischen Sicherheitspolitik* (pp. 57–72). Center for Security Studies (CSS), ETH Zürich. https://doi.org/10.3929/ethz-b-000317784.

Logg, J. M. (2017). Theory of machine: When do people rely on algorithms? *Harvard Business School Working Paper Series # 17-086*. https://dash.harvard.edu/handle/1/31677474

Logg, J. M., Minson, J. A., & Moore, D. A. (2019). Algorithm appreciation: People prefer algorithmic to human judgment. *Organizational Behavior and Human Decision Processes*, *151*, 90–103. https://doi.org/10.1016/j.obhdp.2018.12.005.

Lösel, F. (2018). Evidence comes by replication, but needs differentiation: The reproducibility issue in science and its relevance for criminology. *Journal of Experimental Criminology*, *14*(3), 257–278. https://doi.org/10.1007/s11292-017-9297-z.

Loukina, A., Madnani, N., & Zechner, K. (2019). The many dimensions of algorithmic fairness in educational applications. In *Proceedings of the fourteenth workshop on innovative use of NLP for building educational applications*, 1–10. https://doi.org/10.18653/v1/W19-4401.

Lum, K., & Isaac, W. (2016). To predict and serve? *Significance*, *13*(5), 14–19. https://doi.org/10.1111/j.1740-9713.2016.00960.x.

Lynch, M. J., Barrett, K. L., Stretesky, P. B., & Long, M. A. (2017). The neglect of quantitative research in Green criminology and its consequences. *Critical Criminology*, *25*(2), 183–198. https://doi.org/10.1007/s10612-017-9359-6.

Marda, V., & Narayan, S. (2020). Data in New Delhi's predictive policing system. In *Proceedings of the 2020 conference on fairness, accountability, and transparency*, 317–324. https://doi.org/10.1145/3351095.3372865.

Mastrobuoni, G. (2020). Crime is terribly revealing: Information technology and police productivity. *The Review of Economic Studies*. https://doi.org/10.1093/restud/rdaa009.

Mazerolle, L., Antrobus, E., Bennett, S., & Tyler, T. R. (2013). Shaping citizen perceptions of police legitimacy: A randomized field trial of procedural justice. *Criminology*, *51*(1), 33–63. https://doi.org/10.1111/j.1745-9125.2012.00289.x.

Meijer, A., & Wessels, M. (2019). Predictive policing: Review of benefits and drawbacks. *International Journal of Public Administration*, *42*(12), 1031–1039. https://doi.org/10.1080/01900692.2019.1575664.

Miles-Johnson, T. (2015). "They Don't identify with us": Perceptions of police by Australian transgender people. *International Journal of Transgenderism*, *16*(3), 169–189. https://doi.org/10.1080/15532739.2015.1080647.

Miller, L. (2020). LAPD will end controversial program that aimed to predict where crimes would occur. *Los Angeles Times*. https://www.latimes.com/california/story/2020-04-21/lapd-ends-predictive-policing-program

Morgan, R., & Thompson, A. (2021). *Criminal Victimization, 2020* (NCJ Number: 301775; Criminal Victimization). https://bjs.ojp.gov/library/publications/criminal-victimization-2020

Muftić, L. R., Finn, M. A., & Marsh, E. A. (2015). The victim-offender overlap, intimate partner violence, and sex: Assessing differences among victims, offenders, and victim-offenders. *Crime & Delinquency*, *61*(7), 899–926. https://doi.org/10.1177/0011128712453677.

Murray, A., & Giammarise, K. (2020). Pittsburgh suspends policing program that used algorithms to predict crime 'hot spots.' *Pittsburgh Post-Gazette*. https://www.post-gazette.com/news/crime-courts/2020/06/23/Pittsburgh-suspends-policing-police-program-algorithms-predict-predictive-hot-spots-crime-data/stories/202006230059

Newman, M. E. J. (2001). The structure of scientific collaboration networks. *Proceedings of the National Academy of Sciences*, 98(2), 404–409. https://doi.org/10.1073/pnas.98.2.404.

Newman, M. E. J. (2004). Coauthorship networks and patterns of scientific collaboration. *Proceedings of the National Academy of Sciences*, 101(Suppl. 1), 5200–5205. https://doi.org/10.1073/pnas.0307545100.

Nilsson, P. (2018, November 26). First UK police force to try predictive policing ends contract. *Financial Times*. https://www.ft.com/content/b34b0b08-ef19-11e8-89c8-d36339d835c0

Noble, S. U. (2018). *Algorithms of oppression: How search engines reinforce racism*. NYU Press.

Obermeyer, Z., Powers, B., Vogeli, C., & Mullainathan, S. (2019). Dissecting racial bias in an algorithm used to manage the health of populations. *Science*, 366(6464), 447–453. https://doi.org/10.1126/science.aax2342.

Ongweso, R. Jr. (2020). Police and big tech are partners in crime. We need to abolish them both. *Vice*. https://www.vice.com/en_us/article/8898g3/police-and-big-tech-are-partners-in-crime-we-need-to-abolish-them-both

Oosterloo, S., & van Schie, G. (2018). The politics and biases of the "crime anticipation system" of the Dutch police. In *Proceedings of the international workshop on bias in information, algorithms, and systems – CEUR*, 2103, 30–41. https://dspace.library.uu.nl/handle/1874/377356

Overby, L. M., Brown, R. D., & Bruce, J. M. Jr. (2004). Justice in Black and White: Race, perceptions of fairness, and diffuse support for the judicial system in a southern state. *Justice System Journal*, 25(2), 159–182. https://doi.org/10.1080/0098261X.2004.10767716.

Palmater, P. (2016). Shining light on the dark places: Addressing police racism and sexualized violence against indigenous women and girls in the national inquiry. *Canadian Journal of Women and the Law*, 28(2), 253–284. https://doi.org/10.3138/cjwl.28.2.253.

Peeples, L. (2019). What the data say about police shootings. *Nature*, 573(7772), 24–26. https://doi.org/10.1038/d41586-019-02601-9.

Peterson, R. D., & Krivo, L. J. (1999). Racial segregation, the concentration of disadvantage, and Black and White homicide victimization. *Sociological Forum*, 14(3), 465–493. https://doi.org/10.1023/A:1021451703612.

Pierson, E., Simoiu, C., Overgoor, J., Corbett-Davies, S., Jenson, D., Shoemaker, A., Ramachandran, V., Barghouty, P., Phillips, C., Shroff, R., & Goel, S. (2020). A large-scale analysis of racial disparities in police stops across the United States. *Nature Human Behaviour*, 4(7), 736–745. https://doi.org/10.1038/s41562-020-0858-1.

Pridemore, W. A., Makel, M. C., & Plucker, J. A. (2018). Replication in criminology and the social sciences. *Annual Review of Criminology*, 1(1), 19–38. https://doi.org/10.1146/annurev-criminol-032317-091849.

Prins, S. J., & Reich, A. (2018). Can we avoid reductionism in risk reduction? *Theoretical Criminology*, 22(2), 258–278. https://doi.org/10.1177/1362480617707948.

Quinn, M. J. (2006). On teaching computer ethics within a computer science department. *Science and Engineering Ethics*, 12(2), 335–343. https://doi.org/10.1007/s11948-006-0032-9.

Quinney, R. (1973). Crime control in capitalist society: A critical philosophy of legal order. *Issues in Criminology*, 8(1), 75–99.

Quinney, R. (1977). *Class, state, and crime: On the theory and practice of criminal justice.* https://doi.org/10.2307/2066331.

Rafter, N. H. (1990). The social construction of crime and crime control. *Journal of Research in Crime and Delinquency,* 27(4), 376–389. https://doi.org/10.1177/00 22427890027004004.

Raghavan, M., Barocas, S., Kleinberg, J., & Levy, K. (2020). Mitigating bias in algorithmic hiring: Evaluating claims and practices. In *Proceedings of the 2020 conference on fairness, accountability, and transparency,* 469–481. https://doi.org/10.1145/3351095.3372828.

Reichman, A. (2007). The dimensions of law: Judicial craft, its public perception, and the role of the scholar. *California Law Review, 95,* 1619–1675.

Richardson, R., Schultz, J., & Crawford, K. (2019). *Dirty data, bad predictions: How civil rights violations impact police data, predictive policing systems, and justice* (SSRN Scholarly Paper ID 3333423). Social Science Research Network. https://papers.ssrn.com/abstract=3333423

Rosenfeld, R. (2009). *The social construction of crime* (pp. 9780195396607–0050) [Data set]. Oxford University Press. https://doi.org/10.1093/obo/9780195396607-0050.

Sassaman, H. (2020). COVID-19 proves it's time to abolish 'predictive' policing algorithms. *Wired.* https://www.wired.com/story/covid-19-proves-its-time-to-abolish-predictive-policing-algorithms/

Saunders, J., Hunt, P., & Hollywood, J. S. (2016). Predictions put into practice: A quasi-experimental evaluation of Chicago's predictive policing pilot. *Journal of Experimental Criminology, 12*(3), 347–371. https://doi.org/10.1007/s11292-016-9272-0.

Selbst, A. D. (2017). *Disparate impact in big data policing* (SSRN Scholarly Paper ID 2819182). Social Science Research Network. https://doi.org/10.2139/ssrn.2819182.

Selbst, A. D., Boyd, D., Friedler, S. A., Venkatasubramanian, S., & Vertesi, J. (2019). Fairness and abstraction in sociotechnical systems. In *Proceedings of the conference on fairness, accountability, and transparency,* 59–68. https://doi.org/10.1145/3287560.3287598.

Shapiro, A. (2017). Reform predictive policing. *Nature News, 541*(7638), 458. https://doi.org/10.1038/541458a.

Shapiro, B. R., Meng, A., O'Donnell, C., Lou, C., Zhao, E., Dankwa, B., & Hostetler, A. (2020). Re-shape: a method to teach data ethics for data science education. In *Proceedings of the 2020 CHI conference on human factors in computing systems,* 1–13. https://doi.org/10.1145/3313831.3376251.

Sherman, L. W., Gartin, P. R., & Buerger, M. E. (1989). Hot spots of predatory crime: Routine activities and the criminology of place. *Criminology, 27*(1), 27–56. https://doi.org/10.1111/j.1745-9125.1989.tb00862.x.

Signorelli, A. D. (2016). Quando l'algoritmo diventa sbirro: Pro e contro della polizia predittiva. *Vice.* https://www.vice.com/it/article/qk3ynb/pro-e-contro-della-polizia-predittiva

Singh, J. P., Desmarais, S. L., Hurducas, C., Arbach-Lucioni, K., Condemarin, C., Dean, K., Doyle, M., Folino, J. O., Godoy-Cervera, V., Grann, M., Ho, R. M. Y., Large, M. M., Nielsen, L. H., Pham, T. H., Rebocho, M. F., Reeves, K. A., Rettenberger, M., Ruiter, C., de, Seewald, K., & Otto, R. K. (2014). International perspectives on the practical application of violence risk assessment: A global survey of 44 countries. *International Journal of Forensic Mental Health*, *13*(3), 193–206. https://doi.org/10.1080/14999013.2014.922141.

Slobogin, C. (2018). *A defense of modern risk-based sentencing* (SSRN Scholarly Paper ID 3242257). Social Science Research Network. https://doi.org/10.2139/ssrn.3242257.

Sollund, R. (2006). Racialisation in police stop and search practice – The Norwegian case. *Critical Criminology*, *14*(3), 265–292. https://doi.org/10.1007/s10612-006-9012-2.

Sommerer, L. M. (2017). Geospatial predictive policing – Research outlook & a call for legal debate. *Neue Kriminalpolitik*, *29*(2), 147–164. https://doi.org/10.5771/0934-9200-2017-2-147.

Stop LAPD Spying Coalition. (2018). *Dismantling predictive policing in Los Angeles*. https://stoplapdspying.org/wp-content/uploads/2018/05/Before-the-Bullet-Hits-the-Body-Report-Summary.pdf

Sunstein, C. R. (2018). *Algorithms, correcting biases* (SSRN Scholarly Paper ID 3300171). Social Science Research Network. https://papers.ssrn.com/abstract=3300171

Tankebe, J. (2013). Viewing things differently: The dimensions of public perceptions of police legitimacy. *Criminology*, *51*(1), 103–135. https://doi.org/10.1111/j.1745-9125.2012.00291.x.

Taylor, R. B., & Ratcliffe, J. H. (2020). Was the pope to blame? Statistical powerlessness and the predictive policing of micro-scale randomized control trials. *Criminology & Public Policy*, *19*(3), 965–996. https://doi.org/10.1111/1745-9133.12514.

Thomas, E. (2016). Why Oakland Police turned down predictive policing. *Vice*. https://www.vice.com/en/article/ezp8zp/minority-retort-why-oakland-police-turned-down-predictive-policing

Toro, J. D., Lloyd, T., Buchanan, K. S., Robins, S. J., Bencharit, L. Z., Smiedt, M. G., Reddy, K. S., Pouget, E. R., Kerrison, E. M., & Goff, P. A. (2019). The criminogenic and psychological effects of police stops on adolescent Black and Latino boys. *Proceedings of the National Academy of Sciences*, *116*(17), 8261–8268. https://doi.org/10.1073/pnas.1808976116.

Turanovic, J. J., & Pratt, T. C. (2013). The consequences of maladaptive coping: Integrating general strain and self-control theories to specify a causal pathway between victimization and offending. *Journal of Quantitative Criminology*, *29*(3), 321–345. https://doi.org/10.1007/s10940-012-9180-z.

Turanovic, J. J., Reisig, M. D., & Pratt, T. C. (2015). Risky lifestyles, low self-control, and violent victimization across gendered pathways to crime. *Journal of Quantitative Criminology*, *31*(2), 183–206. https://doi.org/10.1007/s10940-014-9230-9.

Ugwudike, P. (2020). Digital prediction technologies in the justice system: The implications of a 'race-neutral' agenda. *Theoretical Criminology*, *24*(3), 482–501. https://doi.org/10.1177/1362480619896006.

UNICRI, & INTERPOL. (2019). *Artificial Intelligence and Robotics for Law Enforcement*. http://www.unicri.it/sites/default/files/2019-11/Artificial%20Intelligence%20and%20Robotics%20for%20Law%20Enforcement.pdf

Urman, J. E., & Blumenthal, R. (2018). An undergraduate ethics course for promoting common good computing: A progress report. *Journal of Computing Sciences in Colleges*, *34*(2), 39–45.

Valentine, C. L., Hay, C., Beaver, K. M., & Blomberg, T. G. (2013). Through a computational lens: Using dual computer-criminology degree programs to advance the study of criminology and criminal justice practice. *Security Informatics*, 2(1), 2. https://doi.org/10.1186/2190-8532-2-2.

Veale, M., & Borgesius, F. Z. (2021). Demystifying the draft EU artificial intelligence Act – Analysing the good, the bad, and the unclear elements of the proposed approach. *Computer Law Review International*, 22(4), 97–112. https://doi.org/10.9785/cri-2021-220402.

Venkataramakrishnan, S. (2020). Top researchers condemn 'racially biased' face-based crime prediction. *Financial Times*. https://www.ft.com/content/aaa9e654-c962-46c7-8dd0-c2b4af932220

Vold, G. B. (1958). *Theoretical criminology* (pp. xi, 334). Oxford University Press.

Weisburd, D. (2015). The law of crime concentration and the criminology of Place. *Criminology*, 53(2), 133–157. https://doi.org/10.1111/1745-9125.12070.

Weitzer, R., & Tuch, S. A. (2004). Race and perceptions of police misconduct. *Social Problems*, 51(3), 305–325. https://doi.org/10.1525/sp.2004.51.3.305.

Werth, R. (2019). Risk and punishment: The recent history and uncertain future of actuarial, algorithmic, and "evidence-based" penal techniques. *Sociology Compass*, 13(2), e12659. https://doi.org/10.1111/soc4.12659.

Woodward, V. H., Webb, M. E., III, O. H. G., & Copes, H. (2016). The current state of criminological research in the United States: An examination of research methodologies in criminology and criminal justice journals. *Journal of Criminal Justice Education*, 27(3), 340–361. https://doi.org/10.1080/10511253.2015.1131312.

Woolley, S. C., & Howard, P. N. (2018). *Computational propaganda: political parties, politicians, and political manipulation on social media*. Oxford University Press.

Wu, X., & Zhang, X. (2016). Automated inference on criminality using face images. *ArXiv*.

Wu, X., & Zhang, X. (2017). Responses to critiques on machine learning of criminality perceptions (Addendum of arXiv:1611.04135). *ArXiv:1611.04135 [Cs]*. http://arxiv.org/abs/1611.04135

Yang, Y. (2019, December). *The role of AI in China's crackdown on Uighurs*. *Financial Times*. https://www.ft.com/content/e47b33ce-1add-11ea-97df-cc63de1d73f4

Yang, Y., & Murgia, M. (2020). China sets up national laboratory for advanced policing. *Financial Times*. https://www.ft.com/content/5cc651a4-48fd-11ea-aee2-9ddbdc86190d

5

CAUSAL INFERENCE IN CRIMINOLOGY AND CRIME RESEARCH AND THE PROMISES OF MACHINE LEARNING

Introduction

Criminology and crime research have a significant opportunity ahead. The increasing convergence between methods for causal inference and techniques borrowed, developed, or adapted from the machine learning eco-system holds important promises for this area of inquiry. On the one hand, machine learning and related machine intelligence approaches are transcending their traditional status of devices solely designed for prediction and forecasting purposes. On the other hand, the econometrics literature, which blends the statistics and economics traditions, is now aided by the flexibility and pattern detection power of statistical learning and deep learning algorithms that can be integrated into more traditional statistical architectures.

This evolving methodological landscape represents an unprecedented occasion to solve many of the challenges and address many of the unanswered questions that characterize the study of crime and criminal behavior. This chapter specifically addresses this topic by offering a compact tripartite overview on causal research in criminology.

First, I will present the main extant methods for causal discovery both in experimental and observational settings, with a specific focus on Matching, Regression Discontinuity Design, Difference-in-Differences, and Instrumental Variables, supporting Sampson's view against the acritical "superiority" of Randomized Controlled Trials (RCTs) as the gold standard for disentangling causal processes in criminology (and the social sciences in general).

Second, the chapter will concentrate on Leo Breiman's seminal paper about the "Two Cultures" existing in statistical modeling. After having examined Breiman's position, I will discuss how, in the last two decades, many things have changed, leading to increasingly less radical differences between statistical approaches emerging in statistics and econometrics and those developed instead in the algorithmic communities, i.e., machine learning and computer science. In particular, I will highlight the role of Judea Pearl as one of the most important scholars in fostering the attention

DOI: 10.4324/9781003217732-5

of the AI field on causality through his works on graphical models and, most importantly, the Structural Causal Model (SCM).

Finally, I will provide a summary of selected works appeared in the last decade exploiting machine and deep learning for causal discovery. This summary will directly concentrate on four macro-topics: the detection of heterogeneous treatment effects, methods for temporal data, the promises and pitfalls of agent-based models (ABM), and techniques to address issues in causal inference and social networks.

Criminology's Quest for Causality

A Complicated Relationship

Criminology and causality have been so far in what I would venture to call a "complicated relationship." The two have now been seducing each other for decades: criminologists flirting with the analytical devices to unfold causal mechanisms in explaining crime, and those who are more familiar with those methods (partly because they contribute to create them), with the many open questions of criminological research. This bidirectional attraction is a key ingredient to understand how the quest for causality in criminology has evolved over the past years: as crime represents a profoundly impactful phenomenon in most societies around the world, addressing it has become important also for scholars coming from other disciplines, such as economics, public health, and statistics.

Causal inference is concerned with estimating the effect that a particular variable – mapping a given phenomenon, characteristic, or intervention – has on a given outcome of interest. Finding and measuring causal effects stands at the core of all those disciplines in which scholars are interested in understanding how changing conditions can modify a scenario under scrutiny or, in general, what processes – either macro or micro – lead to the occurrence of a phenomenon. Virologists and epidemiologists aim at understanding the outcomes of a given vaccine to contain a virus in a population; social scientists seek to capture the consequences of a certain social policy on school dropout; environmental scientists test the consequences of solar-powered devices for water cleaning: causal questions and causality in general are all around science. So much that we often confound them with mere correlation.

In spite of this now relatively longstanding relationship, however, Ridgeway (2019) argues that the causes of crime remain mostly unknown to us, either because questions are too hard to answer or because the tools to solve them have not been sufficiently addressed. In turn, this poses a problem that goes beyond the boundaries of pure research, affecting the ability of empirics to meaningfully influence the policy debate.

The goal of translating evidence into practice has in fact been central for criminologists and crime researchers in the last decades. Ridgeway draws some daring parallelisms with other disciplines in which scientific knowledge on a particular subject, such as agricultural science and medicine, has led to massive improvements in the real world. While recognizing that many questions remain without an answer, I be cautious in comparing criminology and crime research with other disciplines, especially those that are not part of the "social science" landscape.

Crime is complex, and although this may now sound like a slogan or a cliché with just the right among of "buzzwordiness" in it, its complexity is a fact – and this complexity underlines a myriad of concatenated processes, factors, and phenomena that are jointly at play in this scenario. Crime is the product of interrelated social, economic, and political processes that emerge at the micro, meso, and macro levels, with different levels all having an influence and a good amount of randomness being thrown into this undiscovered imaginary equation. It is a matter of individual, atomistic characteristics and fundamental relational processes that exist because we are all to some extent part of a community, which in turn is an evolving, multi-layered entity, impacting us as it changes and being impacted by us when we act. Furthermore, the often-disregarded biological paradigm in criminology, which has lately surfaced after resistance from the discipline, adds another dimension to the quest for causality: a dimension that it is only secondarily related to society, which investigates such causes by looking at our biological, physiological, and neurological characteristics – becoming the other half of the apparently irreducible "nature versus nurture" debate encompassing many fields.

Although we still miss a great deal of "causal certainty" about crime, as Blomberg (2019) calls it, it is undeniable that progress has been made over the years. There are several contributions to these progresses – although, ironically, I cannot causally demonstrate my claim. First, the exogenous demand for more empirical-driven policy recommendations from institutions in the United States and abroad, which prompted more efforts by criminologists and crime researchers to investigate causal questions. Second, the increase in the number of methodological solutions designed to study causal mechanisms. Third, as already briefly anticipated, the parallel interest of scholars from other disciplines (primarily economics) in such topics.

I see and tend to distinct the progress made in two ways. The first way is the traditional way of thinking about progress: the quest for causality in research on crime has produced clear answers, linking interventions or specific phenomena to clear outcomes. The second way is less conventional and concerns those advancements made precisely thanks to the inconclusive or "null" results produced over years of scientific enterprise. On the one hand, we have clearer answers now on what works, what plays a role, what leads to an outcome of interest; on the other hand, we have clear answers about unclear answers. Albeit we are all more prone to be amazed by glaring, shiny, consistent results (and so is the entire publishing industry), I cannot disjoin the latter aspect from the former, as the two put in perspective together can fully testify to the overall progress made and the complexity of the phenomenon in object.

There is still a long way ahead – with many issues to be addressed to fix this complicated relationship. Yet, we should not be tempted to characterize this trajectory only in terms of separated, simplified categories: this works, this does not work; this plays a role, this does not play a role. For those interested in causal mechanisms in the context of research on crime the good news is that we now have more tools, awareness, and dialogue than before and that these ingredients together will contribute to our quest.

The Gold Rush

I could not start this brief review and discussion of the statistical tools available to criminologists and crime researchers for investigating causality with anything different than RCTs. An RCT is an experimental design in which two groups, an experimental group and a control group, are randomly selected from a given population to evaluate the effectiveness of a certain intervention by measuring its causal effect on an outcome of interest. Their most praised feature is the randomization through which participants are assigned to one of the two groups: randomization, if correctly employed, eliminates any population bias that could distort the final outcomes.

The reason why I started with RCTs lies in their massive popularity: RCTs have been widely used in criminology and crime research, but they are very common in a myriad of other fields, such as medicine, economics, physics, biology, and political science.

In the United States, they have exploded in popularity in relation to the analysis and prevention of crime mostly during the 1980s and have been applied to address problems in policing (MacDonald et al., 2016), prison re-entry (Cook et al., 2015), developmental criminology (Farrington, 2006), drug abuse treatment (Gottfredson & Exum, 2002), education and pro-social behavior (Cross et al., 2009), and families' role in preventing delinquency (Piquero et al., 2009), to name a (very) few.

Compared to other disciplines, however, criminology faces various issues that limit the ease of deployment of RCTs. These encompass their often very high costs, ethical problems, and one-third class that is often overlooked: the resistance of institutions to embrace evidence-based policy decisions. While this aspect may be seen as less salient in some places such as the United States or the United Kingdom, it is an important barrier in many other countries (Italy is an unfortunate example), in which policy development is often completely detached from scientific enterprises, especially in the social sciences. Yet, in spite of these limits, RCTs have acquired the highly discussed role of "Gold Standard" of causal discovery and policy evaluation in criminology and crime research as well. RCTs have this role because they are considered to deliver the highest and "purest" level of evidence precisely for their mechanism of randomization, which reduces inherent biases that are common to other study designs, allowing more robust conclusions about what works and what not, or what causes something and what does not.

In spite of this diffused belief, however, I concur with those who have raised concerns about RCTs as the silver-lining of causal discovery, exposing the various problems they pose, both technically, conceptually, and ethically. The line-up of scholars heralding this critical approach is now well populated, counting representatives from a variety of disciplines. In economics, for instance, the term "Randomistas" has been coined to describe all those researchers who have unconditional preferences for RCTs over other methodological alternatives. Recent scholarship attempted to unfold the many inherent issues deriving from this aprioristic attitude both in research and practice, with a notable example of considerable criticism against application in development economics (Deaton & Cartwright, 2018; Ravallion, 2020). Calls against the idealistic supremacy of RCT have also been made by Pearl, one of the most influential thinkers and scientists in the causal inference community in computer science (2018b).

In criminology, one of the most inspiring reflections on the limits of RCTs has been provided by Sampson (2010). In a seminal paper written in occasion of the 25th anniversary of the *Journal of Quantitative Criminology*, Sampson thoroughly reviewed (and confuted) a series of myths surrounding the theory and practice of RCTs. While advocating for more field experiments, and acknowledging the progresses made in our understanding of crime thanks to RCTs, Samspon calls for less ideologized, acritical positions toward this tool positioning himself against the idea that a supposed hierarchy of techniques should tout-court guide research. In the paper, he specifically considers the following three myths:

1 Randomization alone solves the causal inference problem.
2 Experiments are assumption, and therefore theory, free.
3 Experiments are more policy relevant than observational counterparts.

Concerning the first, Sampson claims that randomization should not be seen as the panacea of scientific progress. He notes how while on one side randomization of treatment holds this silver-lining status, criminologists overlook the importance of having random samples, glossing over selection mechanisms. He further points out how heterogeneous treatment effects have been only marginally evaluated as potential issues in experimental results. Furthermore, an additional problem about the idea that randomization alone leads to reliable causal inference regards the prevalence of compliance with experimental treatments. Among other things, noncompliance often violates exogeneity in the "treatment on treated" scenario, as a treatment is often correlated with other changes, reducing exogeneity solely to the "intent to treat" case.

These two aspects are inherently linked to the second myth, which focuses on the idea that experiments do not require assumptions and theory. Sampson, instead, points out that this is not true: experiments, compared to observational studies, simply require different assumptions. He argues that criminologists tend to make implicit assumptions rather than to explicit them, and to further unravel this problematic tendency he addresses the "stable unit treatment value assumption" (SUTVA) problem. SUTVA is concerned with the statistical concept of interference, which in social settings is often represented by social interactions among participants in a given RCT. Social interactions among participants in an experiment go against the core of SUTVA, which proffers that potential outcomes for any unit participating in an experiment are independent of any other unit in the same experiment. In most experimental research setting in criminology, it is unreasonable to argue that individuals are not influenced by each other and that contagion, information diffusion, or other mechanisms such as jealousy do not have any role in shaping the outcomes of a given treatment. Even more, SUTVA is problematic not only when units in an experiment are single individuals, but also when these are neighborhoods or blocks in a given city. Nonetheless, Sampson argues, criminologists have not sufficiently tackled this issue, and notes how SUTVA violations cannot be statistically fixed but, instead, simply require more assumptions, and therefore theory.

The third myth that Sampson concentrates on is the idea that RCTs are more policy relevant compared to observational studies. Assuming the reliability of internal validity in experimental settings (which is, however, indirectly contended if we consider the previous two myths), the author directly targets the problem of external validity, which he outlines as a fundamental feature of policy effectiveness. Particularly, he reasons about the gap between internal validity and policy transfer: not only differences may arise in different settings, for instance when trying to apply the outcomes of an experiment in a certain urban context to another, but significant differences can occur even when a certain experiment is taken at scale in the same macro-level context where it was originally deployed. One example is the case where a given RCT in a neighborhood is used to set up a policy affecting the entire city in which that neighborhood is located. Citing Heckman (1992), Sampson arrives at the conclusion that experimental evidence is not well suited to predict outcomes in environments that are different from the one in which the experiment was conducted in the first place.

Sampson deliberately refuses the idea of a "gold standard" and, in general, that there exists a method which is inherently, universally superior in the resolution of a given problem (something that reminds me of the "no free lunch theorem" in computer science and machine learning, see Wolpert and Macready (1997)). Instead, methods should depend on specific theoretical questions, assumptions, and – I would add – available information. In the concluding remarks of his article, Sampson further recommends experimentalists to more clearly and transparently address the assumptions and limitations present in every specific experimental setting and ask the entire scholarly community, to work harder to integrate observational and experimental methods for basic science and policy development.

I can only subscribe to this appeal: more than 10 years have passed, and the need for both recommendations to be followed is still of paramount importance; more so today, where the toolbox of crime scholars focusing on causal evidence has been plumped up with tools from the machine learning literature. Before reviewing the devices in this toolbox, however, a tour of the alternative routes that are made available by the "traditional" statistical and econometric literature is provided, in the spirit of Sampson's appeal to a tighter integration between experimental and observational methods.

Alternative Routes

The experimental approach, as anticipated and highlighted by Sampson, is not the only strategy allowing us to tackle causal questions. In fact, criminologists (and social scientists) can draw from an increasing number of alternative methods that rely on the use of observational data. These alternatives, implying different costs, assumptions, challenges, are denominated "quasi-experimental methods", from a macro and nontechnical perspective.

Quasi-experimental methods are cheaper and typically involve more assumptions compared to RCTs, and yet when correctly designed and applied they are powerful to push us to causal answers. The main difference compared to RCTs is that in quasi-experimental methods the treated and control groups in a given population of interest are not selected randomly, therefore posing the issue of selection bias as assignment to a certain condition is either decided voluntarily by a participant or the consequence of a third-party selection, such an officer, a judge, or a policy-maker. This bias involves the risk that those who are assigned to a given group are structurally different than those who are assigned to the other one, thus leading to statistical differences that are not explained by a given intervention or phenomenon under scrutiny.

Research in quasi-experimental methods is continuously evolving, and systematically reviewing all the available alternatives and their nuances is not the goal of this work. Yet, I here introduce four approaches that have gained relevant popularity in the social and statistical sciences, referencing to the specific technical literature on each of them. They all concern the fundamental problem of causality: the fact that to estimate cause and effects we need counterfactual information which is impossible to "obtain" in observational data, as data can only directly inform us on a realized state of the world, and not on an alternative scenario that never occurred (Holland, 1986). These four are approaches are Matching, Regression Discontinuity Design, Difference-in-Differences, and Instrumental Variables.

Matching

The goal of matching is straightforward in studies that intend to obtain causal inference on observational data: in absence of randomization, matching seeks to reduce imbalance of the empirical distribution associated with the pretreatment confounders between the two groups under scrutiny, the treated and the control ones. By reducing such imbalance, we reduce bias in the estimated results. In other words, matching approaches seek to approximate a dataset that would have resulted from a traditional RCT. Not only matching is used to reduce bias in the estimation of a treatment effect, but also to select subjects for follow-up studies in temporary absence of an outcome value. Many matching approaches exist which can be roughly divided into two groups: exact and approximate (Cunningham, 2021).

Exact matching simply addresses the problem of balance by matching each treated unit to all the possible control units characterized by the same identical values on all the considered covariates. This leads to the creation of subclasses within which each treated and control unit has the same covariate values. However, exact matching can be problematic as often it is unfeasible to have units with the same covariate values in the two groups. Approximate matching precisely considers this scenario.

Approximate matching concerns the detection of similarity between units as the objective function upon which matching is carried out. To define similarity, statistical concepts of "distance" are usually considered, as in the case of Nearest Neighbor Covariate Matching, where metrics such as Euclidean and Mahalanobis distances are used. Propensity Score Matching, probably the most common and debated matching approach (and criminology is no exception to this trend, see Apel and Sweeten (2010) and Evans (2021)), also falls within the category of "approximate matching." Propensity Score Matching directly addresses the selection on observables problem by using the relevant covariates to estimate a maximum likelihood model for the conditional probability of treatment, using the predicted value as a propensity score, representing the basis of the comparison between treatment and control groups in the data. Recently, it has been shown by King and Nielsen (2019) that Propensity Score Matching actually leads to imbalance, inefficiency, model dependence, and bias, proposing alternative matching methods with higher standards. In spite of this appeal, this approach remains vastly used also in criminology (Leuschner, 2021; Jorgensen & Wells, 2021; Circo & McGarrell, 2021; Lilley et al., 2020; Silver et al., 2021; Wang et al., 2019).

Regression Discontinuity Design

A second approach to estimate treatment effects in nonexperimental research designs is Regression Discontinuity Design (RDD). In RDD, participants are assigned to either intervention or control groups based on a cutoff score measured on a preintervention variable, known as "forcing" or "running" variable. RDD is then used to measure the difference in the outcomes of units under analyses that are clustered around the given cutoff score. The reader should keep in mind that two main families of RDD studies exist. In one case, called "sharp" design, the probability that a unit is treated is either 0 or 1 at the cutoff. "The alternative - which is generally found more frequently in the literature - fuzzy designs", in which the probability of treatment discontinuously increases at the threshold.

Even though this approach has been developed and presented in the early 1960s, its success has come decades after, with an increasing trend in popularity starting between the end and the beginning of the twenty-first century (Cunningham, 2021). In research on crime, RDD has been utilized for decades (Berk & Rauma, 1983), although, as occurred in other social sciences, popularity has grown significantly in recent years, with applications – amongst others – in sentencing (Loeffler & Grunwald, 2015), organized crime (Khanna et al., 2019), schooling and delinquency (Cook & Kang, 2016), immigration and crime (Pinotti, 2017), and policing (MacDonald et al., 2016).

Nowadays, the popularity in the method is generally linked to the softer assumptions needed for causal inference in RDD compared to other nonexperimental methods. Furthermore, RDD is thought to be more reliable than the extant alternatives because, when employing RDD, randomized variation is a consequence of the inability of units (e.g., agents, students, workers, inmates, neighborhoods) to have control over the forcing variable in the cutoff area (D. S. Lee & Lemieux, 2010). Lee and Lemieux elaborate on this aspect as a fundamental feature of RDD and additionally set forth a series of other points that are worth considering concerning RDD. These are:

1 RDD can be invalid if units under consideration are able to manipulate the forcing variable, outlining the importance of considering the role of payoffs or incentives to receive (or not) a certain treatment.
2 Local randomization, a consequence of the inability of units to control the forcing variable in the cutoff area, allows one to analyze RDD as RCTs because all baseline characteristics should have the same distribution above and below the threshold.
3 Presenting a RDD through dedicated visualizations and plots can be informative and convenient. Yet, scholars should implement strategies to reduce the risks of graphical biases inflating or deflating true effects.
4 Nonparametric estimation should not be regarded as a silver-lining for functional form issues in RDD, rather it should be seen as a complement to parametric estimation. Bias may arise in both cases, and therefore consistency over different specifications has to prevail as a reliability criterion compared to aprioristic preference over one method.
5 In light of many different attempts to test alternative specifications, many different estimations may follow. To rule out possibly overly restrictive specifications, goodness-of-fit and statistical tests can help.

Research on RDD has been particularly active in the social sciences, both from the technical and the merely applied sides. Efforts from scholars in different disciplines led to present additional analytical tools (called "supplementary analyses") to assess the credibility of RDDs (Imbens, 2017) as well as empirical evaluations of bandwidth choices to capture discontinuity around a given cutoff (Gelman & Imbens, 2014).

In spite of the enthusiasm for the approach, and to reconnect with Sampson's call to avoid any hierarchy of methods, it should be noted that RDD face a major limitation in their lack of external validity. Although scholarship on this topic has been produced (Battistin & Rettore, 2008; Bertanha & Imbens, 2020), external validity remains to date an open problem.

Difference-in-Differences

The third approach here reported in quasi-experimental methods is Difference-in-Differences (DID), which Cunningham recently labeled as the "single most popular research design in the quantitative social sciences" (2021). DID designs are often connected to the concept of natural experiments, which are variations that naturally occur concerning a specific treatment variable across units.

Originated in the field of econometrics, and being one of the favored tools used in many economics areas, especially microeconomics, DID designs have catched up also in criminology see for instance Larsen et al. (2015) and Chainey et al. (2021), although most contributions have come from economists dealing with crime-related topics (Anderson, 2014; Cui & Walsh, 2015; Daniele & Geys, 2015; Priks, 2015).

Two main typologies of DID exist. The simplest approach, referred to as "2 × 2 DID," seeks to estimate the effect of an intervention by comparing changes in an outcome of interest between a treated and a nontreated group, both before and after the intervention has been put in place. As an example, we may think of a case in which we aim at capturing the effect of a gun control policy on violent crimes in Pennsylvania, using as control unit another state, such as New York. In the first period of observation, neither of the two states receive the intervention (i.e., the policy), whereas in the second the policy is issued in Pennsylvania, with New York still untreated. To find the effect, we will have to compare how violent crime in these two states changed before and after the policy is issued. A second and more complicated type of design is "Staggered DID." Staggered DID concerns the estimation of a given intervention when such intervention applies to several units across distinct time units. As an example, think about a certain welfare policy implemented over Italian regions over different months or years. The overall goal is to estimate a treatment effect comparing changes in outcomes over time between treated and control groups in relation to the considered intervention or policy.

While certainly powerful, the DID design rests on several important assumptions and conditions that, if violated, critically jeopardize the estimated results. In the simpler 2×2 case, three main assumptions should hold, according to Lechner (2011):

1 The first one is the "SUTVA" assumption, which we have mentioned early in relation to Sampson's critique of blind optimism over RCTs in experimental criminology. SUTVA posits that no interference, spillovers, or variations in treatment are in play when considering a given intervention.
2 The second is exogeneity: our covariates should not be influenced by the treatment in order to be able to condition on them.
3 The third is probably the most characterizing of the method, and is known as the "parallel trends assumption" (PTA). PTA states that in the absence of treatment the difference between the treated and the nontreated groups is constant over-time. In other words, PTA implies that units that have received a treatment would have, on average, experienced the same level of changes of nontreated units, had they not be treated. Generally, this is very hard to fulfill, and fostered a line of research intended to solve the issue posed by this problematic assumption by proposing alternative approaches to PTA (Bilinski & Hatfield, 2020; Freyaldenhoven et al., 2019; Rambachan & Roth, 2019).

It should be noted that recent advances in econometrics have fueled discussion regarding potential biases emerging when staggered DID are characterized by treatment effect heterogeneity, calling for strategies to address this problem (Baker et al., 2021). Particularly, the Two-Way-Fixed-Effect DID estimator, the most popular in staggered designs, has been thoroughly scrutinized, demonstrating that the main coefficient of interest in DID can deliver biased estimates that are not consistent with Average Treatment on Treated (ATT) and Average Treatment Effect (ATE), which are the two common estimands of interest in causal inference. The discovery of such pitfalls led to a revived interest in the theory of the method beyond mere application, opening new questions about the validity of previously published papers and stimulating debates on statistical ways forward. For those who are interested in the explosion of recent developments in DID, see Roth et al. (2022) for a review.

Instrumental Variables

The fourth, and final, tool in the quasi-experimental methods here covered is the Instrumental Variables (IV) framework. While ancestors of the methods can be found in the 1920s through the works of Fisher and Neyman. The origins of IV are generally traced back to the works of Phillip and Sewall Wright, an economist father and a geneticist son, and particularly to a book on animal and vegetable oils (Wright, 1928).[1] The use of the IV framework has diffused across many fields over the decades, including research on crime where it has been applied, among other topics, to the relationships between the labor market and crime (Gould et al., 2002), immigration and crime (M. Bianchi et al., 2012), organized crime and ordinary criminality (Aziani et al., 2020), and police and crime (Lin, 2009).

IV tackles the problem of inconsistent parameter estimation due to endogeneity in regression modeling, a problem that prevents us to claim any causal relationship between a variable of interest and an outcome. Endogeneity means that changes in a regressor are associated with both changes in the outcome and in the error term, thus only leaving the option of investigating correlational evidence, rather than causality. In general, by addressing the endogeneity problem in regression, IV enables controlling over omitted variable bias, error-in-variable-bias, and reverse causality. The aim of IV is then to only generate variations that are exogenous in the regressor of interest: this happens through an instrument (generally labeled as z in statistics and econometrics textbooks and surveys) such that changes in the instrument are associated with changes in our regressor of interest, while at the same time they are not linked directly to any change in the outcome of our regression model. This follows that the instrument is not correlated with the error term. Specifically, when we only use a single instrument, two assumptions are fundamental in the IV framework:

1 The instrument is not correlated with the error term.
2 The instrument is correlated with the regressor of interest.

Borrowing examples from research in economics, assume we want to estimate the economical returns to exogenous changes in schooling. Assuming also that we lack data on individual ability, and therefore regressing earnings on schooling leads to an error term correlated with the regressor, i.e., schooling, we would need a valid instrument that is correlated with schooling but not with ability and the error term. One such instrument is proximity to a college or school, as shown by Card (1993). A measure of proximity to college or school would work as those who live distant from such institutions are less incentivized to enroll in a college program, and also satisfies the first assumption, given that the presence of a nearby college is uncorrelated with ability.

Albeit powerful when properly detected, reliable instruments are often difficult to be found. Angrist and Krueger (2001) argue that to find a valid instrument, one must have a detailed knowledge of the mechanisms and institutions that determine or govern the regressor of interest. Somehow, the difficulty to find valid instruments is related to the common "well-developed story or model" that motivates the choice for a particular instrument.

Angrist and Krueger also review a set of potential pitfalls that can affect IV. First, and trivially, the decision to rely on bad instruments that are correlated with the omitted variables would lead to biased results. Furthermore, issues can be generated by the presence of instruments that are only weakly correlated with the endogenous regressor of interest. The third order of issues involves two-stage least squares regression (2SLS), a popular estimator used in the context of IV. 2SLS is exploited when we have more instruments than endogenous variables, such that endogenous variables are "over-identified" (for a technical explanation of how 2SLS works, see Wooldridge (2012)). In relation to 2SLS, the authors warn that using nonlinear regression techniques such as logistic regression in the first stage when the endogenous regressor is binary may lead to problematic consequences. In light of this, they recommend using linear regression also in presence of dummy endogenous variables.

As already disclaimed, the tools here surveyed are by no means comprehensive of the traditional statistical approaches for causal inference in the social science. To exemplify, two major approaches that readers interested in causal inference in the social sciences (and beyond) should consider are the synthetic control approach (Abadie, 2006) and Bayesian Structural Time Series (Brodersen et al., 2015). This latter technique, for instance, has been recently explored in criminology to assess the impact of COVID-19 mobility restriction policies on crime trends (Campedelli et al., 2020, 2021) and the effect of the Alaska Permanent Fund on crime (Dorsett, 2021). Furthermore, and to conclude, it is also important to note that some of these methods may be actually combined together to reduce the risks of unbiased estimates (Linden & Adams, 2012) and hence it is useful to consider these approaches not only as alternatives but, potentially, also as complementary.

Machine Learning: A Culture of Prediction?

Leo Breiman's "Two Cultures"

What do experimental and quasi-experimental methods have to do with machine learning and AI, in general? This question may roam in your mind as you arrived at this point of the book. The contents of this chapter, so far, might sound a bit disconnected to what we discussed and reflected upon so far. This sensation is - directly or indirectly - the product of decades in which the econometrics and machine learning ecosystems (and the different sub-communities that are part of both) remained distant and failed to coordinate, communicate, cooperate. This intellectual, technical, academic separation is the reason why we generally tend to see machine learning solely as a culture of prediction, completely detached with more traditional statistical approaches that are dominant in the social science literature.

To better contextualize this distance between the methods of causal inference and the dominant machine learning narrative, one document is particularly precious: the article "Statistical Modeling: The Two Cultures" (2001a), written by Leo Breiman, one of the most influential scholars of his time in the fields of statistics and computer science, a scientist that many know for some of his critical contributions to machine learning, the most popular being the inventions of Classification and Regression Trees (CART) (Breiman et al., 1984), Bagging (Breiman, 1996), and Random Forests (Breiman, 2001b).

Breiman's article has been the trigger of a longstanding discussion that still endures to date in the fields of statistics, computer science, and beyond. In his article, Breiman calls out a problematic dichotomy between two separate cultures in statistics: the data modeling and the algorithmic ones. In the first case, scholars are mostly concerned with finding causal relationships between different phenomena, precisely as in the tradition of causal inference. Members of the "data modeling" culture founded their scientific enterprises on the hypothesis that a given mathematical process correctly describes and explains the phenomenon under investigation. In the second case, instead, Breiman identified scholars that primarily aim at correctly predicting a given output given a set of available input data, typically with very few theoretical or methodological constraints and without any assumption of validity for the underlying data generating process.

Although Breiman does not argue that there exists a superior culture between the two, he is particularly critical regarding how the "data modeling" side produced questionable conclusions, based on theory deemed as "irrelevant" and, most importantly, has prevented scholars in statistics to focus on a variety of practical problems.

In a very clear review piece written to illustrate Breiman's seminal paper, Raper (2020) more comprehensively lists his six criticisms of the data modeling culture:

1 Data modeling is overly dependent on the untested or incorrect idea that the suitable model has been chosen.
2 Data modeling focuses too much on model fit, hence overlooking prediction which, according to Breiman, should be preferred as a criterion for model selection.
3 Over-reliance on results from a single data model is risky because there may exist many other equally good models leading to different results.
4 Data modeling puts too much emphasis on simple models even when complexity would work better.
5 Data modeling does not focus on solving problems but, rather, on irrelevant theory.
6 The data modeling approach reduces the possibility for statisticians to work on worthwhile projects, especially interdisciplinary ones.

The paper elaborates on these issues, highlighting how algorithmic approaches would tackle and solve them, in a painting of ideas that looks almost Hegelian in its "thesis-anthithesis-synthesis" structure. While he advocates for an increasing diffusion of the "algorithmic" culture, Breiman also recognizes that the "data modeling" culture has its merits and can effectively benefit statistics overall: thus only a combined approach that puts the solution of problems as the main goal should prevail.

The idea that statistics and statisticians should be more concerned about problem-solving entirely characterizes Breiman's thought, in many direct and indirect ways. Remarkably, he saw the urgency of embracing an algo-rithmically oriented culture in light of the increasing availability of massive amounts of digital data that, already in 2001, were quickly produced and distributed in many scientific and commercial sectors. Many of those data sources, he argued, were associated with important problems in genetics, physics, biology, and they all required solutions rather than theoretical spec-ulations. If problem-solving should be the main goal, data – in Breiman's view – is the natural starting point of any project.

Unsurprisingly, Breiman's words caused a great deal of discussion and debates among statisticians, especially those who were representatives of the data modeling culture, right after the article's publication. Four commentaries of various scholars in the field are available with the paper itself: as Breiman recognizes in a rejoinder which is also added at the end of the article, two of them – written by Hoadley and Parzen – mostly expressed agreement with the "two cultures" argument, while the other two were of the opposite sign.

Although both Hoadley and Parzen provide interesting reflections on the topic,[2] I would rather briefly concentrate on the two critical views: the first coming from David R. Cox, whom quantitative social scientists and crimi-nologists should know for his decisive contributions to survival models, and the second from Brad Efron, who is also a prominent figure in the statistical sciences and the inventor of the bootstrap sampling method. Here I will only summarize their counterarguments against Breiman position, but I would suggest everyone to read all the commentaries carefully and not only the main article, as they represent an engaging intellectual journey condensing decades of statistical thinking and practice in very few pages.

Cox begins his response by delineating Breiman's description of statistical thinking as a "caricature," but he notes that the essay is nonetheless thought-provoking and contains a certain amount of truth that deserves further dis-cussion (Cox, 2001). Although Cox agrees with Breiman's call to a more inclusive attitude toward algorithmic modeling in the statistical community, he entirely disagrees on many of the backbone positions that characterize Breiman's appeal. Data, which for Breiman should be the starting point of any attempt to solve a problem, are viewed as less important than scien-tific hypotheses by Cox, who further argues that such an acritical approach involving data to obtain prediction comes at the expenses of interpreta-tion and understanding. Cox warns that by overlooking explanatory pro-cesses governing information, statisticians face the risk of relying too much on black-box approaches, a theme which is absolutely central today, after 20 years of advances in statistics and machine learning. In defense of the "data modeling" viewpoint, Cox highlights how "prediction" does not have a unitary definition. He acknowledges that there are applications and con-texts in which algorithmic practices are favorable (he makes the example of short-term economic forecasting and real-time flood forecasting), yet he points out that understanding the effect of a particular drug on an epi-demic is also a prediction task, which crucially requires knowledge of the underlying processes – and therefore needs a different approach from the algorithmic one. After a quick but informative review of the accomplishments that were made in the "data modeling" culture at the time of writing, Cox provides an illustration from Beveridge, saying that hypotheses in biology led to significant breakthroughs, although such hypotheses later were proved to be false. This parallelism serves the purpose of reaffirming how the investigation of underlying processes – "especially in the social sciences" – should be cautiously addressed but can lead to substantial gains in terms of knowledge production. He concludes his comment with an aphorism that sounds peremptory within the narrative flow of the article: "better a rough answer to the right question than an exact answer to the wrong question."

Efron starts his critique of Breiman's thought by recognizing its stimulating nature while picturing it as a manifesto in favor of black boxes, putting even more emphasis on this point than Cox (Efron, 2001). Efron continues by describing what he believes is the core distinguishing feature of statistical developments in the twentieth century, namely, the advances toward unbiased estimators. He further points out how these efforts led statistics to become the dominant methodology for interpreting knowledge and reality across a myriad of areas. By doing so, Efron implicitly responds to Breiman's concern that statistics, without algorithmic modeling, is getting detached from important practical problems. He then sets forth two rules that inherently allow algorithmic approaches to be fallaciously seen as superior to traditional devices. Firstly, Efron points out, new methods look better than old ones, and this sort of "bias" is difficult to rule out because honest simulations between approaches are challenging to obtain. Secondly, more complicated methods are harder to criticize, diagnose, and understand because of their "black box" nature.

Without taking sides, it is hardly impossible to refuse that Efron's rules still apply today in many fields utilizing statistical and computational models, including research on crime. Even though interpretability has started to become central in the machine learning community, the negative consequences of hype and complexity over clarity still pervade many areas and applications. Efron then joins Cox in clarifying how causal inference is a form of prediction and how causal inference still is the central goal of many statistical applications while prediction, as intended by Breiman, is often not sufficient. He finally concludes his comment by returning to the starting point, the black box threat, by provocatively express the hope Breiman's article is an advocacy device, rather than a confession of a "born-again black boxist," arguing that the goal of science is to understand and illuminate what lies into black boxes for the greater purpose of social good.

The Two Cultures – 20 Years Later

What is left of Breiman's arguments after two decades? The stimulating angles of his work are not certainly confined to the dusty corners of history. In fact, they are relevant still nowadays – and still force us to critically reflect both on the progresses made and the road ahead.[3] Of course, one important thing once one is on the road is to set a direction, even a partial one. From my perspective, the direction of this debate – which Breiman brought to public attention but was already in the hearts and minds of many statisticians well before 2001 – should be the integration of the two cultures, rather than increasing polarization of the two sides.

Fortunately, we are today witnessing this process of blending via a progressive reduction of the distance between the two cultures. Despite the fact that in the scientific community divisions are often exacerbated between different traditions, perspectives, and approaches (one example is the "qualitative-vs-quantitative" feud in the social sciences, criminology included), the renovated, kind, evolving relationship between the "data modeling" and "algorithmic" souls of statistics is encouraging and stands as a good example of scientific dialogue. This does not mean that all problems affecting the two cultures separately have been solved – or even correctly addressed – but is surely a positive sign for statistics and all those fields that are intrinsically connected with statistics in the first place.

On the one side, statisticians from the "data modeling" culture, including especially econometricians, have started to adopt techniques from the machine learning landscape for improving research on unbiased estimations in the quest for causal inference. In some cases, not only they have applied such techniques "off-the-shelf," they have also worked toward the development of ad-hoc algorithmic devices for capturing causality between different phenomena (Athey & Imbens, 2019). Some examples of these efforts will be outlined in the next section, but overall the growing sentiment is that machine learning can be a valuable ally in addressing those problems that until some years ago were exclusively addressed through traditional experimental and quasi-experimental methods.

On the other side, machine learning has finally started to concretely face the limits of systemic indifference toward causal problems. The motivation for which causality has progressively became more important in machine learning is substantially different from the one that pushes "data modelers" to chase it in their research problems. "Data modelers," like econometricians, are interested in causality substantially because causality can allow us to better understand how the world functions, how it may change based on certain interventions, and how we can inform real-world decisions to improve health, the economy, people's safety, political decisions, and so on.

Researchers in machine learning instead see causality as one of the fundamental missing features to achieve human-level machine intelligence. As humans, we are able to predict what will happen if we pour hot coffee on our hand or if we throw a ball from the top of a building, because we are acquainted with certain causal processes, because we understand – in many cases – the concepts of "cause" and "effect." This enables us to better navigate the world around us, it facilitates our decisions and, crucially, helps us keep ourselves alive. Algorithms do not have such capability and in absence of it, fundamental pillars in the attempt to build intelligence machines inevitably fall apart, creating an irreducible gap between humans and machines.

A champion of the shift toward AI methods (and theory) that encode causal reasoning has been (and continues to be) Judea Pearl, whose research efforts have been focused on this goal for decades. In a recent article, Pearl outlines how the algorithmization of causal inference can be achieved, particularly through the so-called Structural Causal Model "SCM" (Pearl, 2019). The SCM is Pearl's attempt to construct a general theory of causality that must be able to accomplish five (four plus one) separate goals. First, it should be able to represent causal questions through the language of mathematics; second, it should be able to offer a language precise enough to communicating the assumptions that are linked to causal questions; third, it must provide a systematic way to distinguish between answerable and unanswerable questions and respond to those which can be answered; fourth, it has to provide a method that can determine the required assumptions to answer to the unanswerable questions. Fifth, and finally, such a theory must address the four questions and also include all the other previously developed theories of causality that would then become "special cases" within a broader, de facto general, framework. How does SCM achieve this last point? By combining elements from structural equation models, the potential-outcome framework developed by Rubin (1974), and graphical models, which were developed by Pearl in the first place (1998).

Among the consequences of the development of the SCM, Pearl argues that it has been able to unify many different approaches to causality, including the probabilistic, decision analytical, and interventional ones. Furthermore, he points out how it forced the community to discard myths and misconceptions about causality and facilitated the comprehension of many statistical concepts that are typically encountered in the lexicon of statistical inference, including "confounding," "mediation," "ignorability."

More specifically, Pearl lists seven tasks that, he argues, can only be achieved surpassing the logic of "associational" (or, say, correlational) learning while embedding causal modeling into algorithmic systems (Pearl, 2018a, 2019). These are:

1 Encoding causal assumptions in a way that preserves algorithmic transparency and testability: transparency allows to verify plausibility of assumptions, and testability permits to assess whether assumptions are in line with data at our disposal.
2 Controlling confounding, that is, the presence of unobserved causes of two or more variables, through the backdoor criterion[4] and, when not possible, the do-calculus.[5]
3 Graphically representing and generating counterfactuals.
4 Enabling mediation analysis, that is, the investigation of mechanisms that involve changes from a cause to the effect, through graphical representation.

5 Solving selection bias and non-adaptability via do-calculus. Do-calculus can be used to recalibrate learned policies following environmental changes and disparities between non-representative samples and a target population.

6 Recovering from missing data by exploiting causal models of the missingness process, going beyond the "missing at random" case, further formalizing recovery conditions to obtain consistent estimates of relevant relationships.

7 Reaching causal discovery through pruning compatible models associated with testable implications, finally leading to the estimation of causal links.

One noteworthy concept which has been highlighted by Pearl in describing the SCM is that while inference require veracity of the assumed structure, the models do not require adherence to any particular form of the distributions involved, a distinguishing feature compared to traditional causal inference methods in the statistics and econometrics literature.

Summarizing Pearl's work in a few lines is impossible, and therefore this paragraph should not be read with such goal in mind. It should be seen, instead, as a way to expose those who are not familiar with causal inference from disciplines other than econometrics and quantitative social science to different traditions which are often overlooked in traditional graduate courses for criminologists and crime researchers in general. Most importantly, it should be seen as an attempt to show how thinking about machine learning as a mere discipline of prediction is a fallacious practice.

Certainly prediction remains one of the core goals of many machine learning applications – especially off-the-shelf applications which ride the hype wave. Yet, causal inference and causal reasoning have increasingly acquired an eminent role in the development of machine intelligence, and much merit has to be credited to Pearl's impressive series of work on the topic. Although statisticians, social scientists, and computer science tackle the causality problem for different purposes, it is fascinating to see how a pattern of convergence emerges, and among the many effects of such convergence is the horizon of possibilities that machine learning offers for research on crime.

Within this convergence, not only technical inputs have been offered from researchers in algorithmic statistics, computer and computational sciences, and machine learning. In fact, the increasing demand for ethical scrutiny of computational systems in high-stakes contexts (such as criminal justice system decisions and predictive policing) forced scholars to think critically and theoretically about causality as one solution for increasing algorithmic fairness and accountability.

In this regard, Barabas and coauthors (2018) have been strong advocates for a shift from purely correlational evidence (and data-driven correlational decisions) to causal inference. They outline an intervention-driven approach that questions the purpose itself of algorithmic systems. Rather than focusing on mere prediction, they favor a new "risk mitigation" strategy that concentrates on the exploration of causal mechanisms in order to detect possible ways to prevent crime by interrupting individual pathways leading to offending. While others have pointed out that causal models can enhance credibility, transparency, and fairness (Kusner & Loftus, 2020; Loftus et al., 2018), Barabas and coauthors also point out how this change would also productively help in identifying factors that can lead to crime, prompting possible solutions to prevent crime commission, and hence incarceration and victimization. Besides the technical reasons for causal discovery, Barabas and colleagues reveal an additional need, an ethical one, which has strong links with both theory and practice and that should force us all to move toward systems that are more credible in statistical terms, more accountable in their architectures and more effective in reducing crime. Approaching these as mutually exclusive targets is a losing strategy.

Research on Crime and the Contribution of AI in Estimating Causal Effects

Arrived at this point, what are the methods arising from the machine learning literature that can help us in inferring causal relationships from observational data? The machine learning attention on the topic, as already mentioned, has increased over the last decade, a trend that is also testified by frequent initiatives and workshops in major conferences dedicated to AI, such as NeurIPS, ICML, AAAI, and IJCAI. This subsection is limited to a select survey of approaches, yet these already illustrate the important progresses that have been made and the direct effects that these may have on research on crime.

Chasing Heterogeneous Causal Effects

One first important area of research in this interdisciplinary landscape is the detection of heterogeneous causal effects or conditional average treatment effects (CATE) (Athey & Imbens, 2017). The literature has generally focused on average treatment effects, which map the average impact of a certain intervention on a given outcome in the entire population, because estimating the impact of an intervention on every unit of analysis could lead to biased estimates. However, in heterogeneous populations, average treatment effects may be poorly informative as one may be more interested in capturing the effects of said interventions across different strata to assess, for instance, the distributed benefits or costs across subjects. Is the intervention having a higher effect on areas of the city with higher poverty? Is the policy mostly affecting people with a criminal history? Answers to these questions require dedicated techniques. Among these stands Causal Trees, a method developed by Athey and Imbens (2016) which builds upon the subgroup analysis framework and it has the goal to partition the covariate space into subgroups with regard to the treatment effect heterogeneity.

Athey and Imbens explain that the method is different from traditional regression trees because of two mechanisms. First, the tree is built based on optimizing mean-squared error of treatment effects, and second, half the sample is used to find the optimal partition of the covariates that generates the tree structure, and the other half is used to treatment effects estimation.

Wager and Athey (2018) also propose a modified version of the Random Forest model that comprises Causal Trees functioning similarly to a nonparametric method as "personalized" predicted values are derived for each value of the treatment. One of the various advantages reported by the authors is that the method easily handles many covariates, and it is reliable even in cases with many covariates that have little influence on the estimation.

In this same line of research, Künzel and colleagues (2019) presented a meta-algorithm called X-learner that exploits typical techniques such as neural networks to estimate CATE with provable efficiency in contexts where the number of units in one group is much larger than the other. The X-learner can transform every supervised learning algorithm into a CATE estimator, and specifically consists of three separate stages, compared to S-learners which only use a single step and T-learners that consist of two. First, it estimates the average outcome of a treatment using a machine learning model. Second, it imputes counterfactuals, namely, the treatment effects for the individuals in the treated group based on the control group outcome estimator and vice versa. Finally, CATE is estimated based on the counterfactual information provided in the second step.

More recently, Nie and Wager (2021) further expanded the list of tools for CATE by developing a method that first works by estimating marginal effects and treatment propensities to form an objective function isolating the casual role of a treatment and then optimize such objective function. The approach enables fully automatic specification of the estimators of the heterogeneous treatment effects and achieve comparable error levels to methods knowing the distribution of the data-generating process (with the exception of the treatment effect).

The area of research on CATE is particularly vibrant and gained momentum exactly due to the many possibilities that machine learning methods offer. An additional set of approaches relies for instance on LASSO regression. LASSO is one of the most common penalized regression methods (along with Ridge Regression and Elastic net): it is designed as a linear model carrying out variable selection and regularization tasks simultaneously. Specifically, LASSO minimizes the sum of square residuals, as in OLS, and also includes a term that penalizes for the magnitude of parameters estimated for the covariates included in the model. This approach leads to sparse models and is generally recommended in case with high levels of multicollinearity or in settings where we need to extrapolate the intrinsic importance of many covariates. More in general, the LASSO and other regularization methods should be considered as methods to address the bias-variance trade-off,[6] a crucial property in many machine learning applications.

Imai and Ratkovic (2013) used a LASSO model interacting the treatment with the available covariates to determine after regularization which of these covariates have more importance. Athey and Imbens recommend to perform robustness checks to evaluate the validity of the inferred coefficients such as splitting the dataset into two instances, checking consistency of results between a first model using LASSO on the first partition and a second using OLS on the LASSO-selected covariates (2017).

Using LASSO as well, Semenova and colleagues (2021) set forth a method for inferring heterogeneous treatment effects in panel data settings with many controls. The approach consists of a two-stage method: in the first, unit-specific reduced forms of the treatment and outcome conditional on controls are estimated, and residuals of these estimates are then used in the second stage, where the treatment effect parameter is inferred by regressing the residuals on the treatment vector. More in general, the authors illustrate how this two-stage approach advances the current literature in three ways: by being able to handle large quantities of treatment interactions even in the presence of larger quantities of controls, by capturing unobserved unit effects and weak time dependence in panel data, and by reaching simultaneous inference on heterogeneous treatment effects through Gaussian bootstrap.

The LASSO has been also considered for estimating average treatment effects. Particularly, Belloni and colleagues (2018) modified the algorithm in order to obtain valid causal estimates. Given that the original method poses problem in this sense because between two highly correlated variables only one will be chosen with the retained one embedding the effects of both, a modification was required to move beyond mere prediction tasks. The authors then outline a double-selection procedure: in the first stage, LASSO is used to select covariates that are correlated with the outcome; in the second stage, LASSO is instead used to select covariates correlated with the treatment. A final OLS model then include both sets of covariates, leading to an approach that controls the omitted variable bias and greatly improves the validity of the average treatment effects. On average treatment effects, another example is the paper by Bloniarz and coauthors (2016).

Finally, Hahn et al. (2019) expand upon previous work by Hill (2011) and Chipman et al. (2010), specifically seeking to contrast the issues arising in the Bayesian Additive Regression Trees (BART) approach – an ensemble method that has demonstrated high performance in different areas of applications in causal research – when regression-induced confounding is in place (Hahn et al., 2018) and the final goal is to estimate heterogeneous effects. In practice, this concerns many settings in which there is a large set of confounders that we need to control for, and a limited set of relevant effect modifiers. Additionally, BART does not involve direct regularization of treatment effects and it does not allow to adjust prior distribution over heterogeneous effects independently of the prognostic or direct effects of the covariates on the outcome. To fix such criticalities, Hahn, Murray, and Carvalho propose two main workarounds. First, they parametrize the model directly in terms of heterogeneous treatment effects. Second, they recommend including an estimate of the propensity score as a covariate in the Bayesian causal forest model they outline, avoiding that effects of confounders are wrongfully associated with the treatment variable.

These are only few of the many approaches that have been developed and continue to emerge in this vibrant area of research. Those who are interested in exploring other cutting-edge approaches in this sphere are recommended to read a recent review by Koch and colleagues, which deals with ways to obtain causal inference using deep learning techniques (2021).

Tools for Temporal Data

Breakthroughs in machine learning and causal inference, however, are not only bounded to settings with i.i.d. data. In fact, another vast area of application regards causality in time-series data, which are very common in the social sciences and in research on crime as well. Causality in time series data mostly tackles the problem of investigating whether temporally ordered sequences of measurements related to a phenomenon (or more phenomena) have a causal effect on temporally ordered measurements of a target variable. Questions that can be answered in this frame concern, for instance, the impact of the trend of drug prescriptions on overdose, or the effect of trends in police misconduct in social unrest events.

One first example of techniques in this space relates to a recent method intersecting statistical physics, complex systems and machine learning proposed by Runge and coauthors (2019). They present a strategy to find causal associations in multidimensional datasets characterized by diffused presence of nonlinearity building upon linear and nonlinear conditional dependence tests. The method is demonstrated to generate causal networks across applications, including earth and climate science, and to outperform existing alternative methods in the ability to detect causality in time series.

Conditional independence tests represent the backbone of another recent algorithmic framework proposed by Malinsky and Spirtes (2018). The authors extend the Fast Causal Inference (FCI) algorithm and the Greedy FCI (GFCI) approach, which in turn combines FCI and Greedy Equivalent Search (GES), to contexts with partially observed multivariate time-series, assuming a structural vector autoregression approach with latent components as the data generating process. The authors highlight that this approach allows for contemporaneous causal inference, a process that describes a situation in which a certain intervention can influence a variable that in turn impact another variable within the same time period. This technical advancement may be particularly suitable for criminology and crime research as it is often difficult to obtain data at the micro-level for multiple time series: in applications in which time units are discretized in largely aggregated periods (e.g., years), contemporaneous causal inference can overcome the burden of unsafely assuming the exclusive presence of one causal mechanism at a time.

Within the same strand of inquiry, Peters and coauthors (2013) analyze a class of restricted Structural Equation Models for time series called "Time Series Models with Independent Noise" or TiMINo in short. TiMINo approach takes time series as the input and generates Directed Acyclic Graphs to recover causal relationships. This class is part of the family of constraint-based algorithms which learn causal graphs satisfying conditional independence in the data based on the faithfulness assumption. Guo et al. (2020a) note how these approaches can be problematic for two main reasons: first, the faithfulness assumption at their core can be violated, especially in limited samples, and, second, causal direction between two variables can remain unknown, severely limiting the usefulness of the results.

To overcome these difficulties, score-based algorithms represent a common alternative: conditional independence tests are substituted by goodness-of-fit diagnostics, such as the Bayesian Information Criterion (BIC), and said algorithms optimize a certain scoring criterion which somehow proxies the validity of the estimated relationships. Among these are the abovementioned GES method (Chickering, 2003) and its extension Fast GES (Ramsey et al., 2017).

Other time-series strategies for causal discovery are instead based on the concept of Granger causality (Granger, 1969). Granger causality is an operationalization of causality defined in probabilistic and predictive terms, which boils down to the ability of one time series to correctly forecast another, conditional on a given set of information. Over the decades, it has been diffusely employed across many areas, including quantitative social science. However, many discussions have been prompted in the statistical, econometric, and machine learning literatures to verify whether Granger causality can be interpreted as an actual form of causal discovery technique. Granger himself started such discussion by admitting that Granger causality should not be considered "real" causality. Pearl also views this approach as statistical rather than causal (2009). More recently, however, efforts have been produced to try to clarify the link between more sophisticated approaches to causality, such as Pearl's General Theory, and Granger Causality, pointing out that there are conditions under which Granger Causality can be applied to verify the effect of an intervention or to establish direct causal links between different time series.

In this respect, two approaches are noteworthy. The first, described in a paper by Liu and coauthors (2010), applies to contexts in which one is interested in learning temporal causal graphs in multivariate time series. Assuming multiple multivariate time series are available along with a relational graph among such time series, the method is engineered through a LASSO-regularized hidden Markov Random Field regression that exploits the information contained in the relational graph to obtain accurate temporal causal structures for all the sequences. Another method presented by Chikahara and Fujino (2018) uses Granger causality to represent causal inference as a classification learning task instead, differently from most literature that characterize this problem as a regression one. Distances between conditional distributions given past variable values are used in a classification setting where causal labels taking one of three values are assigned to each time series. These values map causation from variable X to Y, from Y to X or no causation, taking inspiration from similar strategies previously designed to be deployed in i.i.d. contexts. These algorithmic solutions are certainly valuable and promising, but one important recommendation is that Granger causality should be considered with more caution compared to alternative methods as it poses higher risks for spurious causal associations due, for instance, to omitted variable biases (Eichler, 2013).

Agent-based Models and Causal Inference

ABM have been already introduced and contextualized in Chapter 3. Their popularity in the social sciences as well as criminology has considerably grown in the last two decades (F. Bianchi & Squazzoni, 2015; Bonabeau, 2002; Groff et al., 2019; Retzlaff et al., 2021). Although ABM are not per se an AI or a machine learning method, they could be easily integrated with machine intelligence approaches to estimate the effects of a particular process (or intervention) on an outcome of interest or, in principle, to design the simulation dynamics themselves.

With regard to the former aspect, those tools surveyed in the two previous subsections can be utilized to estimate heterogeneous causal effects in a simulated population or extrapolate causal associations between sequences, for example time series, of measurements of two phenomena of interest.

Concerning the latter aspect, instead, one such approach would be reinforcement learning, which has not been covered in this book, but deserves a brief discussion here. Reinforcement learning (RL) has been (and continues to be) an important area of research in AI that mostly addresses the study of learning how to behave to maximize a certain reward or minimize a given cost in adaptive scenarios with interactions (Kaelbling et al., 1996; Wiering & van Otterlo, 2012). In other words, RL concerns the study of how artificial agents can learn by interacting with the environment surrounding them to achieve a certain goal. Sutton and Barto (2018) highlight the differences between RL and both supervised and unsupervised learning. First, RL is different from supervised learning because interactive problems (as those characterizing RL) do not provide us with examples of desired behavior that can be deemed to be both correct and representative of all the potential situations in which an agent is called to act. Thus, RL does not rely on labeled examples, as a supervised learning classification algorithm would do. Second, RL is different also from unsupervised learning: although both deal with learning without examples of "correct behavior," RL agents seek to maximize a given reward signal, whereas unsupervised learning approaches generally aim at finding hidden internal structure or associations in a given set of data.

Given its nature, RL can be used as the backbone framework to design how agents in a certain environment, e.g., a simulated urban area or a community, act, behave, cooperate, or enter into conflict, avoiding deterministic or probabilistic designs which often constitute the standard in ABM research. Combinations of ABM and reinforcement learning have already appeared in various lines of inquiry, including social segregation (Sert et al., 2020), conflict research (Collins et al., 2014), environmental science (Bone & Dragićević, 2010), market behavior (K. Lee et al., 2018), and medicine (Jalalimanesh et al., 2017). Criminology and crime research have not yet explored the potential of this methodological partnership, which given the importance of concepts such as rationality, interaction, reward, cost, and opportunity in RL might be valuable for different well-known theoretical prepositions extant in the study of crime, including among others Rational Choice Theory (Cornish & Clarke, 1987) and Social Learning Theory (Akers & Jensen, 2011).

The promises associated with the use of ABM are manifold and concern mainly the possibility to artificially simulate behaviors, interactions, and phenomena that are not easily observable in the real world. Yet, this "artificiality" can be considered both the blessing and the curse of ABM. Particularly, the distinction between real-world outcomes that can be detected, tracked, and analyzed in traditional experimental or quasi-experimental studies and artificial outcomes that are the by-product of simulated mechanisms in a fictitious world has been the central topic of a great deal of discussion in epidemiology and other disciplines around the effectiveness of simulation models when investigating causal mechanisms (Casini & Manzo, 2016; Diez Roux, 2015; Macy & Sato, 2008; Marshall & Galea, 2015). In criminology, the attitude toward simulation approaches and ABM in general has been less controversial. In a recent paper, for instance, Groff et al. (2019) write that ABM indeed allows for both mechanism-based investigations and causal analysis.

Casini and Manzo (2016) reviewed the many existing perspectives around the problem of using ABM for causality research, and the resulting picture is much more complex than the one synthesized by Groff and coauthors. They conclude that causality and causal narratives can be derived from ABM only when precise conditions are met, and that the combination of data-driven methods and ABM represents the most reliable strategy to complement evidence that inherently hold different characteristics and nature (i.e., real-world vs. simulated findings). Among the conditions under which ABM can be used to obtain causal evidence, Casini and Manzo list:

1 The use of micro-level theories and indirect empirical evidence to design models' micro-level mechanisms and infrastructure.
2 The models' macro-level consequences must be calibrated through comparison with well-defined and well-quantified empirical evidence.
3 The models must be constructed to guarantee that empirical information is directly injected into simulated micro-level mechanisms.

All these represent challenging and demanding conditions that were already anticipated in the discussion provided in Chapter 3. Criminologists and crime researchers thus must ensure that both micro- and macro-level dynamics in their simulations are adherent to real-world information and solid, testable theoretical premises. I concur that, without such warrants, ABM should not be used to infer causality, as their artificial nature pose problems of internal and external validity as well as testability.

Causality in Social Networks

The study of social networks has arguably become one of the most important areas in criminology and crime research (see Chapter 3 for a discussion on the topic). Scholars have investigated how relationships between individuals are important to explain, describe, or predict crime in a variety of different settings, including co-offending, juvenile delinquency, gangs, terrorism, and organized crime. In spite of the importance of the vast scholarship of the topic, network criminology still has not comprehensively addressed a number of important questions and issues concerning the relational nature of criminal behaviors. Among these open issues stands the study of causation in social networks. In general, this remains an important and challenging context of research for the social sciences as well as for statistics and AI.

Inferring causation in the study of social networks in criminology and crime research is difficult for several reasons, both technical and conceptual. Problematic sampling, biased data, and inconsistent information gathering, for instance, broadly regard the data collection stage. Criminal networks often face the problems of undefined boundaries and do not guarantee information completeness. This not only pertains completeness in terms of obtaining all the relevant information of participants in a criminal network but also relates to the scarcity of accurate longitudinal measurements or the absence of multi-modal or multi-layer measurements as sources for enriching the information portfolio beyond a single type of relationship among individuals.

Besides these aspects that are peculiar of the study of crime, one major limitation to causal discovery in social networks and graphs in general is the implausibility of SUTVA, particularly concerning the absence of interference. As already mentioned in this chapter, SUTVA posits that when a portion of a population is treated with a given intervention, the potential outcomes for any unit are not influenced by the treatments assigned to other units (no interference) and that, for each unit, there are no different forms of each treatment level (consistency). In other words, when evaluating the effect of a policy on a certain population, we have to avoid that contacts between treated and non-treated unit will manipulate their potential outcome through, for instance, social influence. Additionally, we want to make sure that a treatment is consistently defined and administered without difference between units.

As one will immediately anticipate, SUTVA and particularly the absence of interference are highly problematic when considering contexts in which, instead, relationships and connections among individuals are at the core of the analysis. How can we make sure that two friends in a social policy program, one treated and one in the control group, will not communicate and influence each other, thus invalidating the possibility to reliably estimate the effect that the program had on recidivism? The problem within the problem is that interference is a factual issue in both experimental and observational studies.

Several attempts and solutions have been provided to address this issue (see VanderWeele and Weihua (2013) and Frank and Ran (2021) for reviews). These solutions regard both RCTs and observational studies through, among others, IV regression. Yet, as previously stated, these two are not the only two problems affecting network settings. Among others, we also find entanglement and confounding bias.

In parallel with the continuous efforts from the statistical and econometrics communities, machine learning and AI in general have shown to be able to provide relevant contributions in network causal inference in network settings.

Bhattacharya et al. (2019) directly target the problem of causal inference when both interference and network uncertainty, that is the impossibility to obtain fully specified network structures, are at play; their model works by inferring causality on a chain graph model with uncertainty about network structure. Compared to methods in which experiments or tests are carried out on unrealistic fully connected graphs, the authors use sparser networks leading to a better bias-variance trade-off, resting on weak parametric and theoretical assumptions. Particularly, the authors specify that the individual-level causal structure for each unit is known. However, the shape of the networks between units is unknown, and the considered interference is only partial, meaning that there may be spillover effects between individual units, but other types of macro-level interference (such as interference between neighborhoods in which individuals live) do not exist, thus implying a hierarchical i.i.d. structure. In spite of the assumptions and restrictions imposed in the work, the problem remains challenging given the large search space for network reconstruction which is computationally costly even for small graphs. Different algorithms are proposed through a greedy procedure called Greedy Network Search to infer the true chain graph network model by choosing a graph among candidates by optimizing a model score. The experiments presented in the paper showcase the efficacy in both network recovery and estimation of network causal effects, thus opening possible interesting applications also in research on crime, where true information about extant connections in a given community, group, and organizations are often impossible to obtain or too uncertain to be trusted.

Rakesh and colleagues (2018) develop a generative model called Linked Causal Variational Autoencoder (LCVA) to infer causation between pair of units, a phenomenon the authors denominate "paired spillover." The LCVA builds upon advances made in the areas of variational inference and deep learning and extends research on variational autoencoders (VAE) by adopting a causal variant of such method denominated causal effect variational autoencoder (CEVAE). This variant directly treats latent attributes as confounders affecting both treatment itself as well as outcomes. In a setting where X represents a set of coviariates associated to unit u, t is the treatment under scrutiny, y is the outcome, and Z is the confounder, the authors propose a framework where u and $\bar{u}$ are two units such that the spillover effect is modeled enabling the treatment of u to influence the outcome of $\bar{u}$, and vice versa. The approach then learns the confounders Z^u and $Z^{\bar{u}}$ assuming X^u and $X^{\bar{u}}$ to be their proxies. Overall, the encoding network of LCVA samples confounders by conditioning on available information, namely, observed covariates, the treatments of both units and their outcomes. Then, once the latent confounders of a unit are inferred, they are used to capture the spillover effect of $\bar{u}$ on u or u on $\bar{u}$.

Toulis et al. (2018) deal with a phenomenon that is somehow related to interference, namely, network entanglement. In spite of its importance, they argue, the issue has been largely overlooked in the literature on causality and networks. Entanglement occurs when a treatment is not defined on individual units but, instead, on pairs or groups of units. This often occurs when a certain policy, intervention, and treatment in general is non individualistic, but it is instead applied to groups of individuals in a social network, be it a classroom or a group of people living in the same area of the same city. In particular, they address the issue of selection bias in the presence of entangled treatments, where the probability of treatment does not depend on the individual characteristics of a subject. They motivate their work by highlighting how traditional propensity score methods devised to avoid bias as self-selection cannot be deployed. Traditional propensity score methods are unfeasible because in the setting described by the authors the treatment is multivalued, i.e., it is nonbinary, as it is quantified as the number of new connections arising from time t to $t + 1$ after the treatment is put into place. Furthermore, the propensity score approach posits that treatment is applied to units at the individual level, while in entanglement dynamics this does not apply. Toulis and colleagues thus provide a new similarity function capturing the extent to which two propensity score models are different from each other in terms of their causal estimates. From a methodological standpoint, the work offers an algorithm that considers the uncertainty associated with the observed network via a reliable network evolution model, furthermore deriving estimates of individual propensity scores computed through the average of likely network trajectories. Analytical experiments show that similarity between classic linear propensity scores and true propensity scores often lead to invalid estimates of causal effects. Importantly, the authors set forth a number of properties of their model that can be modified to accommodate domain-specific applications, allowing for significant flexibility.

Finally, two papers tackle another problem arising in studies interested in detecting causality in observational data when information is structured as a network. Specifically, they address the problem of confounding bias arising when a variable affects both the treatment and the outcome exploiting network patterns.

First, Veitch et al. (2019) aim at correcting for unobserved confounding in networks in the specific case where a proxy for the unobserved proxy is available but it has a non-i.i.d. structure and information on a well-specified generative model is unavailable. One example of application might be again the case of a social policy program administered to a social network composed by juveniles living in a disadvantaged neighborhood, where latent confounders might be the unobserved information on age, sex, or educational status, and assuming that the latent confounders are themselves associated with the social network, as homophily plays a role in the probability of relationships between individuals. The goal would be to derive average treatment effects for the treated and nontreated individuals, which becomes impractical in absence of a reliable generative model for both the latent confounders and the network structure itself. In order to overcome such difficulty and achieve their goal, Veitch and coauthors transform this problem into a predictive one by employing network embeddings, expanding previous work by Chernozhukov and colleagues in i.i.d. settings (2018). The prediction problem is a semisupervised one, where conditioning on the embedding output should decouple the characteristics and properties of the unit as well as the network structure. A palatable property of the method is the fact that the embeddings are learned through the minimization of an objective function related to the network without the need that such objective correspond to any generative model. The compromise of such approach is to accept a black-box embedding predictor instead of an unreliable or unrealistic generative model.

Second, Guo et al. (2020b) propose Network Deconfounder, a causal inference framework, designed to obtain the influence of hidden confounders exploiting both the feature space associated with each individual (or unit) under analysis as well as the associated network information (e.g., the relationships between units). The aim in this case is then to learn individual treatment effects from such data, without, however, considering the problem of spillovers effects or interference, as done by the previously commented studied. The Network Deconfounder works assuming that individual features (e.g., an individual's level of education, age, and job) and the associated network structure are two sets of proxy variables related to the hidden deconfounders, thus not requiring that the observed features are sufficient to capture all the variations between treated and nontreated units. The framework works in two steps. First, the authors seek to learn representations of the hidden confounders by simultaneously mapping individual features and networks into a shared representation of confounders. Second, the framework learns an output function estimated to learn a potential outcome of a given unit based on the treatment as well as the represented hidden confounders. The first step is achieved through the use of Graph Convolutional Networks, whereas the second, that is, inference on potential outcomes, is reached by obtaining an output function mapping the representation of the hidden confounders with the treatment to the corresponding potential outcome. The framework then revolves around three components of the loss function, namely, the Factual Outcome Inference, Representation Balancing, and L2 Regularization (also known as Ridge regression). Factual Outcome Inference works by minimizing the error in the inferred factual outcomes. Representation Balancing then is carried out to infer the conditional distribution of counterfactual outcomes, as minimizing error in the factual ones alone is not sufficient. Finally, the L2 Regularization component is introduced to mitigate overfitting in the model parameters of the network deconfounder. Given the virtual impossibility to obtain ground truth individual treatment effects due to the fundamental problem of causality, the authors experiment with two semisynthetic datasets. The use such source of information might become useful to be explored also in criminology and crime research, as a partial workaround to the absence of sufficiently rich (or complete) datasets.

Conclusions

This chapter has specifically addressed the main approaches adopted from the statistical and econometrics literature for causal inference, including a discussion on the pros and cons of RCTs and a general review of four alternative methods afferent to observational studies and quasi-experimental settings, such as Matching, Regression Discontinuity, Difference-in-Differences, and Instrumental Variables. Following, I have reflected on the legacies left by Leo Breiman's perspective on the two cultures of statistical thinking, namely, the data-driven and the algorithmic ones, which can be thought as the traditional econometrics tradition and the AI-related tradition emerging from computer science. I highlighted how these two are progressively getting closer and, in the last section, I have illustrated different strands of research in which machine learning and causal research are partnering up with promising results. These are the investigation of heterogeneous causal effects, the detection of causality in temporal data, the promises and pitfalls of ABM for causal research, and the main extant approaches for tackling some of the problems concerning causal inference in social networks.

Criminology and crime research are facing an important methodological challenge that will shape the way in which this multifaceted area of scientific inquiry will engage with crucial theoretical and policy questions concerning criminal phenomena – and the impact that such phenomena have on society. This challenge comprises two major aspects. The first is the core of this book, namely, the critical need to deeply engage with machine learning methods.

As they become more and more central in many disciplines, including the social sciences, criminology and crime research are still lagging behind in the exploration of how these methods can contribute to them.

The second aspect concerns instead the specific core of this chapter, which is the quest for causality. Criminology has been called out to be reluctant, ineffective, or methodologically unprepared to investigate causal links, and in parallel many give credit to economists to take up the role of sophisticated methodologists able to fulfill the causality mission. This view is partial and simplistic, yet criminology must do better in connecting with those "why" questions that still remain unanswered (or unspoken).

One of the main takeaways of this chapter, however, is that seeing the two aspects as entirely separated is detrimental to the broader goal of advancing the empirical understanding of crime. Instead, they both speak to each other, and taking advantage of this interrelation may represent a game-changer.

While I was concluding this chapter, David Card, Joshua Angrist, and Guido Imbens were awarded the 2021 Nobel Prize in Economics for their decisive role in driving the credibility revolution in economics and for their breakthroughs in natural experiments and causal inference. Such prestigious formal award recognizes the immense impact that the works of these three scholars has in their field: honoring them here – besides the interesting temporal coincidence – gives me chance to highlight once again the practical importance of many of the methods reviewed throughout these pages. Impressively good research deploying such methods has been and is currently conducted in criminology and crime research as well, but we need to do better, and to do better we cannot ignore the promising benefits that machine learning could add to our toolbox.

Notes

1 For fascinating historical accounts concerning the invention of IV regression, see Stock and Trebbi (2003) and Cunningham (2021).

2 Of all things, I found particularly funny Parzen's proposal to associate link prediction with "management" – and profit – and causal inference with "science," and therefore truth (2001). Without agreeing on oversimplifying speculations about the state of the ML industry nowadays, this provocative dichotomy is today the source of a great deal of lively discussion. On the topic, see Sample (2017) and Kwok (2019).

3 The enduring legacy of this debate is easily testified by an article written by Norvig (2017) which narrates and discusses an occasion in which, few years ago, Noam Chomsky derided machine learning researchers that only utilize statistically driven machine learning for mimic real-world behavior. The article is intellectually stimulating and – quite an anomaly in scientific research – funny at the same time.

4 In the context of causal graphical models, the backdoor criterion is a solution provided to solve the problem of distinguishing good controls (deconfounders) in a regression setting from bad ones (confounders). For a technical explanation, see Cinelli et al. (2019).

5 The do-calculus is a procedure made of three different rules that allows to map interventional and observational distributions in causal graphs. Unfortunately, the extent to which this can be fully grasped by the readers is dependent on the familiarity they have with graphical causal inference. The overall goal, however, is to probabilistically generate formulas that capture the effect of interventions. These three rules concern as many central points in the analysis of causal processes: when one can ignore an observation, when we can treat a certain intervention as an observation and when we can ignore a given intervention. Regarding the first rule, one observation can be ignored when it does not impact on the outcome through any existing path in the causal graph. Concerning the second, interventions and observations are deemed equivalent when the causal effect of a given variable influences the outcome of interest solely through directed edges. Finally, one intervention can be ignored if there is no path that lead to the outcome. For more details on this topic, see Pearl (2012).

6 The "bias-variance trade-off" is property of a learning model that concerns the relationship between the inherent error present in a model (bias) and its stability in results when a training set is modified (variance). Regularized regression approaches provide tools to achieve this trade-off constraining the estimated coefficient estimates, accepting a certain level of bias to obtain less sensitive results.

References

Abadie, A. (2006). Poverty, political freedom, and the roots of terrorism. *American Economic Review, 96*(2), 50–56. https://doi.org/10.1257/000282806777211847.

Akers, R. L., & Jensen, G. F. (2011). *Social learning theory and the explanation of crime.* Transaction Publishers.

Anderson, D. M. (2014). In school and out of trouble? The minimum dropout age and juvenile crime. *The Review of Economics and Statistics, 96*(2), 318–331. https://doi.org/10.1162/REST_a_00360.

Angrist, J. D., & Krueger, A. B. (2001). Instrumental variables and the search for identification: From supply and demand to natural experiments. *Journal of Economic Perspectives, 15*(4), 69–85. https://doi.org/10.1257/jep.15.4.69.

Apel, R. J., & Sweeten, G. (2010). Propensity Score Matching in criminology and criminal justice. In A. R. Piquero & D. Weisburd (Eds.), *Handbook of quantitative criminology* (pp. 543–562). Springer. https://doi.org/10.1007/978-0-387-77650-7_26.

Athey, S., & Imbens, G. (2016). Recursive partitioning for heterogeneous causal effects. *Proceedings of the National Academy of Sciences, 113*(27), 7353–7360. https://doi.org/10.1073/pnas.1510489113.

Athey, S., & Imbens, G. W. (2017). The state of applied econometrics: Causality and policy evaluation. *Journal of Economic Perspectives, 31*(2), 3–32. https://doi.org/10.1257/jep.31.2.3.

Athey, S., & Imbens, G. W. (2019). Machine learning methods that economists should know about. *Annual Review of Economics, 11*(1), 685–725. https://doi.org/10.1146/annurev-economics-080217-053433.

Aziani, A., Favarin, S., & Campedelli, G. M. (2020). Security governance: Mafia control over ordinary crimes. *Journal of Research in Crime and Delinquency, 57*(4), 444–492. https://doi.org/10.1177/0022427819893417.

Baker, A., Larcker, D. F., & Wang, C. C. Y. (2021). *How much should we trust staggered difference-in-differences estimates?* (SSRN Scholarly Paper ID 3794018). Social Science Research Network. https://doi.org/10.2139/ssrn.3794018.

Barabas, C., Dinakar, K., Ito, J., Virza, M., & Zittrain, J. (2018). Interventions over predictions: Reframing the ethical debate for actuarial risk assessment. *ArXiv:1712.08238 [Cs, Stat]*. http://arxiv.org/abs/1712.08238

Battistin, E., & Rettore, E. (2008). Ineligibles and eligible non-participants as a double comparison group in regression-discontinuity designs. *Journal of Econometrics*, 142(2), 715–730.

Belloni, A., Chernozhukov, V., Fernández-Val, I., & Hansen, C. (2018). Program evaluation and causal inference with high-dimensional data. *ArXiv:1311.2645 [Econ, Math, Stat]*. http://arxiv.org/abs/1311.2645

Berk, R. A., & Rauma, D. (1983). Capitalizing on nonrandom assignment to treatments: A regression-discontinuity evaluation of a crime-control program. *Journal of the American Statistical Association*, 78(381), 21–27. https://doi.org/10.1080/01621459.1983.10477917.

Bertanha, M., & Imbens, G. W. (2020). External validity in fuzzy Regression Discontinuity Designs. *Journal of Business & Economic Statistics*, 38(3), 593–612. https://doi.org/10.1080/07350015.2018.1546590.

Bhattacharya, R., Malinsky, D., & Shpitser, I. (2019). Causal inference under interference and network uncertainty. In *Uncertainty in artificial intelligence: Proceedings of the ... conference. Conference on uncertainty in artificial intelligence, 2019*, 372.

Bianchi, F., & Squazzoni, F. (2015). Agent-based models in sociology. *WIREs Computational Statistics*, 7(4), 284–306. https://doi.org/10.1002/wics.1356.

Bianchi, M., Buonanno, P., & Pinotti, P. (2012). Do immigrants cause crime? *Journal of the European Economic Association*, 10(6), 1318–1347. https://doi.org/10.1111/j.1542-4774.2012.01085.x.

Bilinski, A., & Hatfield, L. A. (2020). Nothing to see here? Non-inferiority approaches to parallel trends and other model assumptions. *ArXiv:1805.03273 [Stat]*. http://arxiv.org/abs/1805.03273

Blomberg, T. G. (2019). Making a difference in criminology: Past, present, and future. *American Journal of Criminal Justice*, 44(4), 670–688. https://doi.org/10.1007/s12103-019-09484-6.

Bloniarz, A., Liu, H., Zhang, C.-H., Sekhon, J. S., & Yu, B. (2016). LASSO adjustments of treatment effect estimates in randomized experiments. *Proceedings of the National Academy of Sciences*, 113(27), 7383–7390. https://doi.org/10.1073/pnas.1510506113.

Bonabeau, E. (2002). Agent-based modeling: Methods and techniques for simulating human systems. *Proceedings of the National Academy of Sciences*, 99(Suppl. 3), 7280–7287. https://doi.org/10.1073/pnas.082080899.

Bone, C., & Dragićević, S. (2010). Simulation and validation of a reinforcement learning agent-based model for multi-stakeholder forest management. *Computers, Environment and Urban Systems*, 34(2), 162–174. https://doi.org/10.1016/j.compenvurbsys.2009.10.001.

Breiman, L. (1996). Bagging predictors. *Machine Learning*, 24(2), 123–140. https://doi.org/10.1007/BF00058655.

Breiman, L. (2001a). Statistical modeling: The two cultures (with comments and a rejoinder by the author). *Statistical Science*, 16(3), 199–231. https://doi.org/10.1214/ss/1009213726.

Breiman, L. (2001b). Random forests. *Machine Learning*, 45(1), 5–32. https://doi.org/10.1023/A:1010933404324.

Breiman, L., Friedman, J., Stone, C. J., & Olshen, R. A. (1984). *Classification and regression trees*(1. CRC Press repr.). Chapman & Hall/CRC.

Brodersen, K. H., Gallusser, F., Koehler, J., Remy, N., & Scott, S. L. (2015). Inferring causal impact using Bayesian structural time-series models. *Annals of Applied Statistics, 9,* 247–274.

Campedelli, G. M., Aziani, A., & Favarin, S. (2021). Exploring the immediate effects of COVID-19 containment policies on crime: An empirical analysis of the short-term aftermath in Los Angeles. *American Journal of Criminal Justice, 46*(5), 704–727. https://doi.org/10.1007/s12103-020-09578-6.

Campedelli, G. M., Favarin, S., Aziani, A., & Piquero, A. R. (2020). Disentangling community-level changes in crime trends during the COVID-19 pandemic in Chicago. *Crime Science, 9*(1), 21. https://doi.org/10.1186/s40163-020-00131-8.

Card, D. (1993). *Using geographic variation in college proximity to estimate the return to schooling* (Working paper no. 4483; working paper series). National Bureau of Economic Research. https://doi.org/10.3386/w4483.

Casini, L., & Manzo, G. (2016). *Agent-based models and causality: A methodological appraisal.* Linköping University Electronic Press. http://urn.kb.se/resolve?urn=urn:nbn:se:liu:diva-133332

Chainey, S. P., Serrano-Berthet, R., & Veneri, F. (2021). The impact of a hot spot policing program in Montevideo, Uruguay: An evaluation using a quasi-experimental difference-in-difference negative binomial approach. *Police Practice and Research, 22*(5), 1541–1556. https://doi.org/10.1080/15614263.2020.1749619.

Chernozhukov, V., Chetverikov, D., Demirer, M., Duflo, E., Hansen, C., Newey, W., & Robins, J. (2018). Double/debiased machine learning for treatment and structural parameters. *The Econometrics Journal, 21*(1), C1–C68. https://doi.org/10.1111/ectj.12097.

Chickering, D. M. (2003). Optimal structure identification with greedy search. *The Journal of Machine Learning Research, 3*(null), 507–554. https://doi.org/10.1162/153244303321897717.

Chikahara, Y., & Fujino, A. (2018). *Causal inference in time series via supervised learning.* In Proceedings of the 27th International Joint Conference on Artificial Intelligence (IJCAI '18). AAAI press, 2042–2048. https://dl.acm.org/doi/10.5555/3304889.3304943.

Chipman, H. A., George, E. I., & McCulloch, R. E. (2010). BART: Bayesian additive regression trees. *The Annals of Applied Statistics, 4*(1). https://doi.org/10.1214/09-AOAS285.

Cinelli, C., Forney, A., & Pearl, J. (2019). *Causal analysis in theory and practice: Back-door criterion.* http://causality.cs.ucla.edu/blog/index.php/category/back-door-criterion/

Circo, G., & McGarrell, E. (2021). Estimating the impact of an integrated CCTV program on crime. Journal of experimental criminology, *17*(1), 129–150.

Collins, A., Sokolowski, J., & Banks, C. (2014). Applying reinforcement learning to an insurgency agent-based simulation. *The Journal of Defense Modeling and Simulation, 11*(4), 353–364. https://doi.org/10.1177/1548512913501728.

Cook, P. J., & Kang, S. (2016). Birthdays, schooling, and crime: Regression-discontinuity analysis of school performance, delinquency, dropout, and crime initiation. *American Economic Journal: Applied Economics, 8*(1), 33–57. https://doi.org/10.1257/app.20140323.

Cook, P. J., Kang, S., Braga, A. A., Ludwig, J., & O'Brien, M. E. (2015). An experimental evaluation of a comprehensive employment-oriented prisoner re-entry program. *Journal of Quantitative Criminology*, *31*(3), 355–382. https://doi.org/10.1007/s10940-014-9242-5.

Cornish, D. B., & Clarke, R. V. (1987). *The reasoning criminal: Rational choice perspectives on offending*. Transaction Publishers.

Cox, D. R. (2001). Comment to "Statistical modeling: The two cultures." *Statistical Science*, 16(3). https://doi.org/10.1214/ss/1009213726.

Cross, A. B., Gottfredson, D. C., Wilson, D. M., Rorie, M., & Connell, N. (2009). The impact of after-school programs on the routine activities of middle-school students: Results from a randomized, controlled trial. *Criminology & Public Policy*, *8*(2), 391–412. https://doi.org/10.1111/j.1745-9133.2009.00555.x.

Cui, L., & Walsh, R. (2015). Foreclosure, vacancy and crime. *Journal of Urban Economics*, *87*, 72–84. https://doi.org/10.1016/j.jue.2015.01.001.

Cunningham, S. (2021). *Causal inference: The mixtape*. Yale University Press.

Daniele, G., & Geys, B. (2015). Organised crime, institutions and political quality: Empirical evidence from Italian municipalities. *The Economic Journal*, *125*(586), F233–F255. https://doi.org/10.1111/ecoj.12237.

Deaton, A., & Cartwright, N. (2018). Understanding and misunderstanding randomized controlled trials. *Social Science & Medicine*, *210*, 2–21. https://doi.org/10.1016/j.socscimed.2017.12.005.

Diez Roux, A. V. (2015). Invited commentary: The virtual epidemiologist – Promise and peril. *American Journal of Epidemiology*, *181*(2), 100–102. https://doi.org/10.1093/aje/kwu270.

Dorsett, R. (2021). A Bayesian structural time series analysis of the effect of basic income on crime: Evidence from the Alaska Permanent Fund. Journal of the Royal Statistical Society: Series A (Statistics in Society), *184*(1), 179–200.

Efron, B. (2001). Comment to "Statistical modeling: The two cultures." *Statistical Science*, 16(3). https://doi.org/10.1214/ss/1009213726.

Eichler, M. (2013). Causal inference with multiple time series: Principles and problems. *Philosophical Transactions of the Royal Society A: Mathematical, Physical and Engineering Sciences*, *371*(1997), 20110613. https://doi.org/10.1098/rsta.2011.0613.

Evans, S. Z. (2021). Propensity Score Matching. In *The encyclopedia of research methods in criminology and criminal justice* (pp. 859–864). John Wiley & Sons, Ltd. https://doi.org/10.1002/9781119111931.ch166.

Farrington, D. P. (2006). Key longitudinal-experimental studies in criminology. *Journal of Experimental Criminology*, *2*(2), 121–141. https://doi.org/10.1007/s11292-006-9000-2.

Frank, K., & Ran, X. (2021). Causal inference for social network analysis. In R. Light & J. Moody (Eds.), *The Oxford handbook of social networks* (pp. 288–310). Oxford University Press.

Freyaldenhoven, S., Hansen, C., & Shapiro, J. M. (2019). Pre-event trends in the panel event-study design. *American Economic Review*, *109*(9), 3307–3338. https://doi.org/10.1257/aer.20180609.

Gelman, A., & Imbens, G. (2014). *Why high-order polynomials should not be used in regression discontinuity designs* (Working paper no. 20405; working paper series). National Bureau of Economic Research. https://doi.org/10.3386/w20405.

Gottfredson, D. C., & Exum, M. L. (2002). The Baltimore City drug treatment court: One-year results from a randomized study. *Journal of Research in Crime and Delinquency*, *39*(3), 337–356. https://doi.org/10.1177/002242780203900304.

Gould, E. D., Weinberg, B. A., & Mustard, D. B. (2002). Crime rates and local labor market opportunities in the United States: 1979–1997. *Review of Economics and Statistics*, *84*(1), 45–61. https://doi.org/10.1162/003465302317331919.

Granger, C. W. J. (1969). Investigating causal relations by econometric models and cross-spectral methods. *Econometrica*, *37*(3), 424. https://doi.org/10.2307/1912791.

Groff, E. R., Johnson, S. D., & Thornton, A. (2019). State of the art in agent-based modeling of urban crime: An overview. *Journal of Quantitative Criminology*, *35*(1), 155–193. https://doi.org/10.1007/s10940-018-9376-y.

Guo, R., Cheng, L., Li, J., Hahn, P. R., & Liu, H. (2020a). A survey of learning causality with data: Problems and methods. *ACM Computing Surveys*, *53*(4), 1–37. https://doi.org/10.1145/3397269.

Guo, R., Li, J., & Liu, H. (2020b). Learning individual causal effects from networked observational data. In *Proceedings of the 13th international conference on web search and data mining*, 232–240. https://doi.org/10.1145/3336191.3371816.

Hahn, P. R., Carvalho, C. M., Puelz, D., & He, J. (2018). Regularization and confounding in linear regression for treatment effect estimation. *Bayesian Analysis*, *13*(1), 163–182. https://doi.org/10.1214/16-BA1044.

Hahn, P. R., Murray, J. S., & Carvalho, C. (2019). Bayesian regression tree models for causal inference: Regularization, confounding, and heterogeneous effects. *ArXiv:1706.09523 [Stat]*. http://arxiv.org/abs/1706.09523

Heckman, J. J. (1992). Randomization and social policy evaluation. In C. F. Manski & I. Garfinkel (Eds.), *Evaluating welfare and training programs*. Harvard University Press.

Hill, J. L. (2011). Bayesian nonparametric modeling for causal inference. *Journal of Computational and Graphical Statistics*, *20*(1), 217–240. https://doi.org/10.1198/jcgs.2010.08162.

Holland, P. W. (1986). Statistics and causal inference. *Journal of the American Statistical Association*, *81*(396), 945–960. https://doi.org/10.2307/2289064.

Imai, K., & Ratkovic, M. (2013). Estimating treatment effect heterogeneity in randomized program evaluation. *The Annals of Applied Statistics*, *7*(1), 443–470. https://doi.org/10.1214/12-AOAS593.

Imbens, G. W. (2017). Regression Discontinuity Designs in the econometrics literature. *Observational Studies*, *3*(2), 147–155. https://doi.org/10.1353/obs.2017.0003.

Jalalimanesh, A., Shahabi Haghighi, H., Ahmadi, A., & Soltani, M. (2017). Simulation-based optimization of radiotherapy: Agent-based modeling and reinforcement learning. *Mathematics and Computers in Simulation*, *133*, 235–248. https://doi.org/10.1016/j.matcom.2016.05.008.

Jorgensen, C., & Wells, J. (2021). Is marijuana really a gateway drug? A nationally representative test of the marijuana gateway hypothesis using a propensity score matching design. Journal of Experimental Criminology, 1–18.

Kaelbling, L. P., Littman, M. L., & Moore, A. W. (1996). Reinforcement learning: A survey. *Journal of Artificial Intelligence Research*, *4*, 237–285. https://doi.org/10.1613/jair.301.

Khanna, G., Medina, C., Nyshadham, A., & Tamayo, J. A. (2019). *Formal employment and organized crime: Regression discontinuity evidence from Colombia* (Working paper no. 26203; working paper series). National Bureau of Economic Research. https://doi.org/10.3386/w26203.

King, G., & Nielsen, R. (2019). Why propensity scores should not be used for matching. *Political Analysis, 27*(4), 435–454. https://doi.org/10.1017/pan.2019.11.

Koch, B., Sainburg, T., Geraldo, P., Jiang, S., Sun, Y., & Foster, J. G. (2021). Deep learning of potential outcomes. *ArXiv:2110.04442 [Cs, Econ, Stat]*. http://arxiv.org/abs/2110.04442

Künzel, S. R., Sekhon, J. S., Bickel, P. J., & Yu, B. (2019). Metalearners for estimating heterogeneous treatment effects using machine learning. *Proceedings of the National Academy of Sciences, 116*(10), 4156–4165. https://doi.org/10.1073/pnas.1804597116.

Kusner, M. J., & Loftus, J. R. (2020). The long road to fairer algorithms. *Nature, 578*(7793), 34–36. https://doi.org/10.1038/d41586-020-00274-3.

Kwok, R. (2019). Junior AI researchers are in demand by universities and industry. *Nature, 568*(7753), 581–583. https://doi.org/10.1038/d41586-019-01248-w.

Larsen, B., Kleif, H. B., & Kolodziejczyk, C. (2015). The volunteer programme 'Night Ravens': A difference-in-difference analysis of the effects on crime rates. *Journal of Scandinavian Studies in Criminology and Crime Prevention, 16*(1), 2–24. https://doi.org/10.1080/14043858.2015.1015810.

Lechner, M. (2011). The estimation of causal effects by difference-in-difference methods. *Foundations and Trends® in Econometrics, 4*(3), 165–224. https://doi.org/10.1561/0800000014.

Lee, D. S., & Lemieux, T. (2010). Regression Discontinuity Designs in economics. *Journal of Economic Literature, 48*(2), 281–355. https://doi.org/10.1257/jel.48.2.281.

Lee, K., Ulkuatam, S., Beling, P., & Scherer, W. (2018). Generating synthetic Bitcoin transactions and predicting market price movement via inverse reinforcement learning and agent-based modeling. *Journal of Artificial Societies and Social Simulation, 21*(3), 5.

Leuschner, F. (2021). Exploring gender disparities in the prosecution of theft cases: Propensity score matching on data from German court files. European Journal of Criminology, 14773708211003011.

Lilley, D. R., Stewart, M. C., & Tucker-Gail, K. (2020). Drug courts and net-widening in US cities: A reanalysis using propensity score matching. Criminal Justice Policy Review, *31*(2), 287–308.

Lin, M.-J. (2009). More police, less crime: Evidence from US state data. *International Review of Law and Economics, 29*(2), 73–80. https://doi.org/10.1016/j.irle.2008.12.003.

Linden, A., & Adams, J. L. (2012). Combining the regression discontinuity design and propensity score-based weighting to improve causal inference in program evaluation. *Journal of Evaluation in Clinical Practice, 18*(2), 317–325. https://doi.org/10.1111/j.1365-2753.2011.01768.x.

Liu, Y., Niculescu-Mizil, A., Lozano, A. C., & Lu, Y. (2010, January 1). *Learning temporal causal graphs for relational time-series analysis.* ICML. https://openreview.net/forum?id=r1bH5oZ_WB

Loeffler, C. E., & Grunwald, B. (2015). Processed as an adult: A regression discontinuity estimate of the crime effects of charging nontransfer juveniles as adults. *Journal of Research in Crime and Delinquency, 52*(6), 890–922. https://doi.org/10.1177/0022427815581858.

Loftus, J. R., Russell, C., Kusner, M. J., & Silva, R. (2018). Causal reasoning for algorithmic fairness. *ArXiv:1805.05859 [Cs]*. http://arxiv.org/abs/1805.05859

MacDonald, J. M., Klick, J., & Grunwald, B. (2016). The effect of private police on crime: Evidence from a geographic regression discontinuity design. *Journal of the Royal Statistical Society, Series A (Statistics in Society)*, 179(3), 831–846.

Macy, M., & Sato, Y. (2008). Reply to Will and Hegselmann. *Journal of Artificial Societies and Social Simulation*, 11(4). https://www.jasss.org/11/4/11.html

Malinsky, D., & Spirtes, P. (2018). Causal structure learning from multivariate time series in settings with unmeasured confounding. In *Proceedings of 2018 ACM SIGKDD workshop on causal discovery*, 23–47. https://proceedings.mlr.press/v92/malinsky18a.html

Marshall, B. D. L., & Galea, S. (2015). Formalizing the role of agent-based modeling in causal inference and epidemiology. *American Journal of Epidemiology, 181*(2), 92–99. https://doi.org/10.1093/aje/kwu274.

Nie, X., & Wager, S. (2021). Quasi-oracle estimation of heterogeneous treatment effects. *Biometrika, 108*(2), 299–319. https://doi.org/10.1093/biomet/asaa076.

Norvig, P. (2017). On Chomsky and the two cultures of statistical learning. In W. Pietsch, J. Wernecke, & M. Ott (Eds.), *Berechenbarkeit der Welt? Philosophie und Wissenschaft im Zeitalter von Big Data* (pp. 61–83). Springer Fachmedien. https://doi.org/10.1007/978-3-658-12153-2_3.

Parzen, E. (2001). Comment to "Statistical modeling: The two cultures." *Statistical Science*, 16(3). https://doi.org/10.1214/ss/1009213726.

Pearl, J. (1998). Graphical models for probabilistic and causal reasoning. In P. Smets (Ed.), *Quantified representation of uncertainty and imprecision* (pp. 367–389). Springer Netherlands. https://doi.org/10.1007/978-94-017-1735-9_12.

Pearl, J. (2009). *Causality* (2° edizione ed.). Cambridge University Press.

Pearl, J. (2012). The do-calculus revisited. In *Proceedings of the twenty-eighth conference on uncertainty in artificial intelligence.*

Pearl, J. (2018a). Theoretical impediments to machine learning with seven sparks from the causal revolution. *ArXiv:1801.04016 [Cs, Stat]*. http://arxiv.org/abs/1801.04016

Pearl, J. (2018b). Challenging the hegemony of randomized controlled trials: A commentary on Deaton and Cartwright. *Social Science & Medicine (1982), 210*, 60–62. https://doi.org/10.1016/j.socscimed.2018.04.024.

Pearl, J. (2019). The seven tools of causal inference, with reflections on machine learning. *Communications of the ACM, 62*(3), 54–60. https://doi.org/10.1145/3241036.

Peters, J., Janzing, D., & Schölkopf, B. (2013). Causal inference on time series using restricted structural equation models. *Advances in Neural Information Processing Systems, 26*. https://proceedings.neurips.cc/paper/2013/hash/47d1e990583c9c67424d369f3414728e-Abstract.html

Pinotti, P. (2017). Clicking on Heaven's door: The effect of immigrant legalization on crime. *American Economic Review, 107*(1), 138–168. https://doi.org/10.1257/aer.20150355.

Piquero, A. R., Farrington, D. P., Welsh, B. C., Tremblay, R., & Jennings, W. G. (2009). Effects of early family/parent training programs on antisocial behavior and delinquency. *Journal of Experimental Criminology, 5*(2), 83–120. https://doi.org/10.1007/s11292-009-9072-x.

Piza, E. L. (2018). The crime prevention effect of CCTV in public places: A propensity score analysis. *Journal of Crime and Justice, 41*(1), 14–30. https://doi.org/10.1080/0735648X.2016.1226931.

Posick, C. (2018). Reappraising the impact of offending on victimization: A Propensity Score Matching approach. *International Journal of Offender Therapy and Comparative Criminology*, 62(8), 2374–2390. https://doi.org/10.1177/03066 24X17708179.

Priks, M. (2015). The effects of surveillance cameras on crime: Evidence from the Stockholm subway. *The Economic Journal*, 125(588), F289–F305. https://doi.org/10.1111/ecoj.12327.

Rakesh, V., Guo, R., Moraffah, R., Agarwal, N., & Liu, H. (2018). Linked causal variational autoencoder for inferring paired spillover effects. *ArXiv:1808.03333 [Cs, Stat]*. http://arxiv.org/abs/1808.03333

Rambachan, A., & Roth, J. (2019). *An honest approach to parallel trends*. https://www.semanticscholar.org/paper/An-Honest-Approach-to-Parallel-Trends-Rambachan-Roth/d8791bdbd616a6cff80ad2ccf0832359982178d3

Ramsey, J., Glymour, M., Sanchez-Romero, R., & Glymour, C. (2017). A million variables and more: The fast greedy equivalence search algorithm for learning high-dimensional graphical causal models, with an application to functional magnetic resonance images. *International Journal of Data Science and Analytics*, 3(2), 121–129. https://doi.org/10.1007/s41060-016-0032-z.

Raper, S. (2020). Leo Breiman's "Two cultures." *Significance*, 17(1), 34–37. https://doi.org/10.1111/j.1740-9713.2020.01357.x.

Ravallion, M. (2020). *Should the randomistas (continue to) rule?* (Working paper no. 27554; working paper series). National Bureau of Economic Research. https://doi.org/10.3386/w27554.

Retzlaff, C. O., Ziefle, M., & Calero Valdez, A. (2021). The history of agent-based modeling in the social sciences. In V. G. Duffy (Ed.), *Digital human modeling and applications in health, safety, ergonomics and risk management. human body, motion and behavior* (pp. 304–319). Springer International Publishing. https://doi.org/10.1007/978-3-030-77817-0_22.

Ridgeway, G. (2019). Experiments in criminology: Improving our understanding of crime and the criminal justice system. *Annual Review of Statistics and Its Application*, 6(1), 37–61. https://doi.org/10.1146/annurev-statistics-030718-105057.

Roth, J., Sant'Anna, P. H. C., Bilinski, A., & Poe, J. (2022). What's trending in difference-in-differences? A synthesis of the recent econometrics literature. *arXiv:2201.01194* https://arxiv.org/abs/2201.01194

Rubin, D. B. (1974). Estimating causal effects of treatments in randomized and non-randomized studies. *Journal of Educational Psychology*, 66(5), 688–701. https://doi.org/10.1037/h0037350.

Runge, J., Nowack, P., Kretschmer, M., Flaxman, S., & Sejdinovic, D. (2019). Detecting and quantifying causal associations in large nonlinear time series datasets. *Science Advances*, 5(11), eaau4996. https://doi.org/10.1126/sciadv.aau4996.

Sample, I. (2017, November 1). "We can't compete": Why universities are losing their best AI scientists. *The Guardian*. https://www.theguardian.com/science/2017/nov/01/cant-compete-universities-losing-best-ai-scientists

Sampson, R. J. (2010). Gold standard myths: Observations on the experimental turn in quantitative criminology. *Journal of Quantitative Criminology*, 26(4), 489–500. https://doi.org/10.1007/s10940-010-9117-3.

Semenova, V., Goldman, M., Chernozhukov, V., & Taddy, M. (2021). Estimation and inference on heterogeneous treatment effects in high-dimensional dynamic panels. *ArXiv:1712.09988 [Stat]*. http://arxiv.org/abs/1712.09988

Sert, E., Bar-Yam, Y., & Morales, A. J. (2020). Segregation dynamics with reinforcement learning and agent based modeling. *Scientific Reports*, *10*(1), 11771. https://doi.org/10.1038/s41598-020-68447-8.

Silver, I. A., Wooldredge, J., Sullivan, C. J., & Nedelec, J. L. (2021). Longitudinal Propensity Score Matching: A demonstration of counterfactual conditions adjusted for longitudinal clustering. *Journal of Quantitative Criminology*, *37*(1), 267–301. https://doi.org/10.1007/s10940-020-09455-9.

Stock, J. H., & Trebbi, F. (2003). Retrospectives: Who invented instrumental variable regression. *Journal of Economic Perspectives*, *17*(3), 177–194. https://doi.org/10.1257/089533003769204416.

Sutton, R. S., & Barto, A. G. (2018). *Reinforcement learning, second edition: An introduction*. MIT Press.

Toulis, P., Volfovsky, A., & Airoldi, E. M. (2018). Propensity score methodology in the presence of network entanglement between treatments. *ArXiv:1801.07310 [Math, Stat]*. http://arxiv.org/abs/1801.07310

VanderWeele, T. J., & Weihua, A. (2013). Social networks and causal inference. In *Handbook of causal analysis for social research* (pp. 353–374). Springer.

Veitch, V., Wang, Y., & Blei, D. M. (2019). Using embeddings to correct for unobserved confounding in networks. *ArXiv:1902.04114 [Cs, Stat]*. http://arxiv.org/abs/1902.04114

Wager, S., & Athey, S. (2018). Estimation and inference of heterogeneous treatment effects using random forests. *Journal of the American Statistical Association*, *113*(523), 1228–1242. https://doi.org/10.1080/01621459.2017.1319839.

Wang, E. A., Lin, H., Aminawung, J. A., Busch, S. H., Gallagher, C., Maurer, K., Puglisi, L., Shavit, S., & Frisman, L. (2019). Propensity-matched study of enhanced primary care on contact with the criminal justice system among individuals recently released from prison to new haven. *BMJ Open*, *9*(5), e028097. https://doi.org/10.1136/bmjopen-2018-028097.

Wiering, M., & van Otterlo, M. (2012). *Reinforcement learning: State-of-the-art*. Springer.

Wolpert, D. H., & Macready, W. G. (1997). No free lunch theorems for optimization. *IEEE Transactions on Evolutionary Computation*, *1*(1), 67–82. https://doi.org/10.1109/4235.585893.

Wooldridge, J. M. (2012). *Introductory econometrics: A modern approach* (5° edizione). South-Western Pub.

Wright, P. G. (1928). *The tariff on animal and vegetable oils*. Macmillan.

6

CONCLUDING REMARKS

Final Notes

As this book has come to an end, it is finally time to layout some conclusions. I would like to think about these conclusions as notes that I leave both to the readers of today and tomorrow, as well as to myself. There is a non-negligible probability that this book will become outdated in a relatively short amount of time, yet I hope that some of the reflections and reasonings herein will remain longer than the mere evolution of the methodological, theoretical, and practical landscape in criminology and crime research.

The ability of research on crime to improve its societal role cannot prescind from the ability of the whole community to leverage the promises and govern the risks posed by the diffusion of machine learning across fields, along with its rapid developments through a wide array of new tools, approaches, and techniques. If we will be able to exploit the possibilities offered by the transdisciplinary links connecting criminology, those social sciences interested in crime (e.g., economics), computer science, and statistics, then we will have on our side an important ally to target new research questions and answer to old unresolved ones.

This on the one side will contribute to advance our understanding of crime in all its facets. On the other side, it will help us develop or propose instruments, interventions, and strategies to reduce its negative impact on society. The challenge of crime reduction is immensely though, as it is intertwined with manifold social phenomena through myriads of micro- and macro-level factors, therefore calling for the use of all the available tools at our disposal to be meaningfully addressed. I have no doubt that machine learning and artificial intelligence (AI) in general can be useful in this regard.

Yet, as I have written – both directly and indirectly – several times in this book, my point of view is not a mere optimistic apology of these technological and methodological paradigms. There are indeed risks and pitfalls to be carefully managed and governed. And again, these both relate to the research and practice components of the intersection between machine learning and

DOI: 10.4324/9781003217732-6

research on crime. This book is mostly about the research dimension, as I see it as often prodromal to the practice dimension, but in these concluding reflections, I would like to reason about the prevalence of risks in both.

Concerning research, it is imperative to avoid the acritical embracing of machine learning and other AI methods as silver linings to solve the most pressing issues emerging in research on crime. The tendency to ride the wave of the AI hype can lead to overlook aspects of research that have been and should continue to be central in our quest for answers we do not have yet. No off-the-shelf algorithm deployed in few lines of code can be a substitute for informative and reliable data, testable hypotheses, confutable theoretical premises, and transparent assumptions. These are the pillars that as a diverse, dynamic community we should look after. The pressure determined by the need to be published, awarded, funded, and recognized by our peers may become a risky temptation to put aside such pillars in favor of the shimmering lights of (superficial) machine intelligence. It will be fundamental for the research of the future to resist this temptation. Critical, mindful perspectives should guide the way in which we will decide to take advantage of the tools that we will have at our disposal. No algorithm is a shortcut to the long path ahead.

Concerning practice, we shall keep in mind that the fact that machines alone will easily create a better society has so far been a false myth, and this false myth does not only apply to crime reduction and control alone. The examples are abundant, from social media to digital government; the idea that algorithms will solve our problems at no cost is dangerous and has been proven wrong already many times. In areas such as policing and criminal justice, algorithmic systems have been so far under scrutiny concerning many issues related to their impacts on society. Discrimination, bias, and low accountability have become problems and expressions we have all become familiar with in the last years. The hope is that this vigilance continues. Again, I genuinely believe that machine learning and related technologies will help us in our attempt to provide directions for safer, more equitable communities and societies, but again this will take time, an incredible amount of resources (tangible and intangible), and a closer collaboration between fields, institutions, and individuals. The hagiographic attitude toward algorithmic systems of scholars, practitioners, members of the institutions, and politicians has already produced damages to many people around the world. Only a sequence of scandals has helped us open our eyes and address the problem. Let us not dare to close them, again.

This book humbly sought to unfold all these challenges (and the corresponding promises) through various lenses. Through the past, to better understand the origins of the tools we use today, and the origins of the ideas, expectations, and illusions we currently continue to reflect upon. Through the present, to orient ourselves in the interpretation of the complex picture standing in front of us. Through the future, to imagine or anticipate the directions we may (or should) take to ensure that this will not turn into a gigantic, missed chance for research on crime.

The pioneers of AI offered us new paradigms to think about computing, intelligence, causality, reasoning, and new techniques to approach problems that could only be addressed in dreams until recently. At the same time, those who first imagined a role for machines in the fight against crime, broadly intended, helped us preparing the ground for ideas that seem now ground-breaking but are rooted in a decades-long history. Today, the heterogeneous communities of researchers working on crime problems via machine learning and AI draw a scenario that is characterized by fragmentation of topics, fragmentation of collaborative trends, and sparsity of contributions, leaving in the background research on the ethical dimensions of this transdisciplinary and historical process. What about the future, then?

The good news is that, paraphrasing William Ernest Henley, we are the "masters of our fates" and "captains of our souls." Developing research that can have positive social impact is possible, and I proposed in this sense two goals and four pathways to go in that direction. They are not exhaustive, but they may be a starting point. Furthermore, from a technical perspective, the integration of tools from the statistical and machine learning traditions can significantly aid our quest for disentangling causal processes in crime, victimization, delinquency, and deviance, taking us all a little bit closer to the answers for which we struggle during our daily lives as scholars, scientists, and researchers interested in criminal behaviors and phenomena.

There is a mixture of hope and drama in the tension between the past, the present, and the future, and I wish the readers who got to this point have perceived it throughout the book. This continuum and this clash of feelings have been the driving forces behind every page, and if they prompted you to reflect deeper about the perspectives in research on crime, I guess I have achieved my goal.

INDEX

Note: *Italicized* folios indicate figures, **bold** indicate tables and with "n" indicates endnotes.

171

Sweeten, G. 134
Symbolic AI 28

Tafoya, W. L. 6
temporal data, tools for 149–151
test set 35–36
theoretical reasoning 10–11
Time Series Models with Independent
  Noise (TiMINo) 150
Toulis, P. 155
training set 35–38, 159n6
transparency 11, 80, 146; crisis 98;
  discrimination and 94; and reform 97
Turing, A. 22–23; Computing
  machinery and intelligence 25
Turing test 25
two-stage least squares regression
  (2SLS) 139; *see also* regression
Two-Way-Fixed-Effect DID 137; *see
  also* Difference-in-Differences

United Nations Interregional Crime and
  Justice Research Institute (UNICRI)
  109
United States (US) 109–112; courts
  97; criminal justice institutions 6;

government 27; police departments
  56
unsupervised learning 13, 37–40; *see
  also* machine learning; supervised
  learning

variational autoencoders (VAE) 155
Veitch, V. 156
victimization surveys 101
Vollmer, A. 85n1
von Neumann, J. 23

Wager, S. 147
weak AI 12, 29–32; *see also* artificial
  intelligence (AI); strong AI
Weisburd, D. 81
Weizenbaum, J. 6
Wiener, F. B. 6
Wiener, N. 23
Wolpert, D. H. 132
Wooldridge, J. M. 139
Woolgar, S. 11
Wright, P. 137
Wright, S. 137

Zhang, A. 41